RETREAT FROM TRUTH

RETREAT FROM TRUTH

By

G. R. G. MURE

Warden of Merton College, Oxford

OXFORD
BASIL BLACKWELL
1958

PRINTED IN GREAT BRITAIN BY
BILLING AND SONS LIMITED, GUILDFORD AND LONDON

CONTENTS

PREFACE

THIS book grew, slowly and intermittently, from a mood of deep depression. In the years between the wars I had watched without enthusiasm the return of British philosophy to its native empiricist tradition. After the last war it appeared to be reducing itself from naïveté to absurdity with such speed and such conviction that I began to think it might soon be time to cry stinking fish. I did not hurry, because I hoped that my mood and the cause of it might pass away with better times, but after a dozen years, during which I asked myself often and anxiously whether I might not have become a mere praiser of the days of my youth, I could find no reason to repent. Against a background of bitter practical stress, all our non-practical activities, our poetry and our philosophy in particular, seemed continually to deteriorate, while natural science flourished and progressed by leaps and bounds.

Between practical conditions and spiritual sterility one could hardly doubt a causal link, but I could not, in the case of philosophy, see at once what it was. I was faced with the fact that British empiricism and positivism had originated and developed in relatively happy times, and that their modern forms, though they represented a complete break with the idealism of the nineteenth century, a period when the prestige of British philosophers, at least in Great Britain, was at its height, were merely a return to the past and an intensification of the old tradition. We were only reverting to the worm's-eye view. Gradually, however, I came to accept, though with qualifications, the view of Benedetto Croce that science is an essentially practical activity, and that empiricism is an *ersatz* philosophy which falsely identifies in kind philosophical and scientific thinking, and therefore cannot envisage any connection between reason and intrinsic values. On this assumption, it was easy to connect the traditional philosophic attitude of this country with the essentially practical bent of its inhabitants —a connection which has always been less obvious to themselves than to their continental critics—and to see in the rapidly accelerating twentieth-century reversion to empiricism the effect of cruel practical stresses working upon a native tendency.

That is, briefly, the theme of this book and the reason for its title. The specimens of empiricist and positivist thinking which fill most of Parts I and II appear in a more or less chronological order, but I have been more concerned to produce fair random samples than to trace development exactly or completely. Had space permitted, I should have liked to compare the latest phases of British philosophy with French existentialism, another, though a very different, philosophical or semi-philosophical product of spiritual sterility and despair.

The idealist musings of Part III—they are not much more than that—are somewhat in the nature of an appendix. They are not offered as a substitute for the philosophical views which I have attacked. There is little in them that is new, and every age must work out its own philosophy. But the history of philosophy is a large factor in all fruitful philosophizing, and to recall the speculations of the last British thinkers who were in earnest when they spoke of value might, I thought, be a stimulus to some who are not wholly content with the ways in which our modern philosophers think and talk.

If this book seems filled immoderately with gloom, let me say that I hold good and evil to be far too mutually dependent to make either optimism or pessimism as an ultimate view of human life a rational attitude.

My thanks are due to Professor Brand Blanshard and Mr. W. H. Walsh for reading and commenting on some of the earlier chapters. Mr. Walsh in particular pointed out faults some of which I have tried to remedy.

PART I

The Background of Modern British Philosophy

CHAPTER I

THE AGE WE LIVE IN

IT was a central commonplace of Greek thought that speculation and the non-utilitarian arts rose and flourished only
when man's labour had won him some leisure from the
struggle to exist; that despite their late emergence in his history
they were foremost among his definitory characteristics; that,
having no end beyond themselves, they were the worthiest of his
activities.

If this view is in general a true one, as I shall assume it to be, it
would seem to follow conversely that in periods of history when
mankind, or when particular nations, were losing ground in the
struggle for existence or exhausted by it, speculation and the
unpractical arts would dwindle and deteriorate. In prosperous
epochs these luxuries born of leisure might be judged more really
necessary to man than the most exquisite satisfactions of his material needs, but in days of disaster and fear, of material shortage
and frustration, they would decline in general repute, diminish
in vigour, and contract in scope.

To become plausible, however, this hypothesis needs two
qualifications. In the first place—it is again a commonplace—
there have been epochs of leisure and material prosperity in which
the non-practical occupations have been quite busily pursued but
have produced little of permanent importance. The relation of
the theoretic to the practical life is subtle. Leisure is not the only
condition, after natural ability and energy, of non-practical
achievement. There is, at least in European man, a need that
some urge, some prick of exhilaration or confident hope, be
transmitted to him from the world of action before he can accom-
plish something great in a world of vision which exists for no
practical end. He achieves greatness not in epochs of mere prosperity and leisure but rather in times when the glow of some
practical triumph is yet undulled and the future still looks

glorious if not secure—in an Elizabethan rather than in an Alexandrine or an Antonine age. It is a further commonplace that genius may burn brighter in the darkness of adversity. In that there is some truth. Plato worked with the greatness of Athens behind him and with no very rosy prospect for Greek civilization ahead. Milton wrote *Paradise Lost* in blindness and impoverishment amid the wreck of his earthly hopes. It needs, however, to be added that material poverty is seldom the spur to achievement in the theoretic life. Artists and thinkers do not as a rule do their best work while starving in garrets.

In our own times this hypothesis seems fully confirmed by Soviet Russia, where the conception of truth in any form as being of value for its own sake is officially dead, where history and the arts as well as the sciences are rigorously enslaved to support a creed which styles itself philosophical but is in fact a fanatically held religion of action. For it can scarcely be doubted that the state of things in the Soviet Union is mainly due to total absorption in the struggle to live, to disaster and fear, to material shortage and frustration. But Russia has never been an integral part of western civilization, and she affects us now as an impact rather than as sharing with us a common experience. It is the plight of speculation and the non-practical arts in our own country which urgently demands our diagnosis. Here the picture is less dark than the Russian scene, but it is grim enough. Milton and Plato both lived in happier spiritual climes than ours. Milton believed in an after life, and his enemies on earth at least shared some articles of his creed. Nothing comparable to the horrors of the first half of the twentieth century occurred in the lifetime of Plato. He did not witness the monstrous birth of two tyrannies begotten at opposite poles of political thought. He did not see two world wars and live under the threat of a third to be fought with nuclear bombs. He did not find his faith in the Good poisoned at the roots by revelations of evil so abysmal and so ubiquitous that he must wonder whether, if the human race should succeed in extinguishing itself, much would be lost worth the keeping. Plato in fourth-century Athens acknowledged that the good philosopher required the good state to live in and must now take shelter from the storm behind the wall, but behind the walls of the Academy hope for mankind survived and was not altogether disappointed. On the other hand, men who have seen the struggles of the last forty years, though they may be convinced that they have fought on the right side, are apt to wonder whether they are not themselves inevitably tainted by the evils which they have tried to combat. If you lose faith in human nature you cannot long go on believing in yourself. Plato, describing in the *Republic* the genesis of tyranny, is speaking primarily neither as a historian nor as a prophet; rather he is developing logically the possibility of corruption which human nature entails. And the tyranny which Plato describes is only the tyranny of a single perverted city state. But the same logic applied to the modern world makes George Orwell's *1984* an almost unreadably horrible book. The self-enslavement of the human race may not in fact occur, but what has already happened in Europe makes it so real a possibility that to reflect upon it brings not only terror and nausea but, to many minds, a sense of helpless involvement, even perhaps of complicity. There is a darkness against which even genius cannot shine.

My chief object in this book is to test the ancient hypothesis by examining samples of the philosophy produced in this country during the first half of the twentieth century, and I do not doubt that they will reveal the crippling influence of economic stress and of the consequent frustration and spiritual infertility of the times. On the other hand, modern British philosophical thinking is utterly reactionary in character. It is an intensification of a philosophical attitude—or rather, perhaps, of an attitude towards philosophy—which prevailed in this country long before the twentieth century. We were never very good philosophers and, as I see it, our troublous times have aggravated old maladies rather than produced anything very new, good or bad. We must, as it were, in this case study the previous medical history of the patient before we can diagnose. Let us, however, before we begin that task, glance at the simpler case of the arts. On them the impact of economic storm and stress has been more direct. Here there is much which is comparatively new as well as bad. I shall talk first and mainly of poetry, and then a little, for a different reason, of architecture. I select poetry not only because it is the greatest of the arts. Our music, like our cooking, has always been a minor affair, and for a long time it has had little especially native in it. Of great painters we have had only a few. But poetry has been our supreme non-practical achievement. If we fail in that we fail in what is most our own. Poetry, moreover, being ampler in its scope than the other arts, is linked more closely with its environment than they. The poet bears surer witness to the world about him than the composer or the painter. He talks before he writes poems, and all his life he uses words for a multi-tude of purposes besides poetic creation. He learns his technique not only in the conscious study of other poets but also, un-consciously, in daily intercourse with all types of men. The other arts, in their disciplines as well as in their creations, are more withdrawn, more wholly occupied in their own special businesses. The composer and the graphic artist can hardly evade a long training in technique which brings them into intimate communion with their predecessors, but there are no schools of poetry. Regarded as materials, notes and pigments are relatively stable. New use of them springs largely from the study of old methods: Renoir was not joking when he told a pupil who said he meant to pass his vacation communing with Nature to spend it in the galleries instead. But the suggestiveness of words is always subtly shifting, and in great part it is not the poets who work the changes. Poetry has of course its own internal development, too, and its reaction upon current speech, but the winds which fill its sails and alter its course blow from a far wider world. Lastly I select poetry for the converse reason that this same greater reciprocation between the poet and the world makes the ordinary educated man a better judge of poetry than of painting and music.

The ordinary man must, of course, judge with caution. Few modern poems are widely quoted, but any creative artist is apt at first to scandalize the critics, even to excite derision, because his work springs from an experience enlarged and expanded beyond the ken of his contemporaries, because at first the old rules he breaks are more obvious than the new rules he makes. There is a factor of revolution and liberation in nearly all progress of art, which conceals its positive element from the eye of prejudice. When a painter or a sculptor feels that the formulae of design which governed his predecessors' work have become exhausted and can now produce only clichés and banalities, he has no option but to struggle towards a new formula. What he desires, consciously or unconsciously, is a new *basic* design. One might call it a new foundation to build on, but it is more nearly a new principle to develop, a new theme to elaborate. Nearly always, therefore, his new formula first emerges as a simplification and not a complication of the old. Here, I think, is the source (or one of them) of 'abstract art' and also of the vulgar misunderstanding of a new formula as sheer crudity. A naturalistically minded public which has never realized that the progress of painting and sculpture has always been a movement within the art itself from one principle of design to the next, easily mistakes a Matisse nude or a recumbent figure of Henry Moore for a childish failure to copy the actual shapes of things, or as at best the wilful perversion of styles to which (in their exhausted and degenerate forms) it has become so completely habituated as to believe them natural. On the same lines it may be plausibly argued that the ultimately inevitable rejection of traditional metres compels the modern poet to create a peculiar rhythm for each poem, which the conservative ear, unable to apply the old rules, will probably mistake for bad prose. Certainly, to judge it fairly, one must read a new poem more often than one need read an old one which one happens not to have come across before.

I fancy, however, that the average sympathetic and unprejudiced reader of English verse finds in the bulk of the poetry written during the last thirty years something which baffles both his head and his heart,[1] and I do not believe it is because he misses some inner and fuller meaning impenetrable to the vulgar. Modern poetry bears, unhappily, all the marks not of an expanded but of a narrowed experience. The modern poet works in a world which sometimes exasperates and inflames his sensibility but more often chokes it and contracts its expression. His song is in general not sustained. The old themes, the old forms, and the old swelling or at least continuous rhythms are not his; not because he has transcended them but because the old emotions are dead or barely alive in him. At the time of the Spanish civil war communism supplied some impetus, because circumstances allowed it to wear a liberal mask; but to most contemporary poets communism has shown itself a false dawn to be hailed with no ode. Now the future is a cloud of fears and the past has left no exultant emotion to be recollected in tranquillity; nothing is there, even in the cold triumph of a victorious world war, for epic celebration. Physical

---

[1] I am not thinking of poets like De la Mare, Blunden, or Sassoon, who are rooted in an older tradition. They have reacted to the present age rather than been produced by it.

courage, military and civilian, has reached an unexampled height in this half-century, but it would not occur to most of us to call the present age 'heroic'. We may have lived our finest hour in 1940, but by V Day we had, spiritually, forgotten it, and the modern poet, even when he treats the eternal lyric themes of love and nature, which are in some sort the poet's private affairs, can scarcely escape the repressive chill which creeps in from the outer world, frosting his passion and his moral force.

I would call the distinctive character of modern verse its 'prematurity'. The poet of our time seems so often not to work fearlessly in full self-consciousness but to retreat into an inner and a lower, in the sense of a less developed, self. He seizes and exploits the nascent image, even sometimes the hardly more than foetal image. He lacks the power to ripen it, and it comes to us, like Richard Crookback but without his sinister force to compensate, 'Deformed, unfinished, sent before its time Into this breathing world scarce half made up.' The modern poet's half-rhythms, his inchoate metrical divisions, the caprice of his sporadic rhyming, his assonances, designed perhaps but often hard to tell from accidental jingles, the unemphatic lay-out of his poem on the page with its paucity of capitals and stops—these are not for the most part affectations but external forms appropriate to their matter. These are the swaddling clothes that wrap a brood of half-formed images which would look merely ridiculous tailored in the traditional prosody and punctuation. If you gave a modern critic a modern poem hitherto unknown to him which you had typed out in prose form and asked him to divide the lines correctly, what would be the percentage of his hits?

We should perhaps here ask in what special sense good poets are mature poets. The answer lies in the relation of imagery to language. But this, beyond the fact that imagination in the bare sense of 'imaging' is a lower and less developed activity than language, is not perfectly easy to analyse. It must be remembered first that imagery is not confined to one special sense, nor even to two, but belongs to all the senses; secondly that imagery is never purely cognitive in function. Treated as merely subservient to thinking, it is an abstraction which belongs to a certain sort of abstract thought.[1] In actual experience, at least to begin with and before abstraction is made, there is an emotional factor

[1] See p. 229.

inseparable from the cognitive factor within the nature of any image, and in aesthetic experience the emotional factor or moment is equipollent or dominant. The poetic act of vision is formally, I suggest, nothing but the maturing of imagery in this broad sense into speech. It is never a substitution of the word for the image. It is true that the transformation of imagery can never in the nature of human experience be complete: we always 'image' as well as speak, and the sound of the word, too, even when speech is merely inward, does in some measure come as additional, and so far contingent, to the matured image. Transformation, nevertheless, and not substitution nor addition is the clue to the poet's passage from imagery to language.[1] You may call the poetic act 'expression', but only if the term is allowed to carry no suggestion of describing or of translating into quite fresh symbols an original which is not changed in the process. You may better call it 'creation', if you remember that no creation is *ex nihilo*. The poet's *nisus*, then, is towards this consummation of imagery in speech, and the great poets of the past have on the whole been those who have most nearly reached it. It is they for the most part who have come nearest to success in maturing the image and thereby annulling the severance of imagery and language, and in subduing to their single purpose the external sound of words. Shakespeare has this almost absolute eloquence:

> And in the spiced Indian air by night
> Full often hath she gossiped by my side,
> And sat with me on Neptune's yellow sands,
> Marking the embarked traders on the flood;
> When we have laughed to see the sails conceive
> And grow big-bellied with the wanton wind;
> Which she, with pretty and with swimming gait,
> Following—her womb then rich with my young squire—
> Would imitate, and sail upon the land
> To fetch me trifles, and return again,
> As from a voyage, rich with merchandise.

I have deliberately chosen a passage of low emotional intensity, and this full maturing of the image in words of utterly appro-

---

[1] Because the transformation is a partial transition from one activity to another, or rather a partial development of one activity into another. It is fatal to forget that images and words are not implements that we use or prefabricated materials that we construct with, but phases respectively of the activities of imagination and speech.

priate sound is of course not the whole criterion of greatness in a poet. If it were, we should have to set Pope with Homer and Tennyson near to Sophocles. Doubtless the range and quality of the inchoate world of emotion and imagery which the poet has brought to fruition is a factor of greater import when we come to judge the stature of a completed poem. But that world becomes a veritable world only when the image veritably matures in the word, and in this maturation lies, though not all the greatness of the great poet, yet his specific formal function as a poet. In the past it has been assumed, and not merely by pedants, that language has certain principles of structure which poets will develop, but must not violate without evident justification in the aptness of a novel phrase if the image is to ripen as it should. Grammar and syntax merely record this development for pedagogic purposes, but if the record (so it would have been thought) were to become impossible to keep, the eloquence of language would have perished alike in poetry and prose. The great poets bear out this assumption. Their full and coherent eloquence, their 'maturity' in the sense I have given the word, seldom fails, even when the intensity and volume of their emotion becomes immense. Titania's fairy prattle is not more eloquent than Lear's rage:

> And thou, all-shaking thunder,
> Smite flat the thick rotundity of the world!
> Crack Nature's moulds, all germens spill at once,
> That make ingrateful man.

These gigantic lines touch the limit alike of emotion, imagery, and utterance. Shakespeare in his later plays, like Beethoven in his later quartets, can be obscure; but it is the obscurity of a force and concentration which almost shatters the medium of expression —you feel the rushing of a gale. It springs from a development which thrusts and drives beyond the maturity of his earlier and classically eloquent poetry, not from an adolescent weakness in fashioning speech.

It might perhaps be claimed that the modern poet is trying to overcome the severance of imagery and words at a lower level, and that this, if not Shakespearian eloquence, is new and valuable. It might be said that he is using his supple, half-formed material to create something analogous to the work of a deliberately non-representational painter, and such a claim might be supported by appeal to the painter's 'innocent eye' and to the current notion of abstract art.

I do not know whether modern poets have actually urged this analogy, but their practice so strongly suggests it, and it would be so interestingly false an analogy, that I shall venture to spend a little time in rebutting the claim, whether or not it has actually been made.

In the first place, the terms themselves need to be made more precise. Any modern artist knows, and the serious artists of the past assumed implicitly, that a painter must possess what since the days of the impressionists has been called 'the innocent eye'. Something of the same sort is true in every art, not least in poetry, and Benedetto Croce generalized this truth when he made absence of any distinction between fact and fancy the differentia of art in the sense of aesthetic experience. Innocence of eye in a painter means ability to eliminate from his vision all that is aesthetically irrelevant, in particular a large, mainly intellectual accretion which the man in the street commonly believes to be a part of what he actually sees. The ordinary man uses his sight so much for practical purposes that it determines the habitual nature of his vision to a far greater extent than he is aware. He 'sees' and recognizes this book on that shelf, or that tool in the kitchen drawer, as the one he wants; this tree which can serve him as a guide to that house at which he has to call; this or that cloud-mass or sunset which warns him of the storm to come. If his object is not a familiar thing, he will at least recognize it as a member of a general class, and he will call that 'strange' or 'odd' which he cannot quickly classify. The feelings which accompany his practical seeing are those naturally evoked by what is judged useful, useless, harmful, and so forth. He can, however, on occasion look at a tree, a house, a cloud, a sunset, or any other sort of visible object, and, with the different feelings appropriate to aesthetic perception, find in it not use but beauty. But he will continue to a large extent to 'see' his object as it appeared to him in his practical looking. Its elements will to that extent still be for him particular instances of classes distinguished and interrelated in a practical interest. If he now tries to paint a picture in order to express and fulfil his rather rudimentary aesthetic emotion, it will present certain tell-tale features. Emphasis will tend to fall where his practical experience has habitually isolated and individualized a familiar thing. He will try to complete an outline for each of these, and for each one of its 'important' parts which is not blatantly invisible. His half unconscious respect for these familiar boundaries will not only make his composition little more than aggregation, but lure him to put in a great deal that he does not actually see. The surest sign that his practical vision persists will be the banality of his colours, which will be mainly those by which he recognizes and classifies things every day of his life. The sky will be just blue, the clouds just white or grey, and the pillar-box just pillar-box red. Only in the most obvious cases will he notice a reflected colour. If he tries to finish his picture at home by memory because it has come on to rain, his omissions and irrelevant additions will rapidly multiply.

If a good professional painter were then to treat what we should ordinarily call the same subject, the difference in vision would become very obvious. His picture would be articulated on quite a different principle. One element, standing out with a unity of its own, might consist, if analysed in practical terms, of a bit of tree-trunk, a fleck of light on a wall well this side of it, and a distant patch of cloud, and the unity knitting these would rest on kinship and constrast between their shapes, which would be shapes not of familiar things but of what we might provisionally call fugitive *visibilia*, and between their hues and tones, which would not be recognition signals but significant in their own right. He would of course use colour to indicate solidity, and he might set a rock beside its reflection in water. But he would not then be contrasting the real with the less real, since fact is to him irrelevant. His picture as a whole would not be an aggregate of things but a pattern of masses and a harmony of hue and tone.[1] This description is full of gaps, but it may come near enough for our present purpose to defining a painter's innocence of eye. With a little effort and a little knowledge of what to look for—and what not—one can readily discover it in all good painting, and with rather more effort one can modify one's own vision in that direction.

Innocence of eye, then, is a prerequisite of any artistic creation, but it is merely a negative condition and affords no excuse for caprice. A painter can create nothing of value out of 'innocently' seen or imagined colours and shapes unless he at once elicits

---

[1] A painter rebelling against 'naturalism' may very well deliberately depict the cancellation of the practical vision. The popular verdict will then be 'distortion'.

from them and imposes on them order and design. The world of art is autonomous *vis-à-vis* the practical world, but it is not for that reason anarchic. The ultimate material source of all art is actual sensation, and if sensation develops into imagination in independence of practical exigencies it does not thereby acquire any right to be incoherent. That is equally true of 'abstract' and of 'representational' art. The distinction is apt to confuse, because artists have come to abstraction by different routes and have not always been able to describe the journey very clearly, but the vital point to grasp is that it is a relative distinction which can never conceivably become absolute if innocence of eye is a condition of art. A work of art is not a facsimile, and the most strictly representational picture, if it really is a work of art, exhibits an ordering of colour and shape which is not 'given' in our everyday, mainly practical, vision.[1] Equally the most abstract pattern of shapes and colours is still representational in the sense that it has an origin, traceable or not, in actual sensation. Be this, moreover, remembered. Abstract art may have been a restless and sometimes erratic or deliberately sensational reaction to a troublous half-century; its safe arrivals may have been fewer than the wrecks which strew the uncharted seas it has attempted to navigate; yet the best abstract painters (unlike most modern poets) have begun by showing themselves powerful and accomplished exponents of more conservative styles. A nude by Matisse or Picasso cannot be fairly judged except by someone familiar with the past history of nude painting. If the greatest pictures are still the relatively representational masterpieces of the past, it is because the formulae of abstract art are, as I have already said, mainly simplifications, new beginnings which have not yet grown into principles of design capable of comprehending and ordering any very wide content of human experience. A new principle of really universal range has come rather rarely in the history of art, but there is no reason whatever that it should not happen again.

Thus the innocent eye of the artist in general and his more abstract creations in particular could not provide the poet with any excuse for anarchy and caprice. But the fundamental fault

[1] One would say 'not immediately given in Nature', but it is hard here to speak precisely, because although our everyday vision of Nature is largely practical it is not wholly so, and in the case of people accustomed to looking at pictures and statues art has usually reacted upon it.

in the analogy to which I have suggested that the modern poet might be tempted is this. The distinctive formal character of painting is the designed expression of colour and shape, whether in abstract or representative pictures. Colour and shape are the specific medium of the painter's art. The poet's medium, on the other hand, is language, and there lies all the difference in the world. No doubt colour and shape, indeed the content of all the senses, are the stuff of poetic imagery, but the formal act of poetic vision is the maturing of imagery into speech. If the poet arrests the transition halfway his poem will be no more than half-verbalized sensuous content. Words can lift and sublimate imagery, but language has its own principles which simply cease to operate if it is dragged down to the level which it exists to transcend. Colour and shape develop their own discipline through the painter's brush, but speech at that stage of crudity can scarcely have any discipline at all.[1] Simply as musical sound, a modern poem will give far less satisfaction than an ode of Pindar read aloud to a man who is ignorant of Greek but has a sensitive ear; and the supra-sensuous element, for which poetry provides a far greater scope than any art tied to a special sense, will enter only to increase confusion, because it will emerge even less mature than colours, shapes, and sounds. Suggestion is no doubt a larger element in a poem than in a picture, and the poet perhaps has the right to demand more imaginative co-operation from his public than the painter. But the immature speech of the modern poem too often simply fails to move the mind strongly, not only when it makes no sense but because even when it does its emotional content is too raw and confused to create any powerful and lasting impact. I read modern verse eager to mark new birth throes of the power to feel, imagine, and create in words, hoping that I may at last be dazzled by 'the flash and outbreak of a fiery mind' and acclaim a triumph which compensates for the battle casualties of bold experimentation; but nearly all I read I find no more than forcible-feeble.[2] By ingenious surrealist juxtapositions the modern poet may sometimes administer a mildly stimulating shock, but

[1] In prose form James Joyce has at least demonstrated this.
[2] I was brought up to handle words, not clay, but it strikes me that British sculpture offers the spectacle of a far more vigorous revolution. It has its failures, but its successes shame the flaccid sentimentalities of the nineteenth century. Our sculptors may be temperamentally tougher than our poets, but the reason more probably is that, like painters and musicians, they are better educated than poets in the techniques which they deliberately reject.

it is momentary. He may present a chiaroscuro which flickers and beguiles for an instant, but it is a mere atmosphere which swiftly disperses because it is not a world. When Dylan Thomas wrote, something was as a rule evidently stirring in him. He can sometimes, as in *Over Sir John's Hill*, create a scene and an incident effectively. But if you set his *Ballad of the Long-legged Bait* beside *The Ancient Mariner*, which it perhaps very faintly recalls, the latter stays burning in the imagination but the former does not. Coleridge's poem was not quite great enough to escape becoming hackneyed, but is any poem of the last thirty years likely to win even that high second-class distinction? This too is notable. Dylan Thomas does not follow those moderns who use chips of colloquial idiom to give a sense of authenticity. In terms of sheer sound he can be rhythmic, melodious, and effective. But he is not then modern: his vocal effectiveness seems nearly always traceable to the sounds of older-fashioned verse which it recalls.

This poetry has its prose analogue, perhaps to some extent its actual source, in works like *Ulysses*, in which the author deliberately tries to bring to the surface the half-shaped thoughts, images, and emotions of his characters, even their transient organic sensations, before these either grow up or evaporate under the criticism of full self-consciousness. The 'stream of consciousness' is not presented by Joyce as a background to amplify and explain action—the novelist's normal technique— but for its own sake. The 'stream of consciousness', the shifting mass of more or less contingently linked ideas and feelings, has often been prized above its worth. Laws of association have been supposed to govern it, and have been dignified with the title of necessary connections. But a diversity of sensuous and imaginative material under the merely formal control of intelligence cannot, as it here and now presents itself, possess much logical coherence, and the laws, under scrutiny, quickly resolve themselves into an endless multiplicity of mere general rules. The lower levels of consciousness have, too, at times been regarded as the focus of divine inspiration, because credulous people have found it exciting to ascribe a divine origin to visions, dreams, and 'hunches', which seem to come without effort and for no obvious reason. But in fact there is nothing of particular interest in the raw stuff, as such, of human experience, and it serves the artist very ill when he takes it from the background and

gives it a central position in his work. In particular, it helps the
novelist very little towards fixing and depicting his characters.
The key to a man is not the dregs of his mind nor even its undis-
ciplined musings, and when you do drag these up to the daylight
you illuminate, paradoxical as some may think it, not this individual man but his type. *Ulysses* contains a lengthy phantasma-
goria in dialogue form centring round a Mr. Bloom. It may tell
us something about the lower-middle-class Dubliner of the early
nineteen-hundreds, but it does little towards creating Mr. Leo-
pold Bloom as an individual person.

Moreover, in order to write like this the author is compelled
to depress himself imaginatively to the level of experience which
he presents. This need not greatly disadvantage the novelist,
who can when he wishes return to an attitude of detachment
from his own creations. But the poet's mind is far more subdued
to what it works in, and if he unduly exploits its lower levels, if
he forces the subliminal prematurely over the threshold, then the
poetic product will be cretinous. And although these puny
births are in general due to weakness, there is the further danger
that the poet, hobnobbing with psychologists who do not understand their trade, may credulously accept the lower level of his
mind as a treasury of finished jewels instead of the mere mine of
raw materials which it is. He may be tempted to look down
instead of up, and to cry, not 'O for a Muse of Fire', but 'O for a
fruitful subconscious'.[1] Most modern poems are little half-

---

[1] The vogue of psycho-analysis has certainly much influenced modern imaginative writing. The psycho-analyst can sometimes discover and cure diseases which
have their roots deep down in the mind which they distort and disintegrate, but deep
analysis is not the supreme revelation of human personality. When you investigate
the foundations of a building in danger of collapse you are not discovering the
secret of its architectural individuality. Analogously, men at their lowest psychical
level differ least from one another. A Freudian case-history strikes the layman as
very singular, because he is not familiar with that sort of abnormality, but mental
as well as physical diseases are typical rather than individual. Neither do I find it
shocking or disillusioning to be told that we are all rather crudely and monotonously
erotic at the subconscious level. The race would probably die out if we were not.
What matters as a factor in individual character is a man's conscious sexual behaviour.

The modern writer's self-conscious reliance on the subconscious springs partly
also, I suspect, from a certain false ideal of spontaneity. Every athlete, every dancer,
every actor has to learn that the ability to relax irrelevant muscles is a condition of
using relevant muscles correctly, and he often finds it not less difficult to acquire.
In good writing freedom from stale conventions and other bad habits, and from
inhibitions which merely hamper, is an analogous factor. This relaxation is merely
negative, a necessary but not a sufficient condition of creation; but in a time when
the urge to create is weak it may easily pass for the whole creative act.

developed fragments of fancy, ill-nourished offspring of a grimly contracted experience. Because it is fear and frustration which have (not always consciously) narrowed and confined his experience, the modern poet is often an escapist. He does not desert from life to Arcadia—such a flight he would regard with contempt; he retreats to dim inner recesses of the spirit, and it is there that he does his daily work. The office of poetry is, or was, to change all heights and depths of experience into the aesthetic form, but he cannot stretch to a poet's full stature. He cannot let his starved progeny grow up. Because it is so indeterminate, much of his writing, even if it does not actually lapse into *lettrisme*, is not merely impossible to criticize with discrimination but not even communicable except to close associates who have assisted at its birth. Sympathizers not in the know are left to 'botch the words up fit to their own thoughts'.

I might be here again reminded of the innocent eye. I might be told that poetry, which does not state facts, has never a precisely communicable meaning. That, in one sense of meaning, is true, as we have already seen. Poetry, being art, knows no distinction between fact and fancy. Shelley's *Adonais* no more states or argues his pantheism than it asserts or tries to prove his sorrow for the death of Keats. It expresses and fulfils his emotion, transmuting it into something novel and unique. But the world of poetry is rational. *Adonais* sprang in the first place from an experience amply shared, but, even more importantly, its imagery has thrown off in full development the privacy and mere subjectivity of its natal state and grown into a significant, a universal and self-communicating, though not an intellectual, structure;

I venture in summary to offer this opening for a modern *Ars Poetica*, punctuated fairly normally for the beginner:

> De profundis! Plop the irregular mesh of your net
> down the deeps of the layered subconscious;
> hoick the faint swimming images out,
> multitudinous, inchoate, polymath,
> polyglott, polymorph, polychromatic.
> Chuck them to gasp in an alien element,
> flap and flicker inhumanly scrambled,
> touching by chance where they touch at all.
> Don't believe them too young to be printed;
> see in their writhing pure rhythm free-flowing,
> scarcely sublime but profoundly subliminal.
> Throw nothing back, it would simply be criminal:
> F-b-r and F-b-r will vastly prefer to
> publish them just as they are.

C

a very different thing from the raw image, or the cluster of them, most obscurely linked, which is so often the whole of a present-day poem. There are lines in *Adonais* itself which picture perfectly the radiation of full-grown poetry:

> The quick Dreams,
> The passion-winged Ministers of thought,
> Who were his flocks, whom near the living streams
> Of his young spirit he fed, and whom he taught
> The love which was its music, wander not,—
> Wander no more, from kindling brain to brain.

The modern poet's dreams are not for the most part quick or passion-winged; and there is little of love or music in them. Therefore they do not wander far nor kindle many brains before they die. Even when a poet's religion has survived the world's frustration and paralysis, no Miltonic trumpet sounds to overawe us with an allegory there is no mistaking, and no mystical sweetness like George Herbert's is distilled to melt hard hearts. It is certainly significant that in a faithless and unhappy age our most influential poet should be a man of faith, and Mr. T. S. Eliot's *Waste Land* is fair comment. But is it great poetry? When Mr. Eliot rebukes sin we are chastised with fastidious satire, behind which the poet scarcely hides his nausea and despair as he points, a little aloofly, to the way of salvation, and all, save an occasional sharp sword-stroke, is uttered in the manner of a man speaking 'things in doubt that carry but half sense'. Mr. Eliot's expression seems choked by the very paralysis which he combats.

The effect of economic stress on British architecture has been instructively different in form, because architecture cannot be divorced from practical use.[1] Tradition has required a building to mingle beauty and utility. The relation between the two in successful architecture is subtle and hard to analyse, but at least it can be safely said that when an architect fails to blend them truly his design and decoration appear artificial and adventitious; they suggest imposed caprice and not natural form; the building looks not beautiful but beautified. The doctrine of 'functionalism', if it means only that a building cannot be beautiful unless it efficiently fulfils its practical purpose, comes as a healthy corrective of adventitious beautification. It is a truth analogous to the

---

[1] Goethe's phrase, 'frozen music', was not happy.

truth that a completely inefficient man cannot be moral. But the principle which seems now to govern architecture in this country is the converse of this: if a building efficiently fulfils its practical purpose it is *eo ipso* beautiful. That is as false as it is false to say that if a man is efficient he is *eo ipso* moral. A merely necessary condition is mistaken for a necessary and sufficient condition. The fallacy of functionalism so understood lies in the purely economic interpretation of function. A house, or a block of flats, or a hotel, must meet the needs of its occupants by providing shelter, comfort, and domestic convenience; but its occupants are not purely economic creatures, and it is not fully functional unless it is a development and expression of human personality in a suitable environment, and is manifestly such equally to the inmates and to the passer-by.[1] If high costs confine building within strict limits of economic necessity, so much the worse, but it is absurd to make a virtue of that necessity and pervert an aesthetic principle by exalting packing-case architecture.

If we turn now to our philosophical main theme, our task, as I have already hinted,[2] becomes more complex. Modern British philosophy is essentially empiricist or positivist,[3] but so in a less intense and radical form it was in its classical and representative period. The stimuli which provoked and maintained empiricism in the seventeenth and eighteenth centuries were not frustration and fear born of calamity and economic stress; rather they were the calling in question of old political values, which was a *sequela* of religious conflict, and the general weakening of theological dogma before the twin growth of mathematics and natural science. The same empiricist, down-to-earth tendency, moreover, continued well into the nineteenth century, and it is to be found in the nominalism of William of Occam, long before there was any weakening of Christian dogma. As a recent French writer puts it, *un empiriste sommeille chez tout Anglais.*[4]

The answer which I suggest, and shall throughout this book endeavour to defend, is this. It is a truism but none the less true that the Englishman—and the Lowland Scot, too—is essentially a practical man. Even our painting, our sculpture, and our

[1] As is, for example, the Dorchester Hotel in Park Lane, one of the few good twentieth-century buildings in London. The east side of Berkeley Square provides a dismal contrast. [2] See p. 5.
[3] I use the terms at present quite loosely and generally.
[4] Pucelle, *L'idéalisme en Angleterre.*

architecture, though not the best of our poetry, has been, up to the twentieth century, marked more often than not by a certain sober practicality of approach. That there is some connection between empiricism and the practical bent in man nobody would deny, and I shall argue in the next chapter that it is yet closer than is commonly supposed, so close in fact that empiricism can only be called philosophical by a courtesy with which it is perhaps almost time to dispense. There have of course been minor outbreaks of empiricism in all ages and places since man began to philosophize, but when a native spring of speculation began at last to flow continuously in this country, it was bound, if I am right, to be strongly empiricist in flavour. It was further likely that, if an epoch of alternating hot and cold war were to bring on us unparalleled material and spiritual destruction and submerge us almost totally in the struggle to live, the empiricist impetus of our philosophical thinking would be doubly redoubled. It would be assumed without doubt or question, even without consciousness, that there is no world but the world as the practical agent envisages it in order to act; for that is the full flower of empiricism. And that, I suggest, is what began to happen with the first world war.

Our first task, then, will be to consider the general connection between empiricism and practical activity, and to that we will now pass with a final comment on the age we live in. While poetry wilts[1] natural science and mathematics flourish. Chemists and physicists of the lowest ability run no risk of unemployment. The word 'scientific' is more energetically and profitably exploited in commercial advertisement and other forms of propaganda than it ever was. In the next chapter we will draw a conclusion.

[1] I have said that our best poetry is not tinged with practicality. That is also true of our worst. Modern poetry has merely been strangled by the direct impact of hard times. There is, on the other hand, evident kinship between (a) the great British poets and the British nineteenth-century idealist thinkers, and (b) the 'Augustan' poets and the classical empiricists. In reading Pope one can never forget the verse-maker, the infinitely ingenious technician.

CHAPTER II

THE PRESUPPOSITIONS OF ECONOMIC ACTION

I AM committed to examining and defending the thesis that empiricism and practical activity are intimately connected and, more particularly, that empiricism, whether or not it knows its own foundations, is based on the assumption that there is no world but the world as the practical agent envisages it in order to act.

To make this thesis clear, two distinctions must be drawn within practical activity. The first and more familiar is the difference between moral activity and utilitarian or, as Benedetto Croce called it, economic activity. Secondly, we must distinguish and consider by itself that ascertainment of fact which is a *sine qua non* of all efficient action and an essential part of economic activity.

The difference between economic and moral action is as deep a difference as human experience affords, but although Thomas Hobbes was not the only thinker who has come near to conceiving man as a purely economic creature, no man's whole life, nor even any brief stretch of it, was ever sheer economic activity. In what follows[1] the term 'economic agent' will signify an abstraction. It will mean no whole man whether primitive or civilized, but man in so far as his *nisus in esse suo* is egoistic, is directed to the end of maintaining, expanding, and enjoying his own life as a singular individual. I shall accordingly try to endow him only with such capacities as he needs in order to desire, envisage, and pursue his end. It is, however, easy to distort and misrepresent any element provisionally abstracted from a complex, and I know that I may not always succeed in keeping him in focus.

---

[1] My debt to Croce will be obvious, although I cannot accept a good deal of his doctrine. Plato and Aristotle had already worked out the contrast, and to a considerable degree the more precise relation, between economic and moral action.

That which in particular the economic agent aims at getting is what Aristotle called a μέριστον ἀγαθόν, a 'divisible good', something such that the more there is for him the less there is for anybody else. His end is his private end, and if he co-operates with other men and at first sight appears to pursue an end common to himself and them, really he is pursuing an end which is merely conjoint with theirs: the coincidence of advantage which makes his co-operation prudent is for the economic agent merely contingent.[1] A tradition which we accepted in Chapter I as on the whole true makes economic agency the dominant characteristic of primitive man still absorbed in the struggle to exist.[2] Something like it, its analogue at a more instinctive level, has been commonly supposed to characterize brute animals, and this analogy is at once suggested when Croce uses the word *vitalità* to express the economic moment of spirit.

In civilized man economic action takes very various shapes as his conception of the life he desires to maintain and expand alters and develops. It never disappears, but it comes normally to subserve activities of another kind, moral activities, which transform its nature because their end, though always the agent's own end, is no longer solely his own;[3] and in so far as it is not so transformed but continues to dominate instead of becoming subservient, its hitherto naïve and amoral egoism is perverted to immorality. Here, then, is our first distinction. It is familiar enough, but it is not always well understood. In the *abstract* economic agent, pursuing his own individual end, there is nothing moral or immoral in what he does. The only criterion of value which can be applied to his actions is extrinsic: it is efficiency. We can only ask, Do they or do they not serve his purpose well? But the converse is not true, and a great deal of bad ethical theory has sprung from the mistaken belief that it is. The question whether the action of a moral agent is morally

---

[1] Action by a herd of wild animals or Germans constitutes no exception, for in such action the agent is the herd-under-its-leader rather than the members of the herd as individuals.

[2] The economic character of primitive peoples has perhaps been exaggerated, but this does not affect the present argument.

[3] To act morally is not normally to sacrifice, nor even to disregard as indifferent, one's private economic ends. It is to transform them by integration in an end which is at once wider and of a higher kind. Morality may entail economic self-sacrifice in a given situation, and the ability to face it resolutely when the occasion demands is a pre-requisite of the moral life, but if you equate the two you leave no stuff to make the moral life out of.

good or bad does not exclude the question whether it is efficient or inefficient: it contains it. Economic action does not presuppose moral action, but moral action does presuppose economic action; for you cannot will and do a moral action without willing and doing, as an integral element of it,[1] an economic action, and it is just as false to suppose that it makes no difference to the morality of your action whether it is efficient or inefficient as it is to judge the morality of an action solely by its results. That is why Hell is paved with good intentions. To pursue this ancient topic of debate, however, would take us too far afield. From time to time we shall be compelled to resume it, but the distinction as I have drawn it will, I hope, have set the abstraction of a purely economic activity in a clearer light.

The economic agent has emotions. He desires an ideally imagined end which he sets before himself. But if he is to realize it, if he is to act efficiently, he must adopt a much more purely cognitive attitude. Before he selects what means to his end he shall take, he must ascertain the actual situation in so far as it is relevant to his purpose; he must find out how the land lies; he must look before he leaps. His desired end will decide initially the limits of relevance, and it will help to guide his selection of means; but if it is to do that effectively he must apprehend it intellectually as a target rather than emotionally as what he loves and longs for. Desire, that is, must determine only the antecedent of the hypo-thetical imperative. Within the relevant actual situation the economic agent will select and attend to this and that thing, apprehending it in economic terms as helpful or harmful, or as for the time being indifferent. The colours and shapes of things and their other physical qualities will all be significant to him only as specifying these general economic characters. Because he is a strictly economic creature, he will not experience things as possessing any intrinsic value, but strictly as means and not ends. He will not, for example, feel and perceive them aesthetically; but because they are fraught with meaning for his economic destiny, his perception of them will be charged with feelings of hope and fear, confidence and mistrust. But his success depends upon his coolness, and he must again divest himself of emotion. The situation which confronts him is contingent, but it is hard fact. It can perhaps be changed, but it must first be known as it

---

[1] Without which it would not be an action at all.

actually is. It is the reality which he ignores at his peril.[1] He must colour it neither with his terrors and repugnances nor with any wishful thinking. He will succeed through knowing the economic characters of things, not through feeling them. If we seize him in this strictly detached and cognitive activity and make a second abstraction, we may call him 'the economic observer'.

We have met the economic observer before. He was embodied in the would-be artist whose picture turned out to be less a work of art than a rudimentary sketch-map,[2] and that artistic failure offers a good initial clue to the object-world of the economic observer. In that world the most important elements are the particular 'things' which he selects or, more precisely, constructs selectively, within a context limited by relevance to an economic end. These things, although they are particulars, present an internal diversity of qualities and relations. If, however, we first view the economic observer's world broadly and generally, we shall find that the things it consists of, whatever their internal analysis, are for him all members of classes. As we saw in the case of the would-be artist, he recognizes things as instances of classes which he has already determined at least provisionally. Classification is in fact a constant factor in his activity. Thus his immediately relevant situation has a wider context from the first, and it is easy to see that in a certain sense this wider context is limitless. He may construct a class of things with a known or an unknown finite number of members, the stars, for example, of the Great Bear, or the stars of the Milky Way. But a finite class is always selected by him within a wider class which has possible as well as actual members, and a class containing possible as well as actual members is indefinite if not infinite. Without classes containing possible as well as actual members the economic observer could not recognize a single *new* instance, and *a fortiori* his estimate of the situation could never be a basis for predicting probabilities, since it would carry no implication that the future would in any degree resemble the past, nor even that a verb in the future tense bore any meaning.

Primarily the economic observer classifies things as things. He classifies them, that is to say in sophisticated language, taking

[1] Reality as Mr. Bertrand Russell conceives it when he writes: 'The feeling of reality is a feeling akin to respect: it belongs *primarily* to whatever can do things to us without our voluntary co-operation.' *Analysis of Mind*, 1921, p. 186.
[2] See pp. 11-12.

as the intension of the class those qualities which he finds he can with fair safety treat as the defining properties of a thing, as a group of qualities whose coincidence in a new instance will pretty certainly enable recognition of that thing. But he can perfectly well, and often must, classify things in respect of a single quality, or a single relation in which they stand. To be particulars in some respect similar to one another is the only qualification required for membership of a class.[1] Moreover, the economic observer's things, although they have a certain persistence, change in quality and relation, and this means that although his first concern may be the classification of things as things, yet he must, if he is to predict probabilities, also classify things in respect to the events which happen to them; and he may find it convenient to abstract altogether from things and to classify events simply as instancing types of happening. When one remembers that events, if they are to have practical significance, must be apprehended in some sort of causal series, it is easy to see that the object-world of the economic observer is limitless. Philosophers of a certain way of thinking may argue about first causes, but causal series as it presents itself to the economic observer is essentially indefinite regress into the past and indefinite progress into the future. He takes just so long a stretch of it as he needs.

This bare sketch may suggest that the economic observer's object-world is a mere unlimited and monotonous radiation of class-members from a centre of perceptual attention. We shall see that it is not quite so indeterminate as that, but we shall also see that the element in it of determinate order and system is always relatively local. There is always a limitless 'beyond' which the economic observer cannot order and systematize. Meanwhile this sketch requires both expansion and filling in.

A world 'radiating from a centre of perceptual attention' has a subjective, even a solipsistic, ring. It sounds like the vision of a Robinson Crusoe stripped of any past experience of other human beings and quite unable to recognize the significance of Man Friday's footprint. But neither the economic agent nor the economic observer is as abstract as that. They are both aware of

[1] There is no logical reason against constructing a class which has no members. A finite class is not a sort of containing pigeon-hole of limited volume, and a null class is not a container contracted to vanishing point. Classes are not things but classes of things, and classes contain other classes in a sense quite different from that in which they contain things.

persons as well as of things, and although we have yet to consider the nature of this awareness, one obvious consequence of it is that the economic observer takes his world of things as common to himself and other persons. Nor does the economic observer classify at random. He can if he chooses set up a class wherever he finds two similars, but his ultimate purpose in classification is to make useful inferences. He can only do that on a basis of relation between the characters which constitute the intensions of his classes. The latter must therefore fall into some sort of order, and the word 'classification' itself implies this. His general method of ordering classes is that which springs naturally from the fact that his world radiates from a centre of perceptual attention directed on concrete particular things. His scheme will expand from the concrete to the abstract, the complexity of the intension diminishing as the class grows wider and the number of its members greater. The ordering of Nature in genera and species is the most familiar product of his method, and equally familiar is the fact that the indefinite multiplicity and diversity of particular individuals defies exhaustive classification in *infimae species*. To classify things at all the economic observer is compelled to select some of their properties as definitory and treat others as relatively accidental. Even so, he can often only escape cross-division in constructing his class-order by deciding which of two equally possible *fundamenta divisionis* is likely to work best in practice. The very nature of his perceptually centred observation forbids his world the unity of classification in a single order; but his business does not require it. All that he needs is local class-orders provisionally but usefully determined within an indefinitely extending context.

To infer and predict, the economic observer must do more than classify and order classes. He must *connect* the characters which things or events instantiate into a system within which fresh connections can be inferred. Such a system of characters has a tighter unity than an order of classes. The concept of the human organism, for example, has a much closer knit unity of coherence than the concept of the order of mammals. It is a whole of mutually determining elements, and within it relations are for the most part internal to their terms; whereas within any order of classes the relations of class to class and of member to member are taken as purely external. Such a system is not, of course, a perfectly coherent whole, a fully and transparently intelligible unity in difference, and every connection of characters in it is subject to verification in an experience of the instantiating particular thing or event; for because he is concerned with action, a particular situation and particular things and events in it remain always the centre of the economic observer's world. Taken apart from the empirical test, a decision which the economic observer accepts as presented without grounds but permitting no appeal, the connections within his system are hypothetical and the connected characters are indefinite, not determinate but merely determinable, and so far like classes. But even hypothetical connection of characters is more concrete than inclusion or co-ordination; it is connection of universals, not ordering of classes. To speak of 'universals' in the plural is reasonable, I think, in trying to describe the empirical thinking of the economic observer, but this plurality is symptomatic of the limitation of the economic observer's horizon by a practical purpose, and even he has a glimpse of the universal as more than a plurality of universals. Speaking more strictly, universals become a plurality only as severed from system and taken as intensions of classes. Characters connected in systems are more truly described as the universal differentiating or, if we borrow class terminology, specifying itself towards an individuality which is not singular. Because the system is a connected unity and not a class of classes, it is itself the universal; or, in other words, the universal is not a class, because it is identity in difference. But in the world of the economic observer a system is still one among other and unconnected systems, and it is still something hypothetical and abstract which he has to take as complemented by, or realized in (it is hard to say which), the particular occurrent instance, the actual thing or event. The two factors remain unreconciled: the particular thing or event apes the individuality of system, while the universal is broken into a plurality of universals which reflects the mere multiplicity of empirically experienced singular things or events.

To exemplify system in the economic observer's world I took the concept of the human organism, and it will be obvious that we have been watching the economic observer pass from empiric to scientist. It will also be obvious that I took a favourable, perhaps the most favourable, example to support my contention that in system the universal is, even for the economic observer, rather more than a class or a class of classes. It was indeed once common among philosophers to call any system of closely connected elements an 'organic whole', but we must not exaggerate the extent to which the economic observer recognizes system as identity in difference. In sciences more abstract than physiology system is less of a concrete whole and approximates more nearly to a mere order of classes. Possibly in mathematics the universal vanishes in the class, but there lies a controversy beyond our present scope. It is in any case perfectly clear from the progress of scientific inquiry that the economic observer tends more and more to simplify his subject-matter in the direction of class-order and mathematics. The biologist seeks aid from the chemist, the chemist from the physicist, and the physicist almost turns into a mathematician. The decision in favour of this steady swing towards abstraction rests with the economic observer and with no one else. If by envisaging the relevant situation more simply he can more easily find the signal he is looking for, if by this means he can more quickly and accurately predict the event and more successfully serve action, then he is so far more faithfully observing his world. What is real to the economic observer is what it pays to know, not anything which has value in itself. To complain that the biologist is missing something when he treats organism in mechanical instead of teleological terms is beside the point, unless it can be shown that what he misses is a better chance of success in predicting and acting.

Clearly the question whether this coincidence of science and economic observation is complete or partial, necessary or accidental, is beginning to become pressing, but before it is answered we shall do well to revert for a moment to our first abstraction, to the complete economic agent from whom we abstracted the economic observer.

Economic action presupposes a basis—if I may use the word without prejudice—of sense, which is not a basis merely of cognition. This is not easy to describe, but it may provisionally be called an immediacy of sensuous feeling which develops itself into an appetitive and a cognitive factor or moment. These are at first hardly distinct from one another within an experience which is still predominantly experience of pleasure and pain because it is still not very far developed beyond immediate feeling.

In talking here of a process of development I have in mind not merely the historical transition between infantile and adult experience, or between the experience of a more and a less primitive type of economic man. I am thinking primarily of that rather mysterious sense of passage and development from one mode of experience to another, which we can all become conscious of, if we reflect, at almost any moment of our waking lives, and even in the transition from sleep to waking. We make, for example, a judgment of sense-perception, and if we look back on it we know that before we judged we perceived, and that before we perceived we just sensated. We act, and we know that before we acted we suffered that tension between the actual and the ideally imagined situation which is called desire, and that before we consciously desired we simply felt the pain of an unformulated conflict. In each of these series there is transition from one mode of experience to another and less elementary mode, and there is also a passage to fresh content. Yet the earlier mode persists together with the later and not wholly superseded by it, and the content experienced in the earlier mode, although it develops into and as the content of the later mode, yet does so incompletely and remains together with it not fully absorbed. That is why I felt some hesitation in using the word 'basis' to express the relation of the sensuous to the more intelligent element in economic activity.

In feeling and desiring,[1] in imagining a merely ideal situation, and in the act of will in which he identifies himself with his ideal end, the economic agent experiences in modes which are different in kind from the detached cognitive attitude wherewith, *qua* economic observer, he confronts that relevant actual situation which he must know in order to act efficiently. The content of his cognitive activity is an object which he distinguishes from himself. It is hard objective fact which may help or hinder him. He may be able to change it, but it is no part of his own person. On the other hand, his feeling, desiring, imagining, and willing are experiences, *Erlebnisse*, much more intimately his own. They are the enjoyment, in Alexander's sense, of a content which is

---

[1] I do not wish to suggest that feeling is a specific mode of experiencing, as is, for example, the emotion of desire. Rather it is a phase out of which experience in no mode, even in cognition of an object, ever completely passes. It is the 'basis' of experience viewed genetically, but it also persists both in the aesthetic and the economic feelings which attach to sense-perception, and of course conspicuously in desire itself. See further on this terminologically difficult topic, pp. 63 ff.

always, though in different degrees, *Selbstgefühl*, self-feeling. Of the same kind is his experience in exercising those subrational knacks and skills which are linked with physical capacities and play a vital part in economic action. Between the two in kind, perhaps, lies that deliberation (about both ends and means) which is characteristic of practical activity.

This difference of kind within economic activity is nevertheless subject to a qualification which becomes of very great importance as the scope of the economic observer expands: it does not entail a perfectly rigid distinction of content. The economic agent necessarily makes a certain distinction within the self. His body can be an object to him and he uses it somewhat as he uses with it a tool. But he counts it a part of himself somehow intermediate between (*a*) a periphery of objects quite detached and separate from him, and (*b*) a centrally experiencing element which he calls his mind. The latter he regards as the permanent inner core of himself, but (and this is the important point) his abiding consciousness of particular self-identity does not preclude a constant shifting of the boundary between self and not-self, an alternating contraction and expansion of himself as the practical situation changes, which leads him often to externalize as physical objects certain elements of his body which had been subjective and 'internal'.[1] He may even, while he is using them, regard the pen he writes with, the sword he fights with, or the false teeth he bites with, as parts or extensions of himself, but as mere detached physical objects when he lays them by.[2] We shall see later that by virtue of this fluctuation between self and not-self it becomes possible for the economic observer in a certain sense to treat even mind itself as an object.[3]

It is time once more to abstract the economic observer from the economic agent in whom we have been merging him. The economic agent's world, as we have seen, widens as his purposes expand. An action, like all else in that world, including himself,

---

[1] It is dangerous to forget that these terms, if indispensable, are metaphysical. In the 'external world' things are outside or inside each other in space, but the external world is external to the self only in the sense that for the self it is not-self, and only by the same metaphor can an element of the self be called 'internal'. When I perceive material things as spatially external to my body I am experiencing, economically observing, both them and my body as objects in space.

[2] The attitude of a woman to (*a*) the clothes she is wearing and (*b*) the clothes of last year's fashion which she 'wouldn't be seen dead in' is analogous.

[3] See pp. 74-5.

is primarily a particular. Yet a series of particular actions leading to the realization of a particular end has always in some degree, and in a greater degree as civilization develops, a universal aspect. The actions are connected in a plan which soon extends beyond the immediate end, and many trains of action with different starting-points may converge to one end. The agent thus acquires through experience general rules of action, rules of what modern jargon calls 'know-how'. On the other side, the actual situation must from the very moment it can be called a situation have some context beyond what the economic observer perceives, and his 'knowing-that' soon expands into an accumulation of knowledge which is not immediately needed for action but is likely in various degrees of likelihood to be necessary for future action. Nor is all of this accumulated information a mere catalogue of particular facts. The more important elements of it must, like grain for storage, be dried to preserve it: it must be classified and genera-lized. A convenient division of labour soon separates the collector and researcher quite sharply from the user. Once this economic division is made, the collector in a special field defined by human purpose quickly discovers that he needs more generalized researchers to help him, and there is no theoretical limit to check the activity of research in extent or direction. In discussing classification and system we have seen something of the texture of the objective world which this unreserved exploring of the economic situation brings to light. But its structure, if it has one, has seemed so far very vague and indefinite, and this question of structure now demands an answer.

It appears to me that Kant's account, in the first Critique, of the world as the possible object of human knowledge gives a fair rough answer, provided that we allow ourselves to ignore some of its ambiguities and remember that it is philosophical, whereas economic man, whether as agent or observer, is not a philosopher. Kant is reflecting on the ultimate implications of what he regards as knowledge, on the metaphysical implications of its possibility; but such questions are wholly alien to economic man, because their answer could not possibly affect economic action.

Kant contends that man's experiences, however particular in their emphasis and however diverse and miscellaneous they may be, constitute for him a unity inasmuch as they are for him one and all *his* experiences. This identity of his self-consciousness does not merely unify the objects which he actually and directly experiences: it unifies them together with any possible object which he might experience. It guarantees him, that is to say, a unitary objective world of possible experience. It is a unity of apperception, at once a subjective and an objective unity, and without it man could be aware neither of himself as a single persisting *ego* nor of any coherent objective world.

Kant holds that this unity of apperception explicates itself in a system of elements which are at once forms of human awareness and at the same time structural characters of man's world of possible experience. These are the forms of space and time, and also at any rate the first nine schematized categories, which progressively determine any possible object of knowledge as extensive and intensive quantum, substance and accident, cause and effect, and interaction of substances through their accidents.

It must be noted that Kant's unity of apperception imparts its peculiar character to the forms which more or less systematically explicate it. The objective world, on his account, is a unity only of possible experience, and it is a unity only because every element of it is the possible object of an identical experient. Thus, although subject and object are strictly correlative terms, the unity of apperception does not constitute the objective world as a systematic individual whole. It leaves a quite indefinite multiplicity of possible objects of experience unified only to the extent that all of them are necessarily such as to fall within the field of an identical experiencing subject. And the forms of space and time and the categories, though they do further determine the nature and relations of possible objects of experience, set no bounds to the indefinite multiplicity of those objects and in no way determine the actual specific characters which in empirical experience we find objects to possess. The particular elements of the objective world, apart from their spatio-temporal and categoreal characters, are given in experience as contingent, not as self-conditioned but as determined *ab extra* by an indefinite series of conditions. And the universal which they particularize is a class-concept, which does not dictate the number of its barely identical instances, because it is a concept which belongs only to a world of possible experience.

This Kantian world, which is for Kant the possible and the only possible object of human knowledge in the strict sense of knowledge, is pretty nearly, I think, the generalized situation which the economic observer must grasp in this or that relevant detail if he is to act efficiently, provided that we make allowance for the progress of natural science since Kant's day, and provided that we ignore the philosophical inferences which Kant drew from his analysis of human knowledge. For Kant this objective world of human knowledge is a phenomenal world, a world of appearances which implies a real but unknown world of things in themselves. But for the economic observer no such distinction exists. He contrasts apparent and real only within the Kantian world of appearance, and for him the real is what does not belie its apparent economic significance. Kant holds that the unity of apperception, the categories, and the forms of space and time are *a priori*, since they are conditions of the very possibility of a coherent experience and therefore not inferable from experience. The economic observer certainly accepts them, or something sufficiently like them, as structural characters of his world; but he merely assumes them, and *ex hypothesi* he could not raise any question concerning either their psychological origin or the logical ground on which they are to be assumed—he can be neither a Kantian nor a radically empiricist philosopher—since the answers to these questions could have no bearing on action. The Kantian objective world is permeated with contingency because it is not self-conditioning reality but phenomenon. It is no more than the context of a possible experience radiating indefinitely from a centre which is the generalized human subject of experience. The economic observer, on the other hand, believes that the world extending beyond his perceptual focus exists just as actually as does that part of it which he here and now perceives. He thinks of it as a public world which is everywhere the possible object of his own or any other man's perceptual experience, but is nevertheless actual whether anybody is actually perceiving it or not. This 'naïve realism', as it has been contemptuously called when offered with philosophical pretensions, may not even square logically with his conceptions of class and system, but the economic observer certainly assumes it, and it is not merely an adequate but an indispensable assumption for economic action. With these reservations, however, the Kantian objective world is pretty much

D

the expanded and generalized situation of the economic observer
of Kant's own time.

Kant regarded mathematics and physics as knowledge *par
excellence*. A main purpose of the *Critique of Pure Reason* is to show
how they are possible. The cat whose struggling has long been
obvious to the reader is now out of the bag. If I have truly
described how economic knowledge expands, the 'pure' scientist
and the 'pure' mathematician will not be disinterested theorists
whose results, achieved in quite a different interest, the economic
observer borrows as he needs them, but thinkers—even if they
are apt to forget it—who are themselves engaged in the task
of economic observation. Science will coincide with the industry
of the economic observer not κατὰ συμβεβηκός but ἁπλῶς. The
difference between the scientist and the economic observer as I
first described him will rest simply on an inevitable division of
labour which first separates the collector from the user of information, and then produces fresh types of collector as exploration and
collection spread farther and farther beyond any immediate need
for useful information. In total war, which reveals the economic
agent far more starkly than any primitive society, this centrifugal
expansion from the immediately relevant situation is abruptly
reversed. A military force on active service, if you abstract from
any moral purpose which may inspire it, is pretty nearly the
economic agent writ large. Its intelligence staff exactly exempli-
fies the economic observer. On the outbreak of war the intelligence officer and the technical expert in the field are reinforced by
a vast rear echelon of 'theorists' recalled to a directly relevant
situation from occupations which at first sight, but I think at
first sight only, seem quite different in kind from the wartime
duties now laid upon them. A professor of physics, having
worked out the mathematics of a spinning nose-dive, learns to
fly and tests his results in person, and even the 'pure' mathematician may come to realize that there is nothing in the field of his
peace-time labours which might not possibly have a military use;
for presumably there is some date in history at which the permanent cessation of research in pure mathematics would have
indirectly precluded the possibility of all the subtler modern
means of war. I have none the less, by treating science and mathematics as no more than a part of man's practical adventure,
committed myself to a position likely to excite in orthodox

circles the nearest present-day equivalent to horror at blasphemy against the Holy Ghost. It will seem a shocking and antiquated confusion of science and mathematics with technology, and even Plato, it will be said, knew better than that, at any rate in respect of mathematics. I will try to summarize the outcry in two connected rhetorical questions. Is it not ludicrously parochial to hold that science and mathematics reveal the world merely as the actual or possible arena of human economic struggle, particularly in the case of pure mathematics, which contains only *a priori* propositions and is quite possibly identical with formal logic? Have I failed to notice the obvious passion of great scientists and great mathematicians, even of decent scientists and decent mathematicians, in the pursuit of truth for its own sake? To the first question, so far at any rate as it concerns science, one might reply that since the geocentric celestial mechanism of Aristotle dissolved before Galileo's telescope, and since science rejected the idea of creation as 'a diapason ending full in man', the inorganic universe in yielding its secrets to ever more subtilized scientific observation has revealed no *raison d'être* whatsoever of its own.[1] The starry heavens, save to the aesthetic eye, have grown duller and duller, progressively more pointless. The effort to sink parochial pride and explore without prejudice—if that is what science is—has produced no glimpse of a metropolis.

The second question may seem to voice a more respectable objection. The answer is crucial. The whole position for which I contend rests upon it. No truth can have value for its own sake except it be the truth about (or, better, of) that which has value in itself. Save where knowledge is power, why should any man desire passionately to study that in which nothing is intrinsically better or worse than anything else? 'Blind to good and evil, reckless of destruction, omnipotent matter rolls on its relentless way,' wrote the youthful Bertrand Russell[2] and, stripped of rhetorical personification, it still seems a fair statement of the scientific view. To explore such a material world, except in order to exploit it where one can and evade it where it threatens irresistibly, would appear to be a quite irrational waste of time.

---

[1] Nor could it, since *ex hypothesi* it has for science no intrinsic value. Ever since science diverged definitely from philosophy and found its own proper function, the scientist has revealed mechanical causation, or at any rate virtually constant sequence, but he has not attempted to show reasons.

[2] *Philosophical Essays*, 1910, p. 70.

And if matter is devoid of intrinsic value, even more clearly so is the world of pure mathematics.

Why, then, is it believed that science and mathematics can be ends in themselves? We will consider two or three possible answers.

The first is easily dismissed. The solution of a scientific or mathematical problem is sometimes called 'beautiful', the suggestion being that it gives the author and his appreciative colleagues aesthetic satisfaction. I suspect that 'beautiful' in such a context means nothing more specific than 'admirable as excellent of its kind', but even if neat solutions of scientific and mathematical problems have an aesthetic and therefore intrinsic value, this is emphatically not the intrinsic value which belongs to knowledge, and only as momentarily turned artists do the mathematician and the scientist enjoy it. The geometer, as Aristotle remarked, is not concerned with the fact that the circle is the most beautiful of plane figures. Few scientists and mathematicians would, I think, rest their claim on this ground.

To mistake means for ends is the commonest infirmity of busy men, and indeed if one were never so deluded, if one could never forget that practical effort has no final end, life were scarcely to be endured. How natural, then, that researchers so remote from the immediate focus of practical action should come to feel their industry as something intrinsically satisfying. I doubt, however, whether this answer is more than partial, although it may well be true that, as the best way to achieve happiness is often not consciously to pursue it, so the scientist who ignores utility in his research is likely in the end to be the most useful.

No one would question the high intellectual integrity of most good scientists, nor their intense conviction that scientific speculation should be free from any authoritarian interference or direction. Neither can it be doubted that the progress of science is bound up with this liberal faith. Yet from the premiss that science owes no allegiance to any type of dictator some scientists may have concluded, falsely as I believe, that science is autonomous in the sense that its nature is undetermined by any relation to practice. But the conviction that science should be free from religion or politics is a moral conviction. The man of science is capable of it because he is a man and not simply a highly specialized and rarefied economic observer. It arises because he knows

that science in the hands of moral men can serve a moral end.
Such a man of science has decided that, although science in itself
is entirely amoral, yet it is morally right that man should acquire
all possible power, morally wrong that he should cease exploring
in order to exploit. Whether in fact he is right, or whether
Samuel Butler's Erewhonians knew better, is quite beside the
point. His decision that the risk ought to be taken is a moral one,
and it incidentally makes very plain the connection between
science and practice. It is none the less more than probable that
men of science do draw the false conclusion of which I spoke.
It is at least a less dangerous error than the belief that the best
hope of escaping the perils of this atomic and immoral age lies
in the advance of the psychological and so-called 'social' sciences
pari passu with the natural.[1]

There is another answer which carries more weight, and to
examine it may also help to define more positively my own position, which must so far have seemed somewhat negative. I take
it, or at least the first part of it, from the lips of an actual scientist.
'The isolated knowledge obtained by a group of specialists in a
narrow field,' writes Professor Schrödinger, 'has in itself no
value whatsoever, but only in its synthesis with all the rest of
knowledge, and only inasmuch as it really contributes in this
synthesis towards answering the demand τίνες δὲ ἡμεῖς; Who
are we?'[2] If, as I presume, 'all the rest of knowledge' is not to be
confined exclusively to scientific and mathematical knowledge,
this statement is not scientific but philosophical. It suggests
that (*a*) some scientists, consciously philosophizing because in
any whole man the philosophic urge is liable to find expression,

---

[1] Very distinguished men of science have voiced that view, forgetting that the
psychological and social sciences, if they really are sciences, are *per se* just as amoral
as their natural sisters or as mathematics, just as useful a basis of information for
brainwashing and the enslavement of men's minds by propaganda as for the pro-
motion of psychical and social health. *Mein Kampf* and *Das Kapital* are full of good
hints for the social scientist. If it is morally right that man should take the risk of
acquiring all possible power, then the psychological and social sciences, if they can
enable prediction and action, have the same claim on our attention as the other
sciences; but to suppose that they *par excellence* can teach us self-control and forti-
tude, wisdom and compassion, or provide us with some equally effective synthetic
substitute, is the very stupidest confusion of the economic with the moral. It is
genuinely tragic, though history offers many parallels, to watch science, which in
the seventeenth, eighteenth, and nineteenth centuries was the most powerful of
weapons against obscurantism and tyranny, become the dominant superstition
of the twentieth.
[2] *Science and Humanism*, Cambridge, 1951. Professor Schrödinger is not here
considering the economic value of science at all.

have seen that although science and mathematics *per se* yield a purely economic view of the world, yet they do *in synthesis with other knowledge* contribute to a philosophical view; but that (*b*) other scientists have been led by their incomplete grasp of this fact to interpret it as meaning that science and mathematics *per se* can yield intrinsically valuable truth. I should like to interpret and elaborate Professor Schrödinger's remark as follows. If the absence of value in the world of natural science were a sheer absence, the natural world would be totally alien to us. We could not know it in order to use it, and a purely theoretical curiosity about it would be not merely idle but impossible, because Nature (and indeed man himself) would be unintelligible to man. But Nature is in fact that out of which man develops, and he remains always himself in a measure natural. Without that basis of identity with Nature he could not distinguish and contrast himself with Nature—it is a necessary though not a sufficient condition of his understanding both terms—and he could not use Nature as a means, whether as nutriment or instrument. Nature as the object of economico-scientific observation lacks not value but intrinsic value. Value as a means it has essentially, and it is a significant, though constantly paralleled, fact that the word 'value' means primarily economic value, value in exchange, and has been exalted to mean 'goodness' in a general sense, because 'good' was tending to acquire a purely ethical meaning.

Thus the absence of value in the world of natural science and mathematics is not a sheer but a significant absence, a privation. It is by contrast with a world of intrinsic values, and by contrast based, as significant contrast must be, on partial identity, that the world of science and mathematics becomes of theoretical interest to man. The interest which we take perforce in the contrast between the actual situation and the unrealized economic end which presupposes it, is practical; but if this contrast is viewed as a first stage in the contrasting of the merely extrinsically valuable world of mathematics and physics with the whole system of human intrinsic values, the interest becomes theoretical and the knowledge attained valuable for its own sake. But the interest is then a philosophical and not a scientific interest. Danger threatens only when a man of science philosophizing, or a philosophical idolater of science, assumes that this interest can be satisfied on this side of the scientific horizon and within the limits of scientific method; when, that is, he remains dominated by the economic conception of things, which is proper to science but not to philosophy.

We have found that the intelligibility of both man and Nature depends upon their partial identity as upon a necessary but not sufficient condition. The sense in which their contrast is based on a privation and not a sheer absence of value in Nature may become clearer if we now further examine this intelligibility, if we consider again what are the terms in which the natural scientist understands Nature.

In the object-world of mathematics and natural science nothing is in itself better or worse, but there is, as we saw earlier in this chapter, some systematic connection. Its precise nature is not here of the first importance. Logicians, and also professional mathematicians and scientists when some intractable problem forces them back to reflect on their methods, may dispute whether events in the world of physics obey rigid laws of mechanical causation or only statistical rules of probability; they may question whether the bulk of mathematical truths follow in deductive sequence from a few self-evident premisses, or whether after all those premisses must be mutually supporting if they are in turn to support the conclusions drawn from them; but in any case there must be principles, types of system and laws or rules of behaviour, to illuminate and make intelligible the world of natural science and mathematics, although these principles do not illuminate their world in terms of intrinsic value.

The suggestion I make is that this mere intelligibility of Nature, which has a necessary but not sufficient condition in the basic identity of Nature and man, has a further and more important source. I suggest that the light thrown on their objects by the laws and types of system is a borrowed light. I suspect that the scientist, even the mathematician, understands his own principles because he understands certain other principles which do characterize something which can be better or worse.

It might be objected that *qua* economic observer the scientist could have no inkling of any such principles. But the economic observer, whom we have treated in abstraction from the economic agent, is only the economic agent in a certain observational capacity. Before the economic observer can exist to be abstracted, the economic agent has had to develop this capacity in himself and shape, so to say, the intellectual tools which *qua* economic observer he is to use; and the principles to which I refer are perfectly familiar to the economic agent. Consider, for example, the causal principle in science. It has been proposed to us by thinkers in many shapes, but would it be intelligible in any shape if we had no experience of volition? Doubtless neither the human will nor causal behaviour in the world of science is fully intelligible, but we could not, surely, grasp causation in science at all save as volition with something left out; more precisely, as at once contrasting negatively with volition and as at the same time a partial abstraction from, and so a privation of, volition. Without this experience of willing his particular ends the economic agent could make no useful sense of the way things happen in the context relevant to his action. At the lower end of the scale I suspect that the probable or statistical behaviour which is sometimes attributed to electrons is a similar privative analogue of more full-blooded types of causal efficacy such as that accepted by Newton and Kant, and it may be that mathematical order palely reflects statistical, and behind it full-blooded causal, series. In all these cases the higher, more concrete, term explains (philosophically) the lower and more abstract term rather than vice versa, although the relation is not, for human knowledge at any rate, purely asymmetrical. The lower term does also throw light on the higher when they are taken together, and it is the business of the philosopher to take them together and, reversing the direction of scientific thinking, which is towards ever greater simplicity and abstraction, do his best to exhibit the partly reciprocal relation between them. This relation is no concern of the scientist and the mathematician as such. *They* make their abstraction when and where it seems to enable efficient prediction and control—they work with it so long as it will serve their scientific purpose, and when it ceases to do so they abstract and simplify again. It may even be true that science began with the decay of a primitive anthropomorphism which simply failed to distinguish between the two terms of the relation.

This criticism of science and mathematics may not at present convince—in particular it may be said that I have treated their mutual relation vaguely and ambiguously—but it has, I hope, at least enabled me to set my thesis in a clearer light. I had said that for empiricism there is no world but the world as the practical agent envisages it in order to act. I have now defined this world more precisely as the object-world of the economic observer, with whom I have identified the mathematician and the man of science. In the following chapters I shall try to show that the thesis for which I contend is more and more clearly attested if we examine actual empiricist doctrines in a roughly historical order.

VALUE AND MODERN PHYSICAL
THEORIES

THERE is a view held in very various quarters that since the 'material' atom of Newton broke down into erratically whirling electrons, and classical physics gave way before relativity, quantum, and indeterminacy theories, the scientific universe has grown more spiritual, and so, I suppose, much better entitled to claim intrinsic value. It is suggested that 'materialists' who believe in a 'mindless universe' are deluded, because their view is based on quite antiquated scientific ideas. It is often argued in support that many distinguished men of science are far from being materialists.

The suggestion that twentieth-century physical discoveries are a windfall for anti-materialism raises questions of importance which demand discussion before we can decide whether there is any truth in it. Roughly the argument is that if space and time are relative to each other and to the observer, then the world of science is much more subjective than was previously supposed; that if the transference of energy is not a continuous passage but an intermittent jumping of discrete quanta, and if the path of the electron is so indeterminate as to be unpredictable within irreducible limits, then there is a random character in the behaviour of the simplest constituents of things which marks them as less 'material', more individual, more spontaneous, and so again, perhaps, more 'subjective', than the dull and stolid, though elastic, atoms of Newton.

The notion that matter, heavy, solid, and hard to the touch, is a base thing and the antitithesis of mind or spirit is very old and very pervasive. It is part and parcel of a universal human evaluation of Nature in terms of sensible character, which also supplies us with language for expressing nearly every other type of value-judgment. We should be everywhere tongue-tied in appraisement if we were denied the metaphorical application of such terms as 'coarse' and 'fine', 'low' and 'high', 'dark' and 'bright', etc. On this same scale Heaven and Hell are in all theologies allegorically sited. The graded scale of matter persists, ludicrously, in the popular conception of a ghost as visible and sometimes audible, but too 'spiritual' to be touched. It appears, magnificently, in Cleopatra's exaltation:

> I am fire and air; my other elements
> I give to baser life,

lines which remind us that Aristotle was the first thinker who attempted to express this universal evaluation as a systematic structure, and that a part of that structure was his scale of the five elements: earth, water, air, fire, aether.

To dwell a little on Aristotle's concept of Nature may not be waste of time. As science it is obsolete, as philosophy not altogether so. In Aristotle's elemental series each term is less gross and tangible, and less heavy, than its predecessor. Each has more, and more regular, motion than the one before it; and although this motion is at every stage passive rather than spontaneous, because it is all imparted by the Prime Mover, yet at each higher stage it is imparted more directly and so approximates more nearly to the everlasting and perfectly regular rotation of the aetherial spheres, upon which the Prime Mover acts directly. Thus the termini of the elemental scale are (a) coarse and relatively solid earth, which exhibits little and extremely passive motion, and (b) the eternally rotating aether. It is a scale of values, and the principle is that fineness is better than coarseness and erratic motion than stolidity, but that regular motion in a circle is better than erratic omni-directional motion.

This scale of values, ascending to the aether and the Prime Mover, in a certain sense bifurcates. The first four elements, earth, water, air, and fire, exhibit a ceaseless inter-transformation, the cyclical character of which reflects its proximate cause, viz. the rotation of the aetherial spheres. But sometimes this process suffers arrest, and then there occur, and remain for a period stable, certain complex combinations of the four elements, which are organisms. Thus at this point of arrest a new and somewhat different scale of values branches off; for organisms exist in three grades, vegetable, animal, and human, and these are not just three new grades of matter in the sense in which I have hitherto used 'matter', a point which necessitates a brief digression.

'Matter' to Aristotle means, not stolid impenetrable atoms, but simply what anything is made of—its stuff, its materials, its constituents—as opposed to its form; and its form is the combinative formula, the structural plan or the function, which orders its constituent elements and gives it its special nature. Thus form and matter are strictly correlative terms. There is no positive and actual universal matter. For if you analyse a very complex thing into form and matter, the matter-factor which results from your first analysis will again yield to analysis in terms of form and matter, and so on until you reach (but theoretically and as a mere ideal negative limit to analysis) 'primary matter', which is not atoms or electrons but the utterly negative and indeterminate. If, however, you look at it the other way as the matter for making all things, you may call it the merely potential. Any complex thing is essentially characterized and defined by its final form, by the form-factor, that is, which emerges first when it is analysed: the lower grades of form which further analysis would reveal are conceived by Aristotle as absorbed and unified in this final form. Thus the essential defining form of the vegetable is the vital function of reproducing its kind, and in that defining function the subordinate functions of assimilating nourishment and growing are absorbed and contained. Further analysis would here reveal grades of physical structure leading down to the combination of the four elements in a certain proportion. Analogously, if we now go a stage higher, the vital functions which defined the vegetable will be what first appears as matter when we analyse the animal organism, the defining form of which is the twin function of sense and appetition. For an animal eats, grows, and reproduces itself, but in an animal these plant functions are modified and subordinated within a higher functional unity. And, again, the sensory-appetitive function of a brute animal, with all its heritage of subordinate forms, is modified as matter subserving the rational function which defines the human being.

If we examine this whole graded system of values, certain fairly obvious points emerge. In Aristotle's physics there is a certain amount of myth and a great deal of false hypothesis, but his biology and psychology (which I have of course very greatly simplified) have stood the test of time a good deal better than his obsolete physical doctrines. On the other hand, to speak of Aristotle as a physicist, a biologist, and a psychologist is to say both more and less than the truth. In Aristotle the distinction between philosophy, which treats *par excellence* of values, and natural science, in which values are ignored, is still far from complete. With incomparable genius he sketched rough boundaries which the sciences were destined to accept, and he is often in fact thinking scientifically; but he is at the same time, and without clear and conscious distinction, constructing a philosophy of Nature, and for that reason thinking in terms of value. Considering the age in which he lived, he was as faithful and unbiased an observer of 'fact' as any later man of science, but his embodied, or 'emmattered', forms are always final causes.

It is not hard to trace in outline on the scientific side the process of differentiation which has gradually severed natural science from the philosophy of Nature. The branches of natural science, as they begin to emerge in Aristotle, still differ as terms in a graded series of values. On his view, the rational, or at least semi-rational, activity of man, the conscious behaviour of other animals, and the mere nutritive and reproductive life of plants necessitate three different special sciences, because the intrinsic value of the subject-matter belongs in each case to a different level. Below plant life, the grades of complexity which he recognized in purely physical combination led Aristotle to a further distinction of levels, which roughly anticipated the difference between chemistry and physics. But the unbroken tendency of science since the passing of Aristotle has been to neglect value as irrelevant and concentrate strictly on the observation of fact relevant directly or indirectly to action. To this end science has gradually simplified by analysis the subject-matter bequeathed by Aristotle, and so step by step retreated from concepts involving value. For example, the physician assumes today, as he always has assumed since long before the time of Hippocrates, that health in the human organism is intrinsically good. Medicine, however, is an art and not a science, and doctors are by the tradition of their profession moral as well as economic agents: they accept the duty to heal as something more than an obligation arising out of contract. But the physiologist and other biological workers upon whom the physician relies for information have found that signals enabling useful prediction are more readily discovered by regarding the organism, not as a teleologically functioning system, but as some sort of mechanism. Abstractive analysis proceeds steadily on its scientific way. The biologist assumes the spectacles of the chemist, because they, so to say, cut out certain rays of light which he now deems unhelpful and therefore irrelevant. The chemist for analogous reasons becomes more of a physicist, the physicist more of a mathematician. In this continual evacuation of value the distinction of one science from another, regarded by Aristotle as rigid, becomes fainter and fainter. Only success in prediction and practice can dictate how far this process will go, but I think it can be safely said that in the whole history of science it has never been reversed. Indeed it has become obvious that the differentia of science is rather this analytic regress than any character of its subject-matter. It seems quite clear that the biologist who still works with a teleological hypothesis is using an obsolete pair of spectacles which are less efficient than the darker glasses of the mechanist. Possibly he does so in mistaken defence of an extra-professional creed, to which he supposes he would be false if he put on the mechanist's glasses.[1] If so, he forgets that one's choice of optical instruments depends on what one wants to see and why, and that what one does see through them may be highly useful without being complete. Good and bad can be known as well as enjoyed and suffered, but not by the economic observer.

That the analytic and abstractive regress of science has never been reversed affords a strong presumption against any sudden emergence of new values in the course of scientific discovery. Moreover, if we assume, though not all scientists are in fact willing to assume it, that the newer physical theories are more than provisional working hypotheses which usefully cover a temporary gap in our information about the conditions really governing the electron's behaviour, there is still nothing very much more spiritual, or good, or generally edifying, in the subjective and random than there is in the rigidly determined. The contrary view seems to rest on a confusion of free will in man with the

---

[1] The organism so obviously in some sense behaves teleologically that the controversy which occupied Kant so teasingly in the *Critique of Judgment* is still alive. An eminent zoologist once told me that he had much sympathy with vitalism. 'But,' he said, 'I can do nothing with it in the laboratory.' Analogously, everybody knows very well that cause and effect is something more than very frequent sequence, but in the physical sciences the assumption that it is not clearly works better.

mere negative freedom of arbitrary caprice, and even if we must reckon caprice better than passive stolidity, it seems on the evidence optimistic to regard the statistically calculated behaviour of electrons as a pre-conscious analogue of human whimsy. If there is any truth in the 'spiritual' view of modern physics which occasions this inquiry, it must be philosophical and not scientific truth, and it may be just worth while to test it against Aristotle's scale of natural values.

In the first place we must note that, although Aristotle is attempting to grade Nature in terms of approximation to mind, none of his elements, not even the aether, is conceived by him as in itself 'mental' or 'spiritual'. If we understand Nature philosophically as a privation and by virtue of our partial identity with her, then I do not doubt, as Aristotle did not doubt, that we must as philosophers somehow grade even inanimate Nature in terms of approximation to mind;[1] but the notion of a physical universe constituted out of a sort of mental matter would have seemed to Aristotle as misconceived as the fluid Nous of Anaxagoras.[2]

Secondly, the erratic antics of the electron might be held to compare with the partly random motion of the Aristotelian elements intermediate between earth and aether, and on this basis of comparison to be at least superior to the solid Newtonian atom, just as water, air and fire were regarded by Aristotle as superior to earth. But we then have to remember that *below* the four elements, as the matter which analysis reveals in them, there come, according to Aristotle, the two contrary pairs of primitive qualities, or rather *qualia*, viz. the hot and the cold, the moist and the dry. These are too formless, too merely material in Aristotle's sense of matter, to be, as the elements are, substantive bodies with qualities and relations. They might be thought, at least in this respect, to resemble the electron, which is not so much a body charged with electricity as itself just an electrical charge, not so much a particle as part of a pattern of undulation. The analogy is perhaps hardly worth pressing, but if it holds at all the modern infra-microscopic physical structure would seem to be something less determinate than the dance of the Newtonian atoms, and so less and not more 'mental' or 'spiritual'.

[1] And not with Croce regard Nature as an economic pseudo-concept devoid of any philosophic significance.
[2] In Mr. Bertrand Russell's 'neutral monism', which we shall later discuss, there is perhaps a touch of the same misconception.

CHAPTER III

THE CLASSIC AGE OF BRITISH
EMPIRICISM

I HAVE so far loosely linked the terms 'empiricism' and 'positivism' to express a general philosophic, or allegedly philosophic, attitude. Plato, aptly foreshadowing the television screen in the well-known simile of *Republic VII*, describes it allegorically but with striking accuracy. 'Suppose', he says, 'that the prisoners had had among themselves a system of honours and commendations, that prizes were awarded to the man with the keenest eye for the passing objects and the best memory for which usually came first, which second, and which together, and who could most effectively conjecture from them what was likely to come in the future. . . .'[1] Here precisely is the economic observer. It will be remembered that the prisoners, chained by the legs and neck, can see nothing but the shadows thrown on the cave wall in front of them by the invisible fire behind them, shadows of themselves and of each other, and shadows of human and animal images and of miscellaneous artifacts which the passers by hold up above the level of a wall crossing the cave between the fire and the backs of the prisoners; and that the prisoners hear only echoes of the voices of the passers by, which (together, clearly, with the sounds of their own voices) they attribute to the anthropoid shadows on the wall in front of them.

The *Oxford English Dictionary* explains philosophical empiricism as 'the theory which regards experience as the only source of knowledge'. It defines 'positivism', a name invented by Comte about a hundred years ago, as 'a system of philosophy which recognizes only positive facts and observable phenomena, with the objective relations of these and the laws which determine them, abandoning all inquiry into cause or ultimate origin'. Once more we meet the economic observer.

[1] *Republic*, 516 C and D.

Plato is not kind to his troglodytes. For him they symbolize the common man (at any rate the common citizen) of contemporary Athens, and Plato tends to undervalue, as we tend to overvalue, the common man. If there are philosophers among the shackled viewers in the cave they are the sophists, who for profit teach their fellows how to attain economic success, and explain away morality against a materialistic background. Plato takes no account of the fact that guessing the future on the basis of usual conjunctions in the past is the only way by which economic action can proceed, whether its ultimate moral end be good or bad. But Plato was not greatly interested in economic action, despite his acute analysis of τέχνη in *Republic I*; he found it banausic. The cave-dweller is sensual, dishonest, and litigious. Greed and self-indulgence have fettered him with the weights of becoming and lowered the gaze of his soul's eye until he can see nothing but his dim world of shadows. Only a painful and at first forcible conversion to the light under philosophic control could lift him up to a true vision of reality and value. I am committed to maintain that the logical conclusion of empiricism as a philosophy is the denial of any value but that of egoistic enjoyment and of the means thereto, but Plato, speaking here as a moralist—and a somewhat puritan moralist, too—is hard on the common troglodyte. The classic period of empiricism in this country began in a more respectable atmosphere. Its leaders were nothing like Plato's cynical sophists. They were genuinely interested in the plain man's mind, which they found to be very like their own, and when their doctrines led them irresistibly to theoretical hedonism, they did their honest best to give it a decent air of morality.

John Locke has often been called the father of British Empiricism. There is a great deal in Locke's philosophy which is not compatible with empiricism,[1] but his paternity is not doubtful, although Francis Bacon and Thomas Hobbes are important names in the pedigree and Occam might be reckoned a rude forefather of the race. In the empiricist element of his thought Locke's practical bent is very obvious. That the sole source of knowledge is experience is precisely the assumption of the economic agent on

---

[1] The works of thinkers are both richer and less consistent than any summary of their doctrines can show. I shall illustrate in this chapter from the classic theories of the seventeenth and eighteenth centuries, but if I attribute a position to Locke or Hume I do not pretend that they would necessarily have accepted it precisely as I state it.

E

the occasions when he sets out as economic observer to ascertain the lie of the land in order to act efficiently. Locke's programme at the beginning of the *Essay* reads very like an account of such an occasion. The proposal to examine the powers of one's own understanding—to treat one's own mind, that is, as an instrument likely to be more effective if one knows how it works—clearly reveals the economic observer's attitude.[1] Locke himself did not believe that all knowledge is of merely utilitarian value, but once you come to conceive the mind as essentially an instrument and philosophy as essentially an account of how it works, that implication is scarcely to be resisted.

Locke is an individualist and so is the economic agent. What exists, the mind of a man and anything of which it is aware, are for Locke particulars, singular individuals. So are the only materials of knowledge which experience on Locke's view provides, the simple ideas through which existents are known. Locke holds, moreover, that simple ideas carry not merely conviction but an intuitive certainty which is the actual equivalent of knowledge, and this he thinks is so because the mind in acquiring these simple data is passive in the sense that it does not make or alter them but accepts them willy nilly as they are.[2] This is roughly the presupposition of the economic observer, too, if we do not press the word 'simple' too hard. A thinker not wholly wedded to empiricism might question whether it is really possible to discover and isolate a simple datum pure of any judgment, be it a datum of external sense or of what Locke sometimes calls 'inner sense', viz. reflection on the mind's own operations. He might argue that any allegedly simple datum will turn out on examination not only to possess internal diversity but also to be the product of analysis and selection within a wider context to which it is related and by which its character is in a measure determined. The economic observer, however—and that means all of us for large parts of our lives—undoubtedly assumes that whenever he undertakes an inquiry into facts he starts with some datum which is certain because it comes to him whether he will or no. Even if he sees a mirage or suffers a pain which he feels as localized in his long ago amputated foot, he is sure that he did see or feel something which the illusory nature of the total experi-

[1] See p. 30.
[2] This is true of Locke's simple ideas both of primary and of secondary qualities.

ence does not falsify: the 'sense data' which some modern empiricists still believe in were devised in order to account for this
veridical residue in sense, this character common to all sense
contents by virtue of which they infallibly present something.
Nor, again, is the economic observer affected by any warning
from a philosopher that on examination his simple datum may
prove to be internally diverse (and so synthetic) and at the same
time a product of analysis and selection related to a determining
context. Such an examination is outside his scope. He will
merely insist that his initial datum is particular, and is infallible
unless he mistakenly includes in it more than is there. He relies
primarily on his senses, and he will assume that the 'this-here-and-
now' of sense perception provides him with a particular and certain starting-point for the observation of fact which competent
action demands. When Locke or any other empiricist attempts
to build up experience out of simple data, the question which
occurs to one is, What makes a datum simple? The answer
implied, but not always stated, by the empiricist is, outside
mathematics, the answer which the economic observer must
give, if we may for the moment consider him sufficiently sophisticated to understand the question. He must reply that it is the
smallest or the qualitatively simplest element which a man could
in principle perceive within a 'this-here-and-now' which his
attention had already particularized. That is the answer of the
practical man for whom data are data only if they are such as
could have reference to action. The economic observer thus
sets a lower limit in principle to analysis, though he cannot
anywhere precisely define it. If he is a mathematician he will
admit that mathematics must use the concept of infinite divisi-
bility, but he will not necessarily conclude that, for example, a
geometrical point is a simple datum of experience. That, I think,
is why empiricists from Locke to modern exponents of sense-data
theories like Professor H. Price appear to feel that no particular
problem is raised by questions such as, What makes a simple
idea? or, What is *one* sense-datum? Nor was there any need for
Hume in the interests of a consistent empiricism to fly in the
face of the mathematicians and maintain that space is constituted
out of points.

Locke derived from experience a great deal which experience
in his sense of the word can easily be shown incapable of yielding.

He believed, for instance, in the possibility of constructing an ethical system as strictly demonstrable as geometry—he, at least, was no hedonist—although he did little towards constructing it; and he believed that proof of God's existence is the most certain of all demonstrations. But apart from these excursions into a realm of more than utilitarian values, the empiricist basis of his system soon revealed its own internal inconsistencies. I shall have to touch on some of these and, with apologies, retell an old familiar tale, but I shall do so because we are concerned to watch the gradual coincidence of empiricism and the economic attitude, and I hope that this special reference may lend the story a certain fresh interest. First, however, we must dwell again on one of Locke's assumptions which his immediate heirs did not at once question.

Locke, as I have said, reveals the economic attitude by assuming from the outset of the *Essay* that the understanding is an instrument which it will pay us to examine in order that we may thereafter make a more efficient use of it. On this view the human mind becomes itself a part of the actual situation to be explored and exploited in the interests of action. It becomes an object confronting the inquirer on much the same terms as anything in the 'external' world which he considers likely to prove useful. This raises a problem. An instrument presupposes a user from whom it is distinct. But if we are to avoid an indefinite regress, the mind must then be thought of as both instrument and user. The mind of Locke, in attempting to pursue the inquiry which he proposes in the *Essay*, must be both self-exploring and self-exploiting. This may in a limited sense be possible; I think it is, and we shall have to return to the point.[1] But an inquiry based on this assumption can never touch the full nature of mind. The operations of the mind are more than the guided functioning of an instrument, and if we nevertheless choose to abstract and consider them as no more than that they will not by themselves provide us with any adequate ground of inference to a guiding mind.

Locke was only dimly aware of the difficulty. To him the simple idea was a perceiving as well as a representation, just as the Cartesian idea had a being as a mode of mind as well as an *esse objectivum*. But Locke conceives the simple idea of reflection, through which we come to know the mind's operations, as

[1] See pp. 74-5.

closely analogous to the simple idea by which we reach knowledge of external things. His use of 'inner idea' as a synonym for 'idea of reflection' indicates this clearly. We are well on the way to treating mind as not even an instrument but a mere Humian stream of perceptions.

Historically, the first serious attack on Locke's system fell upon his external world. If ideas are the sole direct object of the mind they can provide no ground for asserting that they are either representations or effects of anything which is not an idea. Neither by intuition, as Locke held, nor by inference can we know any relation between two terms if *ex hypothesi* one of them is not and never has been present to the mind. That, roughly speaking, is the main blow dealt by Berkeley against Locke, but Berkeley was also responsible for a further step in the development of pure empiricism. Locke had on the whole conceived both his world of ideas and the world of real things which it reflected as consisting of complexes composed by aggregation of simples, but his doctrine had not been entirely consistent. He had allowed ideas of relation, and he had felt it necessary to accept an idea of substance as a *substratum* supporting the divers qualities of material things, although he was much puzzled by the fact that in analysing a material thing he could not find over and above the simple ideas of sensible qualities any residual content to correspond to this mysterious *substratum*. The source of our idea of substance is something real, but we cannot say what. All we distinctly perceive is, in the case of a material thing, its various qualities, in the case of the mind, which Locke regards as also a substance perhaps material, perhaps immaterial, its various operations. Locke had also held that by an operation of abstraction upon simple ideas the mind could come to entertain those universal ideas which reflect the common characters of things and make demonstration possible; yet it must be observed that he did not regard universal ideas as corresponding to any real thing, since in his view every real thing is a particular.

All these relics in Locke of an older speculative tradition, except the notion of mental substance, Berkeley promptly discards. An idea to Berkeley has no being as a mode of mind; it is essentially passive, sensuous, and particular. It is in fact a mental image, though of course not an image in the sense of a copy representing a non-ideal original; and a sensible thing to

Berkeley is not a complex of qualities inhering in a supporting substance but a constant aggregate of ideas in the mind. An idea can be a symbol of other similar ideas (though Berkeley does not explain how) and thus be used in reasoning, but an abstract general idea, such as, for instance, a triangle which is neither equilateral, scalene, nor isosceles, is an absurdity.

That Berkeley supplies his own non-empiricist elements to fill the gaps he has torn in Locke—the notion of relations, the notion of spirit, the explanation of our ideal world by the presence of archetypal ideas in the mind of God—all that is irrelevant to the development of empiricism. It belongs to Berkeley's campaign against the materialism of Hobbes. It does not square with the empiricist element in Berkeley, and none of it comes within the purview of the economic observer. It is time to pass to Hume, the dominant figure of eighteenth-century empiricism and the hero—if they own such a thing—of twentieth-century empiricist philosophers.

If we examine by itself Hume's critical treatment of Locke's empiricism, we are likely to conclude that, if it be sound, Locke's entire position is destroyed, and we shall probably then not quarrel with the traditional view that Hume himself ends as a total sceptic. I propose that we should make this examination briefly and then ask ourselves whether those conclusions really follow.

Hume is a yet more resolute individualist than Locke; he is yet more determined than his predecessor to constitute the universe of atomic singulars, simples which set a bar to further analysis. He has no interest in Berkeley's theology nor in his never clearly explained notions, but he embraces Berkeley's view that the idea is a singular mental image which can somehow in reasoning come to symbolize other similar ideas. He rejects with Berkeley Locke's idea of material substance, and he discards mental substance into the bargain. He accepts Berkeley's view that Locke's doctrines both of representational and of causal relation between ideas and things break down. He further narrows the meaning of the word 'idea' by distinguishing between immediate singular 'impressions' which we perceive and 'ideas' which are the form in which these impressions persist in memory and imagination, and he insists that there is no idea which does not originate in an antecedent impression. He accepts Locke's distinction between ideas of reflection and ideas of sensation, but he reduces the former[1] to a secondary status. The operations of the mind are called forth by impressions of sensation, and they gain their content from the impressions and ideas of sensation. Hence in effect Hume comes to regard the impressions and ideas of sensation as, strictly speaking, the only objects of the impressions and ideas of reflection.[1] On the ground that we have no impression of it, he denies that we have any more knowledge of the mind as a substantive self supporting its operations than we have of a substance supporting the qualities of a material thing. Causation perishes with substance. We have no impression of necessary connection between successive impressions or ideas, and therefore no knowledge of such a relation.

With the disappearance of material and immaterial substance and of necessary connection, and in the absence of any positive guarantee that anything real provokes or corresponds to our impressions, it looks as if experience has been reduced to no more than a succession of particular impressions and ideas with no reference beyond themselves and no mind to unify them into any sort of coherence. Empiricism appears to be exploded and Locke's 'historical plain method' to have ended in nonsense. In this vein T. H. Green and the old text books tend to treat Hume's pretty complete reduction of thinking to memory, his substitution of mere subjective assurance for the certainty which Locke had made the equivalent of knowledge, and his ascription to custom of belief in mind, external things, and necessary causal connection, as mere confessions of bankruptcy, mere naturalistic explanations not to be regarded as serious philosophy. This traditional account of empiricism from Locke to Hume always reminds me of the magical vacuum-cleaner. Some years ago, when vacuum-cleaners were a fascinating novelty, *Punch* published a brilliant little story told in pictures which succeeded one another roughly as follows. In the first, the householder, intrigued but sceptical, stands contemplating his newly purchased machine. In the second he has reaped a noble heap of dust. Then, sucking superbly and far beyond its advertised powers, the cleaner absorbs the carpet and various articles of furniture. The delighted owner rushes out into the street and easily collects several vehicles and a troop of cavalry. Finally, his face alight with the eternal curiosity of

[1] Except the passions.

mankind from Pandora to the sorcerer's apprentice, he peeps
over the edge of the funnel and vanishes.

In this old-fashioned account of the matter, which leads up
to the view that Hume signified philosophically no more than
an alarum clock to wake Kant from his dogmatic slumber,
there is a great deal of truth but not quite the whole truth.
Hume certainly ended as a sceptic in respect of the claims made
for the human mind by non-empiricist thinkers and even by
Locke's more modest theory of its powers, and at times his
conclusions caused him some disquiet. But while Hume denied
knowledge he did not ridicule belief. Whether or not he continued to believe in the value of philosophizing, he did not suggest
that he himself or any man should abandon belief in a real
coherent world because it cannot be known. There is another
side to the picture. The residue of the Lockeian system patched
with naturalism by Hume presents, if we make clear one point
which Hume never, I think, quite explicitly states, a very tolerable account of the economic agent's world, of the general
situation as it appears and must appear to the economic observer
when he examines it before he acts. The point is this. Hume's
reduction of knowledge to belief, science to induction, and the
conclusions of science (even in the last resort those of mathematics) to probability, becomes meaningless unless the ultimate
cause of belief is taken to be not vivacity or force of habit but
practical success or failure.[1] If it is severed from reference to practice, as his traditional critics including Kant tended to sever it,
then Hume's naturalism really is open to the traditional *reductio ad
absurdum*; for it then presents the operations of the understanding
as no more than a process of events. But, to say nothing of thinking which claims to attain to knowledge, not even coming to believe can be a mere process of events. Once Hume's economic
assumption is made explicit, his theory of the understanding
becomes an intelligible account of the cognitive situation as the
economic agent sees it.

If, as I fancy, philosophy in the full sense of the word is a criticism of this or that mode of experience from a level above it, a
criticism which displays the lower level as a privation and not a
mere absence of the higher, then Hume's empiricism is not in the
full sense philosophical but anti-philosophical. Yet we are much

[1] This doctrine is not pragmatism; see pp. 69-70.

in his debt. We may think his nature—that indeed of all empiricist thinkers—'subdued / To what it works in, like the dyers' hand'; yet Hume provides an indispensable introduction to a fully philosophical criticism of economic action. When he upholds the vulgar against the philosophers, he himself comes near to realizing that by substituting belief for knowledge he is making a philosopher out of the economic agent. His attitude to philosophy reaches its logical conclusion in Reid's principles of common sense, the primitive judgments present in the consciousness of all men, such as, for example, that the thinking self exists and that every event has a cause. In Reid's view, these are the foundations of all certainty, but they are indemonstrable and philosophy can do no more than discover them as facts.

As an account of the economic attitude Hume's theory of the understanding may still be open to criticism, but we shall learn more if we turn now to consider the limitations of empiricist philosophy, which become very evident as soon as its exponents attempt to concern themselves with values beyond the ken of the economic agent.

Locke's brave effort to maintain the demonstrability of ethics was an obviously foredoomed failure. The logical attitude of empiricism to ethics is a flat denial of morality. It is the position adopted by Plato's Thrasymachus in defence of his definition of justice as the interest of the stronger and subsequently improved and expanded for the sake of argument by Glaucon and Adimantus. Baron von Holbach in his *Système de la Nature*, which he published in 1770 but not under his own name, urged it ruthlessly on a basis of materialism. But one seldom finds an empiricist openly scouting morality as an illusion and simply substituting an account of human conduct in terms of economic value, depicting it, that is, as motived by sheer self-interest, as nothing but the seeking by individuals of individual enjoyment. When one does it makes very dull reading. What is far more interesting is to watch a brilliant empiricist like David Hume struggling to incorporate the moral world in the economic and yet to keep it moral.

In the First Book of the *Treatise* belief has been substituted for knowledge, and the human understanding, if it has not been quite reduced to imagination, has had its wings severely clipped. Hume has confined its scope to demonstration in mathematics and to judgment and probable reasoning in the sphere of matters of fact.

We discover, therefore, without surprise, when Hume comes to fulfil the promise on his title-page of attempting to introduce the experimental method of reasoning into moral subjects, that morality is rather felt than judged of, and that reason has no influence upon action save as the servant of the passions.

Clearly we are in fact still in the economic and not the moral world. Reason in the service of the passions is reason investigating the lie of the land in preparation for economic action and calculating means to the economic end of pleasurable self-maintenance and self-expansion. Certainly reason plays no part in determining that end. The egoistic impulse is a presupposition of all human behaviour. If you abstract it from the morality which presupposes it but is not presupposed by it, the end upon which it is directed is more like one of two opposite poles in tension than it is like an end of the rational will. The will in action is a conscious development both of its object and of the agent himself, but the egoistic urge consumes its object and leaves the *ego* qualitatively what it was before. The economic agent is not determined to his end by anything outside his own nature, but he does not freely choose his end: he merely finds his appetites in him. The choosing of means to the economic end is doubtless, in man at any rate, something more than automatic response to appetite. It is a rudimentary will. The agent may construct his means into an instrument which can almost become a part of himself, and his acts may develop his efficiency. But only at the moral level, where will is free and rational, can economic action alter the quality of a man; that, however, is because action is then not only economic but also moral. In the pure and abstract economic agent most certainly reason both is and can be nothing but the servant of the passions.

Hume's own account of the will seems at first sight incredibly crude. It becomes clear, however, as soon as one sees that, unconsciously or half consciously, he is working only within the limits of the economic world. He tells us in the *Treatise* Book II, Part III, Section I that the will, though not actually a passion, is an immediate effect of pleasure and pain, which are for Hume synonyms for good and evil. It cannot, he says, be further defined than as the internal impression which we consciously feel when we knowingly give rise to new physical motions and mental perceptions. He then proclaims himself a determinist, taking care to remind us once more that we have no insight into connection between events of any kind, and that 'necessity' is really just the feel of a mental transition between constantly conjoined ideas which has become habitual. His case for determinism is not impressive. Apart from his contention that reason cannot cause action, his argument consists in naïvely assuming determinism to be the only alternative to libertarianism and then pouring an easy ridicule upon the latter. He never thinks to ask the key question, viz. whether the feeling we have in giving rise to something new, or believing that we give rise to something new,[1] is always the same in degree and kind. I twitch; being something of an addict to tobacco, I light a cigarette 'automatically'; I eat when I am starving and come upon food; I perform a routine professional duty; I win a V.C. in an impulse of mad daring; I earn a bar to it by cool and resolute action; I make my will after careful thought in a calm hour. From case to case my power to choose and, much more importantly, my sense of complicity, by which I mean my sense that my act expresses myself and that I am therefore responsible, increase together on a rough ascending scale. This, *pace* Hume, is the experience alike of the vulgar and the refined. There may be something obscure in this union of a sense of complicity with a sense of choice, but it is variation in the degree to which we experience these combined feelings (and variation in their kind also) which convinces us that freedom is of the essence of the will, and that our wills, though never wholly, are always in a measure free. In contending that we believe falsely that on a given occasion we could have chosen otherwise Hume hides behind the impossibility of making the experiment. He is not then any more plausible than he is when he says we sometimes mistake a calm habitual passion for reason. Do we? Why should we? If, however, Hume is in fact working half unawares on assumptions which confine him to the sphere of economic action, where appetite may be strong and skill consummate but will is barely developed, then his account of the will makes tolerable sense.

The reduction of will to feeling and of reason to servitude leaves nothing but the passions to form both the foundation and the superstructure of an ethical system. One is tempted to de-

[1] The phrase 'give rise to' perhaps suggests that Hume is thinking of an act of will as something like a belch.

clare Hume bankrupt and pass on. But for two reasons it is not
quite so easy to throw aside the *Treatise*. In the first place, Hume
was a tolerably if not an heroically moral man. He was not above
the desire to shock the pedant and the puritan, but he was not a
cynic. He was sincerely convinced that it was well—morally
well—for men to live happily together in mutual good will, and
in resting their ability to do so on a natural sentiment he believed
himself to be strengthening, not undermining nor even depre-
ciating, morality. His logic is dubious from the outset but his
purpose is honest. He complains that all authors of moral systems
slip abruptly and without explanation from 'is' and 'is not' to
'ought' and 'ought not', and he proposes to mend the gap by
making moral obligation flow from natural obligation based on
natural feeling. Yet one cannot doubt as one reads that he is quite
sincere in his attempt to strengthen the categorical imperative
by basing it on the hypothetical. He gains credence somewhat
as Eudoxus, who held pleasure to be the supreme good, was
found persuasive by people who were impressed by the remarkable sobriety of his habits.

In the second place, Hume is plausible because morality,
though it is not mere natural feeling, has natural feeling transcended in it. To conceive moral activity as nothing but intellectual conclusions realizing themselves in action is not less absurd
than to regard it as no more than natural feeling. Hume does,
indeed, try to mediate between these two impossible views. He
distinguishes two sorts of passion. Of our original impressions
some are sensations of pleasure and pain felt in the body, and
from these directly arise certain reflective impressions. These
are passions of the first type, namely grief and joy, hope and
fear, despair and security. The second type of passion is indirect. It does not arise without some further cause beyond
these pains and pleasures. Normally, if I follow Hume, the impression of this further cause develops into an idea, but if the idea
is sufficiently vivid and intense it becomes again an impression—
all passions are impressions. Pride, for example, is caused in me
in this indirect way by some quality of some thing which I
possess, love by some quality in another person. Hume in the
Treatise lists these indirect passions as 'pride, humility, ambition,
vanity, love, hatred, envy, pity, malice, generosity, and their dep-
endants'. This list includes passions or sentiments which are

plainly not egoistic. The economic agent is not generous nor piti-
ful, nor does he feel love save as an appetite.

Here begins Hume's effort to reach the moral world. On these
non-egoistic feelings he founds morality, and he soon adds to
them an innate feeling of sympathy. It is natural to man, we are
told, to feel other men's pleasures and pains as his own, and he
feels a peculiar sort of pleasure in contemplating actions which
lead to pleasure, whether it be his own pleasure or that of other
men. To judge a man virtuous is to approve a character from
which such actions proceed, and that means to feel the afore-
mentioned peculiar pleasure. In the *Treatise* Hume holds that
only my own pleasures can excite a passion in me, and that
sympathy converts other men's pleasures into actual pleasures of
mine. In the *Enquiry* he endows man with a feeling of 'benevolence', or 'humanity', which is directly excited by pleasure and
pain in someone else, and he makes that the basis of morality. He
also there paves the way for his ethical successors, the utilitarians,
by laying great stress on utility as the quality for which we
approve actions (or rather the agents who perform them), their
usefulness, that is, in promoting the pleasure of individuals or
of society.

The doctrine is specious. Hume is describing what actually
does happen. There is in men a natural sympathy with each
others' pains and pleasures. It is odd to find Hume, the individualist who would compose the world by aggregating atomic
singulars, making this exception in favour of human morality—
no less odd than it was to hear that a singular idea can do duty
for a universal merely by becoming a symbol; yet it is refreshing.
Sympathy and benevolence, moreover, do actually work in the
moral agent and give him pleasure, or at least escape from the
greater pain of doing wrong; and doubtless they also make
moral approbation pleasant. Against any theory which decrees
an essential divorce between duty and pleasure Hume is convincing. But these natural feelings do not, simply *qua* feelings, make
a man either a moral agent or a moral judge. In moral action they
are transformed by, or perhaps better transformed in and as,
the rational will—it is so easy to forget that the will in action
develops both its object and the agent—and nobody without a
tincture of morality can make a moral judgment. To ignore this
difference of level is to ignore the very essence of a moral act.

'Benevolence', 'humanity', even 'sympathy', on the tongue of a civilized man, are words which signify already moralized sentiments, not natural feelings which mechanically determine us to action. Hume had no right to call them to his aid.

The confusion and collapse of Hume's ethical doctrine becomes obvious if we remain undeceived by his covert if ingenuous importation of contraband from the moral world. Without it not only has his passage from 'is' to 'ought' become null and void, but also his theory of the moral judgment loses all meaning, because the pleasure of approval, the pleasure of acting morally, and the pleasure given to the spectator by someone else's moral action all turn out to be exactly the same. For 'virtuous' and 'vicious' are, on Hume's view, terms which express nothing but a man's pleasure or pain in contemplating other men's actions and inferring thence their characters. Yet Hume's moral judge gets his pleasure of approval from a tendency in other men to promote pleasure indifferently for themselves or others. Is this a subjective or an objective theory of moral judgment? It is usually said to be subjective, but Hume makes nonsense of the question by using 'sympathy' and 'benevolence' to identify (*a*) the pleasure a man promotes, (*b*) the pleasure he feels at promoting it, and (*c*) the pleasure somebody else feels in looking on. By ignoring difference of level he contrives to obliterate all distinction, and his pretty picture of the moral world vanishes in a flat monochrome of natural feeling.

The nature of Hume's influence on his successors provides further evidence that his assumptions are really economic. His friend Adam Smith, though he based his theory of moral sentiments on Hume's 'sympathy', might almost be said to have invented *homo economicus*, and the philosophical radicals actually labelled their ethical systems with the economic title of utilitarianism.

The utilitarians are commonly called hedonists. Can we call Hume a hedonist? And if we find him to be a hedonist, can we truly say that, as he confines man's understanding to the economic agent's cognitive activity, so with logical consistence he equates the moral good of man with the pleasure of man *qua* economic agent? The answer to both questions is, I think, affirmative, but hedonism is a slippery topic. To discuss feeling is always hard. It seems so positive a thing, yet one can scarcely talk of it except in terms of something else. I should not here dwell on hedonism if I did not hope that a discussion of it might incidentally throw some light on the question why it is that the empiricist thinker so seldom realizes that he confines himself *ex hypothesi* to the economic sphere.

In a passage of the *Nicomachean Ethics* Aristotle identifies pleasure with unimpeded activity. In another and more familiar passage he says it is a further perfecting of activity which supervenes upon it like bloom upon the cheek of youth. He insists that the character of pleasure is determined by the character of the activity to which it belongs.

I quote these statements because they still seem to me to be sounder than anything said since about pleasure. From them follow certain consequences. Whether an activity and its pleasure be identical or necessarily linked, all of us in one sense pursue pleasure, since all of us pursue activity. Hence pleasure and pain can *per se* provide no criterion of morality: that must be sought in the character of the activity. But it also follows that no man can make sheer pleasure his end, because pleasure save as qualified by some activity presents no features to aim at; indeed, pleasure abstracted from reference to the presence or absence of impediment is not even definitely pleasure as opposed to pain. Hence Bentham's attempt to base a hedonistic calculus on purely quantitative difference in pleasurable feeling sets the most enthusiastic voluptuary a task he cannot begin to perform. To make the supreme end of man the greatest possible amount of sheer pleasant feeling is equally nonsense, whether you say that it is or that it ought to be his supreme end, and you will not be able to say under examination which it is you do mean. It is equally nonsense whether or not you add, taking a hint from Hume's sympathy, that it doesn't matter whose pleasure it is so long as there is as much of it as possible.

It follows that the voluptuary, if the word has a meaning, is not the seeker after mere pleasure but the man who pursues certain pleasurable activities which other men do not, or pursues them to a greater extent than do other men. It might also seem to follow that there can be no coherent theoretical hedonism of any sort. For if you accept qualitative difference between one pleasure and another and base it wholly on the quality of the activity, you have done more than substitute pleasurable activity for sheer pleasure as an end of action: since the activity gives the pleasure its whole character, you have made the end aimed at simply the activity and not pleasure at all. You have at least come near to criticizing pleasure out of existence.

What, then, really is the relation—if the word here may be taken to cover identity—between an intelligibly describable activity and the pleasant feeling which belongs to its unimpeded exercise? It is easier to say what it is not. Obviously the terms are not ingredients in a mixture. They are not like chemical elements which when compounded qualify each other's natures but do possess some nature of their own when not compounded; for pleasure apart from activity has no definable nature at all. But perhaps we can take a hint from Aristotle's suggestion of identity and say that the pleasure is the whole of the activity *qua* felt as opposed to self-consciously articulated and known for what it is. In that case the distinction between the two would be a distinction between forms or modes and not between ingredients of experience. The pleasure and the activity would be alternative names which we could apply to the same thing, as in some sense we do when we both describe a certain activity as painting in oils and also call it one of Sir Winston Churchill's pleasures, where 'pleasures' quite clearly means pleasant activities and not durations or spasms of sheer pleasurable feeling.

Yet this analysis of pleasurable activity still hardly satisfies. In describing the two factors as two forms we were trying to do justice to the suggestion that they were identical, yet we have in fact contrived to separate them unwarrantably. I do not know my activity for what it is unless I not merely know for a fact that I enjoy it—as I know for a fact that Sir Winston enjoys painting in oils—but know and enjoy it in one act. Conversely, as Plato pointed out a long time ago in the *Philebus*, I could not enjoy my activity if it were sheer immediate feeling without any articulate consciousness of what it is I do. But in that case our two forms or modes of experience seem to be in danger of collapsing indistinguishably into one. Can one act take two forms at once?

I think we may here get help from the voluptuary. We have seen that he deserves his name neither because he pursues sheer pleasurable feeling nor because, like the rest of us, he inevitably pursues pleasure in pursuing any sort of activity, but because he pursues certain specific pleasurable activities, or pursues them to a greater extent than other men. Now we in fact specify these activities as sensual, whatever degree of refinement we think they admit, and we attribute to them certain further consequential characteristics. In the first place, although we may recognize that all unimpeded activity is pleasant, yet we regard sensual activities as more blind or opaque, more *merely* felt, than any others, and we do consider that when they are present to the imagination of the voluptuary as desired ends to be realized the factor of feeling plays a larger part in attracting him than is the case in other activities, though no doubt the feeling only attracts as qualified by the activity. One man may get as intense a pleasure out of mathematical thinking as another does out of drinking, but when the mathematician longs to resume his interrupted studies his ideal end does not present itself in the form of feeling to the extent to which the drunkard's does when he wants to get drunk or the lecher's when his lust is strong. The case of the voluptuary thus suggests that pleasure and activity are forms or modes of unimpeded experience which are always present together, but that their relative dominance differs from one kind of pleasurable activity to another, and also from one phase to another of the same pleasurable activity.

Secondly, we tend to regard experience in which blind or mere pleasure dominates as relatively immature and undeveloped. Here, however, there is need for caution. We do not, unless we are the victims of some intellectualistic prejudice which makes us deny that pleasure perfects its activity, suppose that when, or if, experience becomes a fully rational self-conscious activity feeling has simply disappeared, but rather that it has become the clarified pleasure appropriate to that activity. 'Clarified' is of course a mere metaphor, the aptest word I can think of to contrast with 'blind' or 'opaque'. In a fully rational and developed activity the two forms would be really identical.

It would thus seem that, except in this perhaps merely ideal case, pleasure is always experienced as a form distinguishable from the rational developed form of the active experience, and that it is so distinguishable because it is relatively 'blind' or 'opaque', and relatively undeveloped or immature. Variation of dominance in the course of the same pleasurable activity gives the clue. One can exult suddenly in one's activity, and on another

F

occasion one may say, 'I didn't realize at the time how much I was
enjoying myself.' We are constantly passing from one form to
the other, but the transition is never complete, and inasmuch as
that is so we are in a state which I can only describe, perhaps
paradoxically, as that of experiencing simultaneously at two
different levels of development. In fact it is no unparalleled
paradox. To make the simplest sense judgment we must pass
through some such series of forms or modes of experience as
sensating, perceiving, imagining (or imaging), and judging,
and I doubt whether we can in judging stop short of inferring.
Yet in passing from each to the next we have never completely
passed. In perceiving we still sensate, in judging we still imagine,
and in inferring we still judge.[1]

There is, too, a third characteristic which we commonly
ascribe to the pleasures, the pleasurable activities, of the voluptuary. Not only do we regard their relatively opaque or blind
nature as a symptom of their immaturity, but we also take them
to be *par excellence* selfish pleasures, pleasures confined in scope
to the singular individual subject who enjoys them. Moreover,
apart from any moral implication in the word 'selfish', we do as a
rule correlate the selfishness of these pleasures with their immaturity; and when we do give selfishness a moral implication it
becomes fairly clear that the selfishness and the blindness of these
pleasures are also closely connected, for we can hardly hold that
ignorance plays no part in vice.

If the position which we have reached is sound it helps to
explain two things. We can understand why a particular activity
can be called a pleasure, though in justice to common speech
it must be admitted that the term is usually applied to a man's
less important activities. We can also see how easy it is in
general to stick in the familiar, the γνωριμώτερον ἡμῖν, and rest
content with a definition of an activity in terms of its lower and
less developed form. So Hume almost identifies thinking with
remembering and understanding with imagining, not crudely
mistaking one distinct and separate thing for another, but
taking the nature of a thing to be fully given in its immediately
obvious but less developed form. So also he takes both moral
action and moral judgment as sympathy or benevolence, not
because he cannot recognize morality when he meets it in himself

[1] Cp. p. 29.

or other men, but because he can only envisage it in the form in which it naturally first strikes a genial, unpuritanical man of the world like David Hume. His substitution of the less for the more developed, or (which in effect is the same thing) of the simple for the complex, is of course pre-eminently exemplified in his reduction of the mind to a 'bundle or collection' of singular impressions and ideas, perceptions which are at once acts and contents of perception but justify no inference to a self persisting beyond the given singular perception. In this case he shows no inkling that, taken at a developed level, the mind might really be a concrete unity differentiated in its experiences and not, as he supposes, a fiction produced by confusing the two ideas of (a) identity and (b) a succession of related objects. These two ideas he regards as 'perfectly distinct and even contrary', as indeed he must, since he holds that all complexes are constituted of atomic simples which provide the only true answer to the question what the complex is. All relations are to Hume, the individualist, perfectly external to their terms, because they are in fact nothing but ways in which we customarily associate ideas. Even more remote from Hume's thought is any conception that sympathy might be moralized if minds themselves were not externally related, if individual minds expressed some kind of genuine identity in difference of which man, save as economic agent, is always in some measure conscious.

I should perhaps here add that Hume's reduction of the mind to an unowned bundle of perceptions is a notion so different from the working beliefs of the ordinary man that this discrepancy might seem to testify against our general thesis that Hume, *qua* empiricist philosopher, accepts, consciously or not, the assumptions of the economic agent. We shall, however, see later that a Humian view of the mind can serve practice, that it is a possible assessment of the situation which can enable prediction and action. I am thinking of certain types of empirical psychology which have an avowedly practical purpose.[1] If this is so, Hume's conception of the individual mind is not the quite unplausible nonsense which to some late nineteenth-century critics it appeared to be. It is mind at an undeveloped level, a drastic simplification which makes of mind an observable object on all fours with the objects of natural science; but that is an economic procedure.

[1] See pp. 73 ff.

We can now return to the question of Hume and hedonism. We have seen that to make man's end the pursuit of pleasure taken as sheer feeling which admits only quantitative difference, is a nonsensical endeavour. There is little doubt, I think, that Hume's doctrine of sympathy is at the bottom of the conjuring trick by which Bentham and his utilitarian followers contrived to present anybody's pleasure as indifferently any good utilitarian's object of pursuit, but Hume never asserted or believed that pleasure was susceptible only of quantitative difference. We can therefore find him not guilty of hedonism in this crude shape.

If a coherent hedonism is possible, our discussion of pleasure suggests that it must consist in taking as man's supreme end the pleasurable activities of either (*a*) the voluptuary or (*b*) any purely selfish agent, because such activities are more predominantly pleasurable in form than any other. (*b*) is of course wider than (*a*). It would include the pleasures of the voluptuary and also, for example, the selfish exercise of personal power, whether or not as a means to the former. It would in fact comprise precisely the activities of the economic agent. I am not quite sure whether it is just to charge Hume with this economic hedonism. To advocate it was not his deliberate intention, but he had looked at the human understanding through economic spectacles, and he could not take them off, because he did not clearly know that he had them on. He could not envisage a moral activity save in its economic form as a pleasure or a means to pleasure.

If empiricism can do no more with morality than reduce it to its own economic level, in the face of aesthetic experience its bankruptcy is yet more obvious. It can only substitute technique for artistic creation, which does indeed contain technique transcended within itself but is essentially theoretic and not practical. Aesthetic judgment it must reduce to a taste in pleasure, as does Hume in the analogy he often draws between moral judgment and the taste for beauty. In both cases the interposition of economic spectacles is too clear to need argument. The empiricists, classical or modern, provide us with little to cite in the way of aesthetic theory. Either from prudence or from lack of interest they have mainly kept silence.

CHAPTER IV

INTERMEDIATE EMPIRICISM

BEFORE we consider the trend of empiricism in nineteenth-century England it may be worth while to note briefly in passing two kindred types of philosophical thinking, namely pragmatism and Marxism. Neither is native to this country nor quite in the strict line of empiricist descent, but both reveal that exclusively practical view of the world which I have maintained to be the essence of empiricism.

William James based his pragmatism on the contention of C. S. Peirce that in order to think clearly about an object we need only consider what practical effects it may have. That, so far, seems to be just the attitude of the economic agent to the object which he selects for attention within the situation relevant to action. He asks whether the berry will nourish or poison, and the berry exists for him only in this utilitarian character. But James was chiefly concerned with quite another sort of object. He conceived it the function of philosophy to discover what practical difference it makes to us if this or that theory of the universe is true, and he held that an idea is 'true' so long as to believe it is profitable to our lives. An idea, that is to say, *becomes* true; it is made true or false by events. It was in fact James's main purpose to justify protestant Christianity as a successfully working and therefore 'true' belief, and by a successfully working belief he meant a faith which makes for happiness. Thus his attitude is practical, but it is not the attitude of the economic agent or the true empiricist, because it is moral and not simply economic. If the economic agent believes in a God he endows him with no more than a magnified form of that same economic character which he attributes to things and other men. The pragmatist's conception of truth is further from that of the economic agent or the genuine empiricist than at first it looks. Doubtless the economic agent expresses the truth about his objects in terms of their economic effects, but he regards the truth of a belief as the cause and not the effect of successful action; for he knows that it belongs to the essence of his objects *qua* economic to be largely beyond his control, and he knows that wishful thinking does not make for efficiency. He may on occasion judge it folly to seek the truth where ignorance is bliss (where, for example, ignorance preserves the self-esteem which it is part of his economic end to maintain), but he is then merely refusing to investigate a situation on which he does not wish to act, not identifying truth with delusion. Again, Hume virtually substituted belief for knowledge and probability for certain truth, but when he advised against practical scepticism he did not advocate the arbitrary selection of beliefs according to their likelihood of promoting happiness. He had in mind mainly the obvious fact that if you do not assume causal connection you will get nothing done and will probably suffer more than you bargained for. Hume abandons as impossible any attempt to show that belief is grounded on fact, but he knew much better than James that without the notion of fact the notion of belief disappears.

Dr. Dewey's philosophy of instrumentalism and his substitution of 'inquiry' for truth add little in principle to the pragmatism of James. The divorce of belief from fact and the conception of truth as endlessly made and remade by human effort are perhaps ideas more natural to America than to England. Mr. Bertrand Russell in discussing Dewey remarks very plausibly, 'It has seemed to me that the belief in human power, and the unwillingness to admit "stubborn facts", were connected with the hopefulness engendered by machine production and the scientific manipulation of our physical environment.'[1] In fact, if the classical empiricism of the seventeenth and eighteenth centuries be the basic and typical philosophy, or substitute for philosophy, of the practical British race, modern empiricism in England and pragmatism in America will be its natural variants in different conditions of environment, the former its contraction and impoverishment under intense economic stress, the latter its transfiguration in an optimistic atmosphere of prosperity.

Marxism was begotten in more sombre surroundings. It was inspired by the spectacle of economic distress, and it achieved

[1] *A History of Western Philosophy*, 1946, p. 854.

its startling practical triumph in Russia at a time of political and economic chaos. In its ideological and 'activist' character it has much in common with pragmatism and instrumentalism—the attitude of Soviet propagandists towards hard fact leaves no doubt of that—but Marx's pragmatic faith sprang from desperation rather than optimism. 'Marxism' is a name for some atrociously tangled thinking, but if we first remove its absurd dialectical façade, it reveals factors closely akin to the economico-empiricism which I have been trying to sketch. Marx saw all history, particularly political history, through economic spectacles, but the dialectical shape in which he depicted the class struggle developing out of the methods of production is the merest sham. When he asserts the collapse of capitalism to be as inevitable as the destruction of feudalism by the capitalists, Marx's position is utterly alien to Hegel's. He is really thinking in terms of the rigidly mechanical and necessitating 'laws of Nature' which were fashionable among the natural scientists of his time. Hegel denied the possibility of historical prophecy,[1] and his dialectic is a teleological concept, a theory of values which explains the undeveloped in terms of approximation to the developed. The Marxian inversion of his method into 'dialectical materialism' is a crude contradiction in terms. It could seem faintly plausible at a time when there was a confused but widespread belief that one of the laws of Nature was human progress, but it would have been discarded long ago as an antiquated myth if the violent emotional urge which it attempts to rationalize had not stupefied the critical powers of so many leftist intellectuals.

Stripped of its dialectical mask, the Marxist interpretation of history presents its own peculiar version of the objective situation which the economic agent must know in order to act.[2] What is relevant in that situation is not simply the behaviour of physical objects but technological and social change in man conceived as occurring in accordance with laws as rigidly mechanical as the laws of mid-nineteenth-century physics. Whereas the type of empiricism which we have traced in Locke and Hume comes, without quite knowing what it does, to treat man himself as in *pari materia* with his economic environment and as governed by

---

[1] In the Introduction to the *Philosophy of History* Hegel remarks that the future is the object not of knowledge but of hopes and fears.

[2] How efficient as economic observation to enable action Marxism has been is another question.

the same laws, Marxism does this frankly from the start, and from the start identifies man with the economic agent. But Marx was not a Thrasymachus. He was not in the least disposed—if, indeed, he understood the issue at all—to accept the logical consequence and discard morality, and he would of course have stood little chance as the prophet of social revolution if he had.[1] It is interesting and important to note in Marx the same sort of confusion between the economic and the moral as that which appears in Hume and even more obviously in the liberal utilitarians who derived so largely from him. The reason for this is not far to seek. Marx himself was not a proletarian but a *bourgeois*—an ironic comment on his view that a man's political outlook is inevitably that of his class—and the fantastically improbable climax of Marxian history, the apocalyptic paradise of happy classless individualism which is to succeed the dictatorship of the proletariat, bears the clear stamp of *bourgeois* liberal ideals. Between conclusion and premisses, between this plainly moral fantasy and the rigid economic necessitation of social change, there is the same inconsistency, the same muddled attempt to recapture discarded values, as there is in J. S. Mill's bland identification of moral virtue with the pursuit of individual pleasure. The confusion is the more blatant because of Marx's openly economic initial attitude.

From this digression we may now return to our main topic.

For a hundred years after Hume there is not, from the point of view of this book, a great deal that needs to be said of British empiricism and positivism. Utilitarian ethics and inductive logic were fairly obvious developments from Hume. The former we have already touched upon, and the latter will perhaps call for comment when we come to discuss the logic of the twentieth-century empiricists. They are in any case topics with which every English reader interested in philosophy is familiar. The latter half of the century was dominated by the idealists, though their sway was not uncontested. Idealism was a borrowed philosophy, and when we became engulfed in the miseries of hot and cold warfare, and the expanding physical sciences began to take an ever-increasing toll of the intelligentsia, we rapidly forgot it and

---

[1] To tell the 'have-nots' that they are being immorally exploited is much more effective propaganda than to adopt the cynicism of Thrasymachus and tell them that justice is no more than the interest of the stronger, and that they had therefore better grab all they can for themselves.

returned to our Humian vomit. Yet idealism had its proximate source in the minds of greater thinkers than this country has hitherto produced, and its ultimate roots in the philosophy of the Greeks without whom European man would scarcely have had a mind at all. For half a century and more we consented to break away from our provincialism and learn what we could from those teachers. During that time when empiricism was on the whole a minority view in philosophical circles, its most important development was the growth of the science of empirical psychology. Here again was unbroken continuity with the past, for where philosophy is empiricist, positivist, naturalistic, the distinction between philosophy and science tends inevitably to disappear, and with it any difference between a philosophical and a psychological treatment of mind.[1] A cursory examination of empirical psychology will leave us in no doubt of its essentially economic character.

The empiricist, I have contended, is the man who treats the real as everywhere identical in kind with the situation relevant to future action as the economic agent observes it. In Chapter II I described this situation as an external object which the economic agent distinguished from himself by virtue of a strictly cognitive activity. In the first instance it would be a selection from the sensible environment in which he finds himself, but the urge to explore more widely in the interests of merely possible action has led him to attend to and cognize a great deal more than that; his research has led him to mathematics and natural science. To know how other men's minds work in order that one may predict their behaviour and act accordingly oneself is a need which clearly arises very early in an economic world. But the attempt to observe methodically the mind of another individual agent comes a good deal later. At that point the empirical psychologist appears on the scene, and it is well to be clear what his advent signifies. His attitude will no longer be that of the unsophisticated economic agent; for he represents the economic observer attempting to focus the whole economic agent within his field of view. It will be his purpose to envisage minds as objects in *pari materia* with all the other cognizable objects in the general situation relevant to economic action. He will thus hope to

---

[1] This became much clearer in the twentieth century than it had been in the nineteenth.

provide some help towards the prediction and control of human behaviour, though he will not, if he is prudent, believe that certain prediction is by any method possible even in principle, or that his own method is more than a very partial means to his end. We have seen the beginning of such an enterprise in Locke and Hume.[1] They went very far in laying down the ways of approach to mind still in use by modern psychologists.

When the economic agent first turns psychologist he will probably regard his own mind as the likeliest, though perhaps not the only possible, source of information about minds: his approach will mainly be, in modern parlance, 'introspective'. What he will find when he first attends to his own mental operations has been roughly indicated in Chapter II. We distinguished there between (a) his perceptual cognition of an object which confronts him as other than himself, as no part of his own person, and (b) his other modes of experience such as feeling, imagining, desiring, willing, etc., which are immediate *Erlebnisse*, enjoyments of a content which is always in some degree self-feeling. Hence the general question to be answered is whether he can cognize objectively his own experience in all or any of these modes.

In the same chapter we qualified the sharpness of this distinction. I pointed out that the economic agent ordinarily counts his body as a part of himself somehow intermediate between his mind and the external world, but that these boundaries are not rigid. He treats, we saw, portions of his body, and also material instruments which he uses with them, now subjectively as elements or extensions of himself, now objectively as detached physical things. Hence the more precise question is whether he can, as it were, extrude and objectify elements of his mind as he extrudes and objectifies parts of his body.

The distinction between modes of experience must now be further qualified. Cognition directly concerns what is taken as other than the self, whereas the other modes are all modes of self-consciousness; yet nothing can be cognized as an object save by distinguishing it from the self as subject, and in the other modes there is always a reference of some kind to something beyond the self, always some cognitive factor. These modes would thus seem to fall roughly on a scale between definite cognition and an ideal limit of sheer feeling[2] and to exhibit no absolute

[1] See p. 50.   [2] See p. 29 footnote.

difference of kind. All of them in different degrees seem to be experience both of self and not-self.

If this is so, the task of the introspectionist will be roughly the same in respect of all the modes of his experience, and this continuity between the modes may embolden us to answer the question affirmatively and say that if he can objectify and cognize parts of his body, then he can extend the procedure to elements of his mind; for before he extrudes and objectifies them he does actually experience these parts of his body as mental, or at any rate psychical, elements.

The path of the introspectionist is nevertheless theoretically thorny, though it must always be remembered that his purpose, whether he knows it or not, is practical. Let us first consider perceptual cognition of a definitely external thing. What precisely is here to be the introspectionist's object? Presumably the whole complex of himself cognizing an external thing. But within that complex the external thing is an already cognized object. In cognizing it he would seem to be merely repeating himself, whatever we take to be the relation between the content of a perception and the external thing perceived. This seems to reduce the introspectionist's object to his own subjective act taken in abstraction from *its* object. But here David Hume provides the proper empiricist answer: if you try to observe your own impressions and ideas you will not find among them any impression or idea of a self or subject. Kant retorted by pointing out that the subject is given *a priori* as presupposed in any cognition of an object; but to that a pure empiricist can only reply that in that case it is never known at all.

The same theoretical dilemma confronts the introspectionist when he attempts to spy on other modes of his own experience. If he wants an object he must exclude the subject, but his object will not then be psychical at all. If he retains the subject he will not have before him a genuinely empirical object. So, it would seem, the magical vacuum-cleaner claims another victim.

Yet the introspectionist method is plausible. In particular we seem to experience imagery which is the persistence in memory and imagination of impressions from without, and this imagery at least seems to be at once sufficiently loosened from the external world and at the same time sufficiently distinct from the subject to be taken as a genuinely psychical object. Introspection does, moreover, appear to be a genuine source of practical knowledge, if only because it seems doubtful whether behaviourism, the more truly empiricist form of psychology which we have next to discuss, can fully substantiate its claim to work without any reliance on 'privileged access', on private experience of one's own mind's operations. As a theory, however, introspection has survived because its advocates have compromised a degree ambiguously with empiricism. They have continued to accept the subject, if not as an actual object yet as giving its nature to what they claim to observe, as somehow making it psychical. G. F. Stout, who relied mainly on introspection, held the method of psychology to be essentially subjective and took pains to give the term 'object' a special meaning in psychology.[1] The introspectionists have given various and conflicting answers to the vexed question of the relation (or identity) of a cognitive impression to an external thing: it is a copy; it is an effect partly or wholly dissimilar to its cause; it is a sense-datum which may or may not be an actual part of the external world; it is a phenomenon, but beyond it and behind it we have no knowledge. F. H. Bradley held phenomenalism to be senseless in metaphysics but the only rational attitude in psychology. He defined it provisionally as 'the confinement of one's attention to events with their laws of coexistence and sequence. It involves', he continues, 'the complete abjuration of any attempt to ask in psychology for ultimate truth or consistency, and it involves the adoption as relative truth of whatever serves best to explain the detailed course of facts or those particular ways in which things happen.'[2] Had Bradley added that by relative truth he meant truth strictly in relation to action (though I do not suggest that he did) his philosophical sympathizers might have been less puzzled. How a phenomenalist attitude thus defined could be rational in psychology or any other special science except as the attitude of a man exploring in order to exploit I fail to see.

Viewed historically as a theory which claims to offer something more than merely economic knowledge of the mind, introspective psychology is an unstable hybrid. It is empiricism with a bastard strain from older philosophical views of mind, and it is open to

---

[1] See *Manual of Psychology*, 3rd edn., 1913, Chapter 1, §§ 1–3.
[2] 'A Defence of Phenomenalism in Psychology', *Collected Essays*, 1935, Vol. II, p. 365.

attacks from both sides. Examined as the economic agent's first approach to a practical problem, it seems to show that he can get useful information by looking from a point of view which is not simply that from which a man directly cognizes an object distinct from himself. If that appear puzzling, it is to be remembered that I have been contending, not that the economic agent is a pure empiricist, but that pure empiricism is an attempt to philosophize taking as real only what is one in kind with what the economic agent succeeds in observing as definitely external to himself. Whatever psychological approach the economic agent proper adopts, he does not lose from sight the relatively 'subjective' modes of his experience, and if he does succeed in cognizing his own mind, or by analogy another man's mind, as an object, he still only understands that object by reference to 'subjective' experience. The economic agent is only an abstraction, but he is a less empty abstraction than the economic observer: there is more in him than pure science or pure empiricist philosophy. In any case we need dwell no further on the ambiguities of the introspectionist method. It has long been wilting before the blast of modern empiricist criticism, though it can perhaps never quite disappear.

Everybody knows that by watching other men behave you can get some idea of how they are likely to act, and no psychologist has relied entirely on introspection. But if the economic agent next turns behaviourist he will eschew introspection altogether as a baseless myth. True behaviourism, springing from discontent with the failure of introspection to provide a scientifically observable and measurable object which can be subjected to experiment, is ruthless in pursuit of such an object, and its self-confidence has grown in proportion to the development of scientific apparatus designed for this purpose. Has the behaviourist, then, found his object? If he has, what is it?

Two observations determine the general attitude of the behaviourist. He notes that the operations of a mind are often, perhaps always, stimulated by or through the body. He also observes that the accounts which men, not excluding himself, give after trying to reflect, by whatever means, on their own experience are highly fallible. This turns him to study the outward and visible behaviour not only of men but also of other animals. The brutes at least cannot deceive him with words, and he is led to hope that his conclusions in this field may bear also on the workings of the human mind. In this enterprise he has the aid of the physiologist and the anatomist, of the economic observer, that is, who began investigating the organism, human or animal, in the interest of health. He has always before his mind the picture of the reflex arc: sense organs receiving stimuli from their environment within or without the body, bundles of nerve fibres transmitting electrical impulses which agitate in complex but localized patterns the ten thousand odd million neurones of the brain, until these in turn transmit through efferent nerve fibres the impulses which result in muscular action. The picture, though already very complicated, is still far from complete, but it represents an original which is in principle through and through open to scientific investigation, and there seems to be no theoretical ground for denying that it could be completed.

To the ordinary man, and to a good many eminent physiologists as well—Sherrington, Lord Adrian, Dr. Penfield, for example—this picture seems to present an ancient, tough, and perhaps insoluble problem: What kind of transition occurs between these afferent impulses and the mind which thereupon responds by thinking, desiring, and transmitting fresh impulses to produce physical movement? What, in short, of consciousness? A possible philosophical answer, though hardly a complete one, is to say that the question is senseless, or at least wrongly formulated, because it implies a causal relation between a physical system and a mind or a consciousness which is not physical; that between any sort of cause and effect there must be a certain community of nature; that in this case no such community of nature can be found. The retort of the out-and-out behaviourist is much the same in substantial implication, though different in form because he is not a philospher even in his off moments, but an empirical psychologist. His retort, moreover, if the purpose of empirical psychology is practical, is fundamentally sound, though without this qualification I believe it to be nonsense. The behaviourist replies, somewhat after the manner of Hume, that his observation of human and animal behaviour enables him to predict and control with tolerable success, but that it never presents him with a mind or a consciousness such as the introspectionist pretends to encounter, never with something which is absolutely different in kind from the observable movements of an organism. In short, he solves the problem of connection between a mind and the to-and-fro of nervous impulse by denying distinct existence to mind. Thinking, for example, he will maintain to be nothing over and above its physical expression in speech. It simply is the muscular movement which is fully developed in talking aloud and inchoate in talking silently to oneself; it is a part of man's active or, more exactly, reactive behaviour.

Should it be objected that to develop a psychology on these lines would be merely to do over again the work of the anatomist, the physiologist, and the neurologist, the apostle of behaviourism will reply that, although those disciplines are indispensable to him, the study of behaviour still has its proper and peculiar field. Pavlov's experimental proof that a hungry dog will salivate successively in the presence of (a) food, (b) food and a ringing bell, (c) a ringing bell without food, has led to the discovery that a human babe is born subject to a comparatively small number of types of reflex action, but that these are liable to endless complication as the child grows up. A simple reflex is fairly seldom left to itself to become a monotonous habit of automatic reaction. Much more often a second stimulus becomes associated with the first and after a time elicits the same response even in the absence of the first. The perpetual change of conditioning stimuli by association and substitution constantly modifies and varies a man's or a brute's habits of response. In principle we can account in these terms for all that men do throughout their lives; we can predict what particular men will do; we can by deliberate modification and substitution of stimuli exercise considerable control over the actions at least of brute animals and children.

The practical character of this doctrine is very obvious. Cognition, for example, is not merely reduced (as the introspectionist view also reduces it) to events abstracted from any reference to truth and falsehood; it becomes a muscular action observable directly when a man talks aloud, and at least in principle during his 'sessions of sweet silent thought'. And since nothing nearer to action than physical movement and change can be observed and measured scientifically, behaviourism quite consistently reduces human action to reaction. It is hard to see how one could come nearer to making mind an object of scientific cognition. At first this teaching shocked even empirical psychologists— J. B. Watson was perhaps the only out-and-out behaviourist—

but ever since the first world war the demand for every kind of applied psychology has grown steadily, and with it the use and success of the behaviourist approach. Only psycho-analysis, another practical technique with its own peculiar practical mythology, has had comparable success, and they are not fundamentally in competition.[1]

The discussion of empirical psychology has led us well beyond the nineteenth century into the twentieth, and it provides an appropriate bridge for transition to modern empiricist philosophy. When we cross the bridge we find ourselves in a tangle of philosophical controversy which shows its assimilation to science by working itself out largely in desultory magazine articles. But I think there is little doubt whom we should treat as the central figure, and our task of criticism will be the easier because he is a man still sufficiently old-fashioned to commit himself quite frequently in book form.

For a good many years Mr. Bertrand Russell was the main influence in every branch of British philosophy. If his disciples have passed beyond him it is largely because he has pointed the way for them. Even apart from his travels in the world of mathematics and physics, he has always speculated in a wide context. He was brought up in an aristocratic, though not conservative, atmosphere, but his own liberalism led him to discard his peerage so far as he legally could. His adolescent interest in religion was passionate. He was once a Hegelian, but the common-sense realist, G. E. Moore, dissipated his already failing faith in Hegel. He still delighted in the eternal world of Plato's Forms, but he then learned from Wittgenstein, though with pain, to regard mathematics as consisting of nothing but tautologies. So Mr. Russell had knocked about the spiritual world quite a bit before he began to work out philosophical views of his own, and in doing that he has never feared to change his mind. We can perhaps indicate as follows the broad outline of his *Weltanschauung* ('philosophy' in his sense of the word would be here too narrow a term), though whether we judge it consistent is another matter. Whatever can be known can be known by means of science, and modern analytical empiricism, which has incorporated mathematics and

[1] Psycho-analysis, however, has a special philosophic interest, because it does attempt to grade the mind in levels. It was a happy chance that Freud was not a close student of orthodox empirical psychology.

developed a powerful logical technique, can in regard to certain problems 'achieve definite answers which have the quality of science rather than of philosophy'.[1] But in the field of ultimate values, traditionally included in philosophy, scientific methods are inadequate; science alone, for example, cannot prove that it is bad to enjoy the infliction of cruelty. Ultimate values lie outside the province of science and are, legitimately, matters of feeling. To this we must add Mr. Russell's confession that he has always ardently desired to justify feelings of awe inspired by certain things which seem to stand outside human life—the starry heavens, the vastness of the scientific universe, the edifice of impersonal truth, especially mathematics—but he has nevertheless to confess himself intellectually a humanist. 'Those', he writes, 'who attempt to make a religion of humanism, which recognizes nothing greater than man, do not satisfy my emotions. And yet I am unable to believe that, in the world as known, there is anything I can value outside human beings, and, to a much lesser extent, animals. Not the starry heavens, but their effects on human percipients, have excellence; to admire the universe for its size is slavish and absurd; impersonal non-human truth appears to be a delusion. And so my intellect goes with the humanists, though my emotions violently rebel. In this respect, the "consolations of philosophy" are not for me.'[2]

I shall begin the Second Part of this book, which is to contain samples of modern philosophy, with what may seem a disproportionately full account of Mr. Russell's *Analysis of Mind*. Mr. Russell is the only survivor of the analytic school which he founded who has not totally rejected metaphysics and has produced some sort of philosophical system. After him, and largely because of tendencies already strong in his work, metaphysics and system virtually vanish into mere method. It is, however, impossible to expound a method without initial reference to a system, because in philosophy method is an abstraction from system and not intelligible without it, whatever pure 'methodologists' may suppose. It is in fact just this conscious and deliberate

[1] See *History of Western Philosophy*, 1946, pp. 862–3, on which I am here drawing. 'Philosophy' here clearly means traditional philosophy.
[2] See *The Philosophy of Bertrand Russell* (*Library of living Philosophers*). Evanston, Illinois, 1946, 2nd edn., Vol. V, pp. 19–20. Cp. also p. 35 above. Just how Mr. Russell's intellect can be going with the humanists when he consigns ultimate values to feeling I do not know. Or is it an emotional concession to mathematics?

G

effort to divorce method altogether from system which marks the beginning of the new empiricism, and I know no book which exhibits the divorce proceedings so clearly as *The Analysis of Mind*. It appeared just after the first world war. That Mr. Russell may not now think precisely what he thought nearly forty years ago signifies nothing for our purpose. His *Analysis of Mind* is an essential clue to the spirit of our dismal age.

PART II

The Philosophy of Analysis

CHAPTER V

LOGICAL ATOMISM AND MIND (i)

M R. RUSSELL'S conception of mind descends philosophically from Hume, though there are perceptible
relics of Locke in it. It closely resembles that of the
psychologists whom we discussed in the last chapter; indeed,
although Mr. Russell claims to be interested in psychology more
for the light it may throw on the problem of knowledge than for
its own sake,[1] his *Analysis of Mind* is largely a critical development
of their doctrines on the basis of his own philosophy of physics.
He is, however, far more explicit than Hume or the psychologists
as to the method he proposes to use, and therein lies the main
interest of all Mr. Russell's philosophical work. Mr. Russell's
philosophy has for its chief purpose the justification of mathematics and physics, and since he has called it the philosophy of
analysis, we must try to discover what he means by analysis before
we watch him analysing mind. His source of inspiration is
mathematics, and he states the general nature of mathematical
analysis clearly enough in the beginning of his *Introduction to Mathematical Philosophy*.

We may either start, says Mr. Russell, from the most familiar
notions of mathematics and proceed deductively by construction
towards gradually increasing complexity—from integers, for
example, to fractions, real numbers, and complex numbers, and
from addition and multiplication to differentiation, integration,
and the higher mathematics. Or else we may proceed in the opposite direction by analysis towards increasing abstractness and
logical simplicity, seeking for more general ideas and principles
in terms of which we can define or deduce what was our starting-
point. When Greek geometers passed from empirical rules of

---

[1] *Analysis of Mind*, p. 15. On the question how he relates psychology to the theory
of knowledge see p. 115.

land survey to the general propositions which justified them, and thence to the axioms and postulates of Euclid, they were pursuing this latter analytic course, and their procedure, as compared with Euclid's deductions, was philosophical rather than strictly mathematical. By thus analysing our ordinary mathematical notions, says Mr. Russell, 'we acquire fresh insight, new powers, and the means of reaching whole new mathematical subjects by adopting fresh lines of advance after our backward journey'.[1]

Here a word of cautious comment seems needed. Presumably these fresh lines of advance are deductive and lead in principle to a mathematics yet higher than, for example, that reached through the previous deduction from integers to fractions, etc. But this new deductive enterprise, though it be constructive and, I suppose, 'synthetic', must yet, I suggest, remain on the level of abstraction reached by the analysis which preceded it and made it possible. The God of Jeans forbid that lay ignorance should question the propriety or success of mathematical procedure, but it seems quite clear that a high mathematics is not superseded by a higher because the latter gives an altogether more full and complete account of what was originally subjected to analysis, but because it more plainly reveals certain properties of the original which it is *useful* to know.[2] An equation is not the whole nature of a curve, even if deduction in terms of equations reached by analysis of curves gives such fresh insight into the relevant properties of curves as will subsequently enable fresh prediction in the world of physics. Is it even certain that an integer is nothing but a class of classes? Moreover, even if mathematical analysis and construction were genuinely theoretical, it would still remain to ask whether analysis of mind, in the same sense of analysis, does or could enable us to acquire fresh insight, new powers, and the means of reaching whole new *mental* subjects by adopting new lines of advance after our backward journey.

Although in discussing Mr. Russell one should never forget his belief that solipsism cannot be logically refuted, his theory of mind, like Locke's, is ostensibly causal, and we shall do best to begin by examining his view of causation in science, primarily in

---

[1] *Introduction to Mathematical Philosophy*, 2nd edn., 1920, p. 2. Cartesian geometry was, I suppose, an analytical regress upon Euclid followed by a fresh construction.

[2] And makes them more manageable by solving at its own level problems hitherto insoluble.

physical science.[1] Causal law, we learn, is still the guiding thread of scientific research and interpretation, but it has been much attenuated by analysis in the course of time. Causation is no longer deemed to mean production, nor even change in the accident of one substance by change in the accident of another. In modern physics[2] the nearest approximation to the old idea of cause and effect is the empirical generalization touching observed phenomena which states that event B usually follows event A. It is not held either that B must follow A or that B is more than A's almost invariable antecedent. Such generalizations survive as data for more exact laws, but even this emasculated relic of causation does not bear close analysis. The two events must be contiguous in time; otherwise some other event might intervene to prevent the expected effect. For any observable event turns out on inspection to be a continuous process, and in any suggested case of cause and effect we can rule out one by one the earlier sections of the antecedent event as not truly part of the cause, because what happened next might have been some quite unexpected event. Swallowing arsenic, to take Mr. Russell's example,[3] cannot really be the cause of a man's death, nor can even the subsequent penultimate stage of physiological collapse, because he might be shot through the head at the last moment. The effect as a process can be similarly reduced towards its point of contact with the cause: the corpse might be blown to bits by a bomb at as short an interval after death as you please. Hence causal law, if it is to aim at strictness, can do no more than state the direction of a change at each instant in terms of a differential equation. It can, for example, only state what a particle's acceleration would be in given circumstances, not where it will be at a given moment. But this means that we are now dealing with continuity in terms of infinitesimals, and these stricter laws are neither verifiable by observation nor on any other ground certainly true. Continuity, moreover, if the quantum theory holds, may be only apparent, and if that is so we reach theoretically an event which is not a process.

The laws linking events, then, are of the general type described, and Mr. Russell sets out to build by means of them a psycho-

---

[1] See *Analysis of Mind*, particularly Chapter V. Mr. Russell's view of causation has not since remained perfectly constant, but that is of no consequence to us.
[2] Mr. Russell is writing in 1921.   [3] Ibid., p. 94.

88   PHILOSOPHY OF ANALYSIS

physical world, or what ordinarily might be called a world of mind and matter. Its constituents are to be those events which (a) best survive the test of a Cartesian dubitation,[1] and (b) are minimal in the sense that they are the simplest constituents to which the world at present appears to be reducible. The event which best fulfils these conditions is a 'sensation', a term of which, for reasons which will shortly be plain,[2] we cannot ask whether it means an act or a datum. But certain other events, even though more dubitable, must also be included among these atomic constituents, namely (1) events (if any) which are not experienced and therefore not sensations, but are inferred as similar to and continuous with what is directly given in sense— sensibilia in fact[3]; and (2) psychical images. This introduces a difference in type among causal laws, for Mr. Russell maintains that images obey peculiar psychological laws of causation,[4] though he is careful, even anxious, to gesture with Occam's razor and allow that in time physical laws may replace them.[5] Meanwhile we are to hold that images obey only psychological laws, whereas sensations obey now psychological now physical laws, without any change of intrinsic character and simply according to the relations in which they stand.

These constituent events, atomic so far as present analysis can show, are all evanescent, but they occupy, while they exist, 'a region of space-time which is small in all four dimensions', although they do not have mutually external parts.[6] Mr. Russell's usual generic term for them is 'particulars', and their specification in three types becomes clearer, perhaps, when we learn that the

[1] Those, that is to say, which, if we ignore propositions of logic, are at the top of a hierarchy of dubitables. Cp., e.g., Our Knowledge of the External World, 1914, pp. 70 ff.
[2] See p. 89, footnote 3.
[3] Mr. Russell does not use this term in Analysis of Mind, but it expresses what he means. It must be remembered that, on Mr. Russell's view, a sensibile, in order to become an actual sensation, changes only its relations and not its intrinsic neutral character; for Mr. Russell shows his true descent from Hume by regarding all relations as external to their terms. In Analysis of Mind he is prepared to use the word 'appearance' to cover both sensibile and actual sensation; see p. 90.
[4] Presumably these are empirical generalizations which theoretically might become data for the more exact type of causal law.
[5] On the use of Occam's razor, so religiously venerated by modern philosophers, Mr. Russell comments interestingly: 'There is no very good ground for supposing that a simple law is more likely to be true than a complicated law, though there is good ground for assuming a simple law in scientific practice, as a working hypothesis, if it explains the facts as well as another which is less simple'. Analysis of Mind, p. 132. Italics Russell's.
[6] See Analysis of Mind, p. 286, where this is said of events in the physical world. I presume it applies also to actual sensations and to images.

'stuff' of Mr. Russell's world is neither material nor mental, but a 'neutral stuff' out of which both the mental and the material are constructed.[1] That, it seems, is how an image can be purely psychical, a *sensibile* purely physical, and a sensation material in one relation and psychical in another.

Nothing in this Russellian world can be 'explained' save in terms of reducing particular causal laws to more general ones. Any physical or psychical assemblage of particulars, any systematization, that is, of particulars by causal laws, such as, for example, a piece of matter or a mind, is a 'logical construction', something derivative and not empirically given, for which 'logical fiction' is sometimes offered by Mr. Russell as a synonym. Morris Weitz collects about twenty physical and psychological 'constructions' from Mr. Russell's writings: 'space', 'thing' or 'matter', 'point', 'instant', 'qualitative series', 'space-time', 'interval', 'quantum' (we should add, I think, 'proton' and 'electron'), and in psychology 'instinct', 'habit', 'desire', 'feeling', 'perception', 'memory', 'conception', 'thought', 'belief', 'emotion', 'will', and 'consciousness'.[2] For Mr. Russell Occam's maxim is fundamental in scientific philosophy, and as a good empiricist he slashes always at that which is furthest from sense. He offers 'logical constructions' on the principle that a construction out of known entities, though not something directly experienced and so the object of knowledge by acquaintance, is always preferable to an inference to unknown entities, because it is higher in the hierarchy of dubitables.[3]

The nature of a logical construction will be clearer when we come to discuss Mr. Russell's linguistic and logical doctrines. Meanwhile it will be helpful to observe his reduction of the common-sense 'physical thing' to a logical construction.

When several people 'see' a table simultaneously they all see something different. It is natural but wrong to say that there is a real table which is the common cause of all the appearances it presents to different observers. Such a table is not observed; it must therefore be a hypothesis or a construction. Cause is a

---

[1] Mr. Russell's neutral monism was derived largely from William James and from the American New Realists.

[2] See *The Philosophy of Bertrand Russell*, p. 108, footnote. Weitz's article is most helpful. His list is not exhaustive.

[3] A 'subject of experience' is a logical construction, and it is now clear why 'sensation' cannot be labelled either 'act' or 'datum'; see p. 88 and *Analysis of Mind*, p. 142.

notion too dubious to bear the weight of an inference to something which of its very nature cannot be observed. It is therefore
better to hold that the 'real' table is the set of all the different
observers' sensations, together with certain *sensibilia*. These
sensations of the observers Mr. Russell also speaks of as 'appearances', and as what 'would naturally be called "aspects" of the
table from different points of view'.[1] But he explains that the
word 'appearance' is used for brevity's sake, and does not mean
something which must appear to somebody but an event at a
certain place which is connected with a physical object. A star,
for instance, can be seen and/or photographed from a certain
place, because it transmits light at a definite velocity. This means
that at the eye (or the sensitive plate) something, which on a now
rather obsolete hypothesis would be called a transverse vibration
of the aether, happens in connection with the star. Thus a particular event at a place containing a percipient organism is at once
(*a*) an event connected with the star, (*b*) an appearance, and (*c*) a
sensation. But (*a*), (*b*), and (*c*) are all characters of the particular
qua constituent of the star. It is a part of the nature of the star to
appear and be sensed, although the star has other particular
constituents as well, namely the events connected with it at all
places on the path of its light at which a percipient organism
might theoretically be present but in fact is not. Thus neutral
stuff is constructed here into mental events, sensations, and there
into material events, and both are constituents of the star as a
logical construction.   A physical object or piece of matter may
be approximately defined as the collection of all those correlated
particulars which common sense would regard as its effects or
appearances in different places. But Mr. Russell then attempts a
closer definition. Given any appearance x of an object, we can
construct a system of appearances to which it would belong if
the laws of perspective alone were concerned. But between x
and the object the medium distorts to a degree which lessens as
we approach the object. The series of sets constructed for each
place we so pass through tends to a limiting set where distortion
ceases, and this set may be taken for purposes of physics as the
definition of the physical object or piece of matter concerned.[2]
We may now consider the psychological aspect of Mr. Russell's

[1] See *Analysis of Mind*, pp. 98–101.
[2] Ibid., pp.106–7.

world. Change in the appearance of an object at a given place occurs either (i) through change in the medium, in which case the change is only partial and is minimal in places close to the object; or (ii) through changes which we attribute to the object itself, in which case all or most of the object's appearances undergo a connected change. This is the type of change with which physics primarily deals, stating most of its fundamental laws in terms of matter. Psychology, on the other hand, is concerned not with systems of particular appearances taken as things but with certain of these particulars themselves. Perceptions, for example, are appearances of objects where sense-organs and brains form part of the intervening medium, and they interest the psychologist on their own account. Whereas the physicist classifies particulars by collecting the appearances of one object from different places, the psychologist classifies them by collecting the simultaneous appearances of different objects from one place, and he constructs not a physical object but a 'perspective', which consists of all the perceptions of a given man at one time. Moreover, the causal laws which govern these particular appearances differ from the laws of physics, which treat objects, unbroken systems of particulars, as causal units.

'The stuff of our mental life,' says Mr. Russell, 'as opposed to its relations and structure, consists wholly of sensations and images.'[1] Sensations, as we have already seen, can be either 'material' or 'mental', and they are accordingly subject to either physiological or psychological laws. Images are purely mental. They have no intrinsic reference to an object, and they are subject only to the psychological laws of association. Sensations and images can only be distinguished by their different causal behaviour: sensations are caused by a stimulus external to the brain, images by association with a sensation. Mr. Russell is thus, with reservations, a behaviourist rather than an introspectionist. Images do not obey physical laws (if only because they are often localized in places already physically occupied), and they are 'private'. But they can be scientifically known, because privacy is a matter of degree. On the one hand, even visual sensations are in a sense private, and the visual sensations of one observer must, in order to be known, be correlated with those of other observers. On the other hand, bodily sensations,

[1] Ibid., p. 109.

which seem very private, can theoretically be correlated with the help of physiology.

Mr. Russell now sets about 'constructing' out of sensations and images mental phenomena such as perception, memory, language and meaning, thought, belief, truth and falsehood, emotion, and will.[1]

We shall do best to begin with his general account of 'mnemic phenomena'. Memory, in a broad sense of the term, marks the boundary for Mr. Russell between the realm of physics and the world of living organisms. 'Mnemic phenomena', of which memory proper is only one, appear even in plants, and as a class they include almost everything that interests the empirical psychologist except sensations and, I think, instinct. Their peculiar characteristic is that past occurrences as well as the present stimulus and the present condition of the organism, so far as we can ascertain it, enter into the proximate, not merely the remote, cause of the response.[2] This applies to acquired habits; to images in so far as they are copies of sensations; to association, which is essentially habit; to all the non-sensational elements in perception with which we eke out its central core of sensation; to memory proper, which is definite knowledge of a past event in one's own experience; and finally to 'experience' in the sense in which it modifies behaviour.

The general law of mnemic causation descends very evidently from Pavlov's salivating dog. If a complex stimulus has caused a complex response, a part of the stimulus can on a subsequent occasion provoke the whole response. Mr. Russell justifies the inclusion of a past occurrence as part of a proximate cause on the ground that in science a causal law is no more than an observed uniformity of change, and to ask for any explanation of it beyond its subsumption under a wider law is meaningless. Hence to object *a priori* that what has ceased to exist cannot be a present cause would be to reintroduce an old and false metaphysical notion of cause and effect. Scientifically, the law is sufficiently justified by the observed uniformity of sequence between the past burning of the child and its present dread of the fire, or

---

[1] This is presumably the point at which after 'analysis' of mind deduction should begin (see p. 86), but Mr. Russell continues to 'analyse' ordinary conceptions of mental operations. It is, indeed, not always easy to see from Mr. Russell's practice when he is 'analysing' and when 'constructing', though his net result is always pretty destructive.   [2] Ibid., p. 77.

between the past salivation of the dog confronted with food and
dinner bell together and its present salivation at the bell without
the food. Mr. Russell is prepared to admit that the engram
theory, which accounts for the response as wholly due to a brain
change induced by the past experience, might some day be verified, but he prefers mnemic causation as at present less hypothetical, and also because it avoids any need to suppose that knowledge, images, memories, etc., can lie dormant in a latent and
unobservable mental condition.

We can now pursue further some of these mnemic phenomena.
To reach a definition of perception, Mr. Russell starts from the
point of view of physics. A 'momentary thing' is a set of more or
less simultaneous aspects collected according to the laws of
perspective. The thing itself is the series of these sets collected
according to the laws of dynamics, and it may therefore be said
to possess a 'biography'. But you might instead collect a series of
successive aspects related by dynamics, and then form the set of
these series according to the laws of perspective. You might,
for example, collect the series of an actor's successive aspects or
appearances to one spectator, repeat the process for every other
spectator, and form the set of these series. If a man's mind were
occupied with a single aspect-sensation at a time, we could define
this sensation as his perspective and the dynamically related
series of which it was a member as his biography. But in fact his
momentary perspective is a set of aspects of several things, and
should therefore be defined as the set of particulars simultaneous
with a given sensation. Simultaneity is here not, as might be
thought, too loose a condition: the set of aspects does not include
the whole world at that instant, because on the assumption of
relativity time is local to a given place, here one man's mind.
A man's biography can accordingly be defined as the set of particulars simultaneous with, or earlier or later than, the given
sensation.[1]

Mr. Russell prefers to omit place and rely on time alone in
these definitions, because he is uncertain whether the presence
of two aspects in one place can be defined solely in terms of the
laws of perspective and dynamics.[2] Yet he has previously said,
'In every place at all times a vast multitude of things must be
happening, namely at least one for every physical object which

can be seen or photographed from that place.'[1] But although he thus hesitates to regard the mind as a place, he next proceeds towards a physical definition of perception in which 'place' occurs in a sort of amphibious sense.[2] Every particular considered by physics is a member of two groups, viz. those particulars which constitute the other aspects of the same physical object, and those particulars which have direct time relations to the given particular. For example, my sensation when I look at a star, and equally the spot representing the star on a sensitive plate, is a member of (a) the group which is the star and is associated with the star's place, and (b) the group which is my biography, or that of the sensitive plate, and is associated with my place, or the place of the plate. Thus every particular of the kind relative to physics is associated with two places, (a) the place of that whereof it is an aspect, which may be called its 'active' place, and (b) its own place, which may be called its 'passive' place. But 'active' and 'passive' here imply nothing specially 'mental', since this duality holds throughout the purely physical world. This distinction between the quasi-subjective and the quasi-objective, very characteristic of Mr. Russell's attempted *rapprochement* of mind and matter, enables us, without departing from physics, to collect and distinguish (a) all the particulars actively at a given place, and (b) all the particulars passively at a given place. (a), in the case of a man, is his body or his brain; (b) is his mind so far as it consists of perceptions. In the case of the photograph, (a) is the plate as physics deals with it, and (b) is the aspect of the heavens which it photographs. We can now take the last step within physical confines and define a perception as, 'the appearance of the object from a place where there is a brain . . . with sense-organs and nerves forming part of the intervening medium.'[3]

Psychically a perception is more than this, for such appearances of objects both cause and are caused by mnemic phenomena. They may be remembered and associated; they may influence our habits and cause images; they are themselves different from what they would have been if our past experience had been different. Theoretically we may distinguish within the perception the core of sensation due to the object and the mnemic element due to past experience. But practically this is often difficult. Moreover, perception itself is a vague experience, because the medium may

---

[1] Ibid., p. 100. [2] Ibid., pp. 129 ff. [3] Ibid., p. 131.

so distort an appearance that we are compelled to treat it on its own account. We constantly see as one what the telescope or microscope would dissipate into several objects. Perception is always in some degree confused.

Before passing to further mental operations, Mr. Russell issues a warning. A man could only know anything outside his personal experience, his own biography, either by inference from something within his biography or by some *a priori* principle outside experience. Neither method affords anything like certainty. Belief in things outside one's own biography is only a hypothesis justified by the simplification of scientific laws which it enables. Logic must rank it as a prejudice. For Mr. Russell there is theoretically no sure escape from solipsism.

With Mr. Russell's doctrine of perception enough of his system has emerged to let us vary exposition with comment.

To Mr. Russell, as to Hume, the simple is the clue to the complex, and his whole philosophy rests upon the neutral particulars out of which he builds his universe. These, together with the laws of logic, head the hierarchy of dubitables,[1] and among them the actual sensation takes pride of place; for the *sensibile*, the purely physical event, is an inference, and the image, since it is caused by association with a sensation, may be fairly ranked as so far less primitive. It is, then, the actual sensation which we must first examine. The task is not easy. In the first place, a sensation is not itself a cognition, though it causes cognition. Hence, if we know it as an immediate and virtually indubitable datum, this knowledge is not a part of the sensation itself *qua* datum. In the second place, the sensation is said to be the central core of a perception, the rest of which consists of relatively more dubitable mnemic phenomena; but Mr. Russell confesses that in practice it is difficult to distinguish it from its periphery.[2]

It is hardly possible at this point to resist the suspicion that the difficulty of disengaging the pure sensation is theoretical as well as practical, and that a sensation, as a definite atomic particular, is really nothing but the product of an inference from perception, and of an inference which is very dubious indeed. But Mr. Russell in *The Analysis of Mind* remains undeterred. He knows, it seems, as

---

[1] See p. 88, footnote 1. Deductive construction from the initial products of analysis moves from the more to the less certainly known.
[2] See p. 94.

certainly as he knows anything, that a sensation is an evanescent event which, although not possessing mutually external parts, occupies a small region of space-time. He knows that its intrinsic nature is quite independent of the relations in which it stands, and presumably he knows in a given case that it is, for instance, a visible blue patch of a certain shade. One might object that to know a visible blue patch of a certain definite size, duration, and colour involves a complex judgment of distinction and comparison, that in fact such a patch, if and when it is known, is not an immediate datum but a quite obviously mediated product of sense and thought. Mr. Russell would perhaps reply that some such judgment does take place when we attempt to enucleate the sensation accurately from the perception, but the 'product' of such a judgment is not something changed or developed, as his critic clearly implies, but the particular blue sensation just precisely as it was in the actual perception. To that the retort is, What, then, except an easily remedied absence of attention, prevented us from being fully aware from the start of this indubitable particular?

Mr. Russell, I feel pretty sure, conceives his atomic particular as defying analysis, although it occupies a region of space-time, because he also conceives it as what answers to the demonstrative 'this' of pure denotation.[1] But the truth seems to be that a sensum which we designate as 'this' is no more than the immediacy of a perception which, until it is mediated by some degree of thinking, is neither dubitable nor indubitable, because it is nothing definite enough to admit of either certainty or doubt. It is not an atomic particular which 'must have been there all the time', but a non-cognitive prior phase of perception within a single process of perception. It is only retrospectively recognized as an immediate experience, and indeed it may well on retrospective reflection be taken to contrast with the definite perception as 'blind' or 'brute' rather than as indubitable, if 'indubitable' carries any implication of clear and distinct.

This answer, however, does not quite adequately explain that urge to associate immediacy and certainty which is characteristic of the plain man and of the empiricist who champions him. It ignores two facts. First, we are all of us pretty certain that our sense-perceptions are veridical at least in respect of some element;[2]

[1] See p. 130 and footnote 3.   [2] See pp. 50-1.

and secondly, the content of perception always reveals a field
fading away from a relatively small central area on which some
interest focuses our attention. Usually that area is what we should
describe as an aspect of one physical thing, though it may be an
aspect of a group of things. If the interesting area is too large,
we may have to concentrate our vision, though not for that
reason the whole of our intelligent attention, on a part of it. It
is quite true that fallibility decreases as the centre is approached,
and that when the aspect of the thing, or of a part of it, is fairly
simple, it is easy to assume that here an indubitable particular
datum is reached. In actual fact the fair degree of certainty which
we reach is a judged and mediated certainty, and in actual fact
the area of attention is never an atomically simple particular;
but, while these facts should be clear to any philosopher, we are
none of us in perception philosophers but just simply economic
observers,[1] and these facts do not then concern us. It is economically efficient—it pays us in saving of time—to forget, if we
ever knew, that the immediacy and the definiteness of our perceptions are different phases of a process. We telescope them into
one, and to lapse into this handy approximate truth is as useful
as it often is to forget how we perform some skilled action in
order to perform it freely and competently.

In *The Analysis of Matter* Mr. Russell modifies this view, but
the change is not the revolution it may at first sight appear to be.
Discussing perception, he there confesses that, 'the element of
interpretation can only be eliminated by an elaborate theory, so
that what remains—the hypothetical bare sensation—is hardly to
be called a 'datum', since it is an inference from what actually
occurs'.[2] He concludes that the part of the interpretative element
'which can only be discovered by careful theory, and can never
be made introspectively obvious, ought to be included in the
perception'.

At first sight one might perhaps suppose that by 'interpretation' Mr. Russell here means the process from immediacy to
mediation in judgment which I described, a process to which the
starting-point is no bare particular but an immediate phase of the
whole perceptual content, and of which the mediation is the

---

[1] Unless of course we are artists, but I abstract here wholly from aesthetic experience.
[2] *Analysis of Matter*, p. 189. Thus do the troubles of the empiricist begin, ironi-
cally, with what he accepts as the very source and fount of knowledge.

H

whole perceptual content made definite. If this were his doctrine his whole philosophical attitude would be reversed in the twinkling of an eye. He would be accepting the view that the developed explains the undeveloped, and that structure is not an external relation of its constituents but rather that which gives them their own real nature. He would have seen that as perception reveals what sensation is, so in each higher phase of the mind's activity lies the clue to its predecessor rather than vice versa. He would have realized that the 'hypothetical bare sensation' is not the remainder when theory, however careful, has eliminated interpretation, and not even the conclusion of an inference more dubious than that by which the common man infers the substantial table from its aspects, but a pure illusion, a thoroughbred chimera. But he clearly means nothing of the sort. For Mr. Russell interpretation is quite separate from what it interprets, however hard it may be to distinguished the two. The only result in *The Analysis of Matter*, when Mr. Russell has degraded sensation from datum to inference, is that 'percept' takes the place of 'sensation', and the will-o'-the-wisp bare particular recedes a step farther into the gloom to become an ideal represented approximately by the empirical percept. It remains the basis of Mr. Russell's philosophy.

It should here be said that the particular which the economic agent takes for granted is not necessarily atomic in the sense of having no parts, nor necessarily simple in any sense which precludes it from being an identity in difference. It is in the first instance an individual person or thing; for the world of the economic agent, as we saw in Chapter II, is peopled with individuals, beginning with himself. His individuals tend on the whole for him to be mutually exclusive—he is by definition a selfish man—and they are in that sense particulars. But they do not lack internal diversity. On the other hand, the economic individual is, *qua* particular, essentially amenable to being counted and to other simple mathematical operations—all statistics are essentially economic—and if it is proper, which here means 'useful', to treat the subject-matter of mathematics as simple atomic particulars, the economic observer will of course do so.

Let us consider one or two of the many other difficulties connected with the atomic particular which threaten to wreck Mr. Russell's system at the outset, certainly as a genuine philosophy, perhaps even as an aid to the economic observer. According to Mr. Russell, the causal relations in which it stands are quite external to the intrinsic nature of a particular. Yet only because they stand in different relations do we call event A a purely physical event, and event B a sensation. This must surely mean that an event owes all its interesting qualities—its blueness, hardness, sweetness, 'clanginess' or whatnot—to the external relations in which it stands. In respect of its intrinsic nature, which consists, I suppose, in occupying (or being?) a small region of space-time, it is presumably identical with (or should we say precisely similar to?) a purely physical event. That external relations should add blueness to a momentary bit of space-time is surely odd. Be it remembered, moreover, that Mr. Russell makes his external relations about as innocuously external as they could be. The particulars 'collected' to constitute a piece of matter —the catless grins, so to say, that make up the Cheshire cat— —are originated by nothing. They merely happen in an order of place and time within which it cannot even be said that the position of any one term is due to its predecessor. Neutral monism was introduced by Mr. Russell in order to overcome philosophic dualism, but his world on closer inspection seems to consist of nothing but little space-time occurrences, some of which acquire quite inexplicably a sort of overlay of sensuous qualities. The *rapprochement* of mental and physical seems to be after all wholly a movement towards the physical. Yet on Mr. Russell's view the sensation, or at any rate the percept, gives us the nearest empirical entity we have to an indubitable datum, for the purely physical event is *ex hypothesi* a product of inference which we can never verify in direct experience. If then we press Mr. Russell's reliance on sense, we find him turning into a phenomenalist, or even slipping into solipsism, against which he himself admits that he has no logical defence. When he opts for 'the causal theory of perception', he sounds like a realist, but in fact he reduces causal law to no more than such consecution as an observer records in order, like Plato's cave-dwellers, to base a guess on statistics. Such a concept of cause affords no ground whatever for realism against phenomenalism. It is in fact a methodological device without any direct implication as to the real nature either of what is observed or of the observer. This is very obvious when we come to examine Mr. Russell's view that the subject of experience is a logical construction of causally correlated particulars. If that is offered as serious philosophical theory, we are entitled to ask who makes logical constructions in general and this one in particular. The answer is then plain: a presupposed subject who does not enter into the theory at all, and with that answer the theory is ruined; for Mr. Russell's subject of experience, which is his reconstruction after analysis of the old-fashioned subject of experience, wholly fails to meet Kant's familiar philosophical argument that one cannot make an object of the subject. If, on the other hand, logical construction of a subject of experience is merely a methodological device of the economic observer who is only trying to make an object of mind for practical purposes of prediction and control, then the fact that the observer himself as the subject constructing remains outside the construction presents no problem. Thus Mr. Russell's 'causation' is a very proper concept for a phenomenalist. But phenomenalism is not a serious philosophical position; it is merely the minimal assumption which the economic observer need make.[1]

[1] This was virtually admitted by Prof. A. J. Ayer in a defence of phenomenalism (see *Phenomenalism, Proceedings of the Aristotelian Society*, 1947) against an objection raised by Mr. W. F. R. Hardie which may be put briefly as follows. An unobserved physical event may stand in causal relation to other events observed or unobserved. But if, as phenomenalists hold, an unobserved physical event is a set of possible sensory events, then it cannot be a cause. For the merely possible cannot cause the actual, whether causation is taken as agency or merely as regularity. Professor Ayer replied that, although he himself and other phenomenalists have usually fallen into the error of supposing that sense-data cause sense-data, in fact the occurrence of a sense-datum is not an event in the same sense as a physical event, and sense-data are not causes nor effects and do not depend on one another. They can be correlated, and only because they can be correlated have we reason to believe in causal connection between physical events; indeed, to say that physical events are causally connected is, in the last analysis, to make a complicated statement about correlations of sense-data. But these sense-data need not be actual, and this correlation is always based on a hypothetical proposition to the effect that, given certain conditions, a sense-datum of one type will occur if a sense-datum of another type occurs. To say thus that a categorical proposition would not be true unless some hypothetical proposition were true does not involve the absurdity of making the actual depend on the possible.

Professor Ayer seems here first to assert a dualism of physical events and sense-data, which is hardly consistent phenomenalism, and then to attempt to efface it by equating a statement about physical events with a statement about sense-data; but he would probably reply that the 'dualism' is merely a contrast between two alternative languages. That linguistical lunacy is a subject for our later concern, but in any case Professor Ayer's correlated sense-data are, even more obviously than Mr. Russell's sensations, just observer's records with the minimal orderliness required to produce a statistical basis for prediction.

CHAPTER VI

LOGICAL ATOMISM AND MIND (ii)

M R. RUSSELL has so far been analysing mind in accordance with the title of the work which we are discussing. On the other hand, he has also been reconstructing mind by deduction from the products of his analysis.[1] But this reconstruction has been a very cautious affair. It is curbed by Mr. Russell's firm empiricist belief in the superiority of knowledge by direct acquaintance, in any sphere where that is possible, to any other sort of knowledge. We reach by analysis bare particulars, or at any rate particulars as bare as empirical experience permits, and any inference, even any construction, which we make from them is bound to be more dubitable than these directly known particulars. In mathematics, where there are no empirical data, this diminution of certainty as deduction advances is doubtless far less of an obstacle to progress, but in the sphere of mind Mr. Russell's loyalty to empiricism ties him to a hesitant and often baffling procedure. He achieves his effects more often by ostensible destruction of other views than by any positive advance.

We know, then, pretty well what to expect as Mr. Russell ascends the traditional scale of mental activities. He will call them phenomena rather than activities or operations, because they must be objectified and empirically observed. By the necessity of his initial hypothesis he must construct them out of particular sensations and images in external relation, and these constructions must not be allowed to form any sort of system exhibiting a character of its own not possessed by its constituent particulars. By Occam's principle, which rests on respect for direct observation, he must not only prefer construction to inference, but also be as sparing of constructions as he can, and define each phase of mind at the lowest possible level—or, it might be fairer to say, as near as possible to bare particulars. How, if their relations are

---

[1] See p. 92, footnote 1.

purely external, particulars can even be 'collected' into groups of different kinds, is a difficulty which we have already examined at the base of Mr. Russell's theory. It will not lessen as we proceed. We shall again be left wondering whether Mr. Russell's analysis is followed by any genuine construction at all, whether Mr. Russell succeeds in producing in the sphere of mind anything analogous to the deduction which follows analysis in mathematics.

Mnemic phenomena, Mr. Russell tells us, distinguish the animate from the inanimate world. Memory proper, which is recollection, marks a second boundary, because it involves definite, direct and not inferential, knowledge of a past event. Mr. Russell disclaims confidence in his account of it[1] and is often hard to follow.

Memory involves the belief that a present image is a memory-image, the belief, that is to say, that it is a copy (good or bad) of a past sensation. The dilemma is that (a) the sensation is past when the image exists and is therefore only known by memory, but (b) memory of it seems only possible through the present image. Thus comparison of image with sensation seems necessary but impossible. Mr. Russell finds the beginning of a solution in James's theory of the 'specious present' which includes every stage of a sensation fading into an image. The content of the specious present includes succession, and it enables us to apprehend, for example, movement and time-order. But though the specious present may, he thinks, be called immediate memory and is an experience of succession, Mr. Russell apparently does not regard it as an experience of the past. Just what use it is to him in solving his dilemma is obscure, but in any case he finds that it falls short of true memory, because the truly remembered event is one which has come to the end of its period of fading. So he offers a solution in terms of 'belief-feelings'.

The distinctive character of memory, and the seat of the time-determination which it involves, now turns out to be a peculiar belief-feeling which, by its reference to a reality which is past, differs specifically from the belief-feelings involved in bare assent and expectation. This gives 'meaning' to the image, and we believe 'this occurred', was real, that is to say, in the sense of felt to be capable of affecting us without our co-operation. This belief-feeling must be carefully distinguished from the content believed,

[1] Which occupies *Analysis of Mind*, Chapter IX.

in which there is no time-determination. Feelings of familiarity and of degree of temporal remoteness are also involved in memory, but they are not enough by themselves to constitute memory proper. Mr. Russell comments in passing on a certain ambiguity in our belief, when we remember, that 'this' occurred. 'This' might suggest that the present content is actually identical with a past event, but in fact 'this' is inevitably vague, and it expresses not identity but close similarity, a doctrine recalling Hume's view that the mind is a fiction produced by confusing the idea of identity with the idea of a succession of related objects.[1] The vagueness of 'this', says Mr. Russell, is not falsity but a sometimes misunderstood characteristic of ordinary language. Vagueness is not generality, not the applicability of a word to different objects in virtue of a common property; for judgment of generality *follows* judgment of identity and difference, whereas a vague belief *precedes* such judgment. The difference between vagueness and accuracy depends on difference of response to stimuli, and though vagueness aims relatively low it has a greater chance of truth than precision. Misunderstanding of vagueness has, according to Mr. Russell, caused philosophical mistakes such as Bergson's interpretation of past and present and Hegel's doctrine of identity in difference.

Mr. Russell may well lack confidence in his theory of memory. His initial dilemma is quite insoluble because it rests on the common empiricist assumption that the 'presentness' of present experience is indubitable, whereas 'pastness' is a matter of relatively uncertain inference. This assumption springs from a fairly simple error of incomplete analysis. As we saw in discussing Mr. Russell's theory of perception, a sensation is an immediate initial phase of perception which is only recognized as immediate by retrospective reflection.[2] In actual immediate sensation there is no experience of 'presentness'. In reflecting we judge sensation to *have been* present, which is simply to say that we judge it to *be* past, and we so judge it only by distinguishing it from the 'presentness' of our judgment. In short, immediate experience as such has no time-determination, and we neither do nor could experience 'then' and 'now' save together and in constrast. 'The occurrences,' says Mr. Russell, 'which are *called* knowledge of the past are logically independent of the past; they are wholly analysable into present contents, which might, theoretically, be just what they are even if no past had existed.'[1] But the logic which imposes this naïve severance of past from present is merely Mr. Russell's own logic of particulars in external relation, which offers no escape from solipsism and belongs, not to philosophical nor even ordinary thinking, but only, as we shall later see, to a rather rarefied type of economic observer. The awkward predicaments from which it cannot release us in fact never arise. The specious present, which Mr. Russell drops almost as soon as he touches, provides the clue to memory. Here at any rate is undeniably identity in difference. The whole duration of it is called 'present', but no element of it is purely present save a merely ideal durationless instant in which we conveniently regard it as terminating when we measure it. Mr. Russell himself virtually admits the converse of this when he talks of 'degrees of pastness'; for what are degrees of pastness but degrees of presentness looked at the other way round, somewhat as degrees of cold are also degrees of heat? In memory proper the principle is the same. The gulf which recollection spans is not a total break in identity, and forgetting offers us no less a problem than memory. In our empirical experience there are many gaps besides those which memory involves, and none of them can be theoretically crossed without presupposing some such *a priori* unity of apperception as Kant invokes, some unity such that only within it 'gulfs' and 'gaps' have any meaning at all. The 'this' of 'this occurred' does express identity; it is not 'vague' in Mr. Russell's sense. Theory above the level of behaviourism is bankrupt if we must count the sensation wholly dead when the image has faded away. That no doubt implies a latent and 'unverifiable' mental content. If Mr. Russell dislikes it he would have done better to accept the engram theory, which at least preserves identity at the physiological level, and is quite a good enough hypothesis to base prediction on.

Mr. Russell has something to say later on about belief in general, but I think we may legitimately ask at once just what is the belief-feeling which leaps the chasm dividing past from present. We have seen that feeling is a logical construction,[2] and since feeling is mental this belief-feeling is presumably constructed out of sensations or images or both together. But, if I under-

<hr />

[1] *Analysis of Mind*, p. 160.   [2] See p. 89.

stand Mr. Russell, sensations and images never have any time-determination but 'presentness'. How a structure of them should acquire 'pastness' we are not told and I cannot guess. All Mr. Russell really does is to state the perfectly familiar fact that all of us sometimes 'feel-believe', so to say, that what we are experiencing is past, and we call this remembering. Once again he fills a gap by retaining presuppositions which remain quite outside the system which he is trying to build out of sensations, *sensibilia*, and images.

The rest of Mr. Russell's account of mind is chiefly interesting because it reveals more and more plainly the perversity of his procedure if it is taken to be philosophical in aim. At each stage he introduces a new activity of mind familiar in common experience, and does his best with Occam's razor to slash it into bare particulars. These mutilated shapes remain recognizable only because we continue to assume them as we knew them before Mr. Russell began to subject them to analysis. The sketch-map which he provides may be useful for prediction and control, but as a philosophical treatment of mind it has not even the interest of a caricature. I shall summarize it with only an occasional comment. The account of words and meaning which comes next has importance for modern views of logic and language, which we must ourselves discuss later, but some readers may prefer to skip or skim the rest of this chapter.

A word as a physical thing has two causally connected aspects: it is spoken and heard. *Qua* spoken (the more important aspect for the analysis of thought) it is a class of similar series of movements which develop naturally by habit, only rarely by convention. The needful degree of similarity cannot be made precise. Words relate to things which may be called their 'meanings', but there is no simple one-one correspondence of word and thing, and to determine what the precise relation is we must first analyse both the terms. Mr. Russell offers five types. (A) Proper names. The word 'Napoleon' is a set of series of movements linked by similarities. Napoleon, the individual, may have been a single identical *ego*, but although that cannot be disproved there is no ground for supposing it. Napoleon as empirically known was a causally connected series of appearances, together with various occurrences causally connected with those appearances. Thus neither the word nor the man is a 'particular',

an ultimate atomic constituent of the world. Particulars might
have had proper names if language had been invented by scientists
and not for practical purposes.[1] As it is, we give a proper name
to the individual system—'Jones' for example—and not to the
'ultimate brief existent', the particular appearance of Jones which
interests us. (B) A general name—'man', 'cat', etc.—means 'a
whole class of such collections of particulars as have proper
names', and the collections are assembled by virtue of a
similarity or a common property.[2] (C) Some verbs, such as
eating, sleeping, walking, mean a set of occurrences which are
similar, not causally connected as two instances of 'Jones' are
causally connected. Yet it is hard in practice to distinguish
(C) from (B), because an instance of, say, 'walking' is a process of
causally connected earlier and later parts just as 'Jones' is. We
must not suppose that an instance of walking contrasts with
Jones as something insubstantial. We are apt to think that
Jones walks and that walking could not exist without a walker.
But equally there is no Jones without walking and like movements: actions do not need agents any more than thinking needs
a subject or *ego*. 'Jones walks' is equivalent to 'walking is part
of a series of occurrences which is Jones'. 'There is no *logical*
impossibility', says Mr. Russell, 'in walking occurring as an
isolated phenomenon, not forming any part of any such series as
we call a person.'[3] Hence these verbs may be classed with words
like 'rain', 'sunrise', 'lightning', which are not actions and only
differ from general names because their instances are simpler.
(D), qualities, differs little from (C) save that qualities are states
and not processes. 'White' means a set of particulars similar in
respect of a static quality which is not a process. Whether there is
a universal whiteness, or whether white things are to be defined
as similar to a standard thing such as freshly fallen snow, is a
problem which Mr. Russell regards as insoluble and here irrelevant.[4] (E), words expressing relations, such as 'in', 'above',
'before', 'greater' and so on, are more abstract and logically
simpler than those we have discussed, but they are more important to logic than to psychology and need not delay us. The
present classification is psychological.

   To 'understand' a word is merely to be made (passively) by

circumstances to use it and behave (actively) in a suitable way on hearing it. It is a habit. Knowledge of the meaning of a word comes by subsequent observation and analysis, and its meaning has always a degree of vagueness: what it means is a target of which the bull's eye is only a part. To use a word correctly is to affect your average hearer as you intend, and no more involves knowledge of its meaning than a planet's motion involves its knowing Kepler's laws. The relation of a word to its meaning is a causal law governing our use of, and our reaction to, a word. For example, 'Car coming!' makes an absent-minded Englishman look and jump aside; no idea intervenes and physiological explanation is adequate. Said to a Frenchman, it entails his translating it into his own language before he jumps. Said to a child who does not understand 'car', it is ineffective unless accompanied by pointing. The association produced in the third case gives the word some of the causal efficacy of the object: 'Car!' can make you jump, though it cannot break your bones. Such effects occur by psychological, not physiological, laws, and are mnemic phenomena in so far as they are identical with or similar to possible effects of the object.

These 'demonstrative' uses of words can be explained on behaviouristic lines. Not so narrative and imaginative uses. In narrating a remembered event the speaker does not see but remembers and images, while the hearer does not expect but forms similar images, unless the word-habit telescopes imagery. Thus we talk 'demonstratively' to produce sensations, 'narratively' to produce images. We can narrate (*a*) describing or recalling a memory image; or (*b*) either describing an imagination-image after the manner of a novelist, or creating one in order to give information (which we intend also to create belief in an occurrence). These two narrative ways of talking, including inner speech, cover the use of words in thinking, and a behaviouristic account is here inadequate, because the most essential function of words is to bring us in touch through images with what is remote in time and space.

To explain the function of words in thinking, we must consider the causes and effects of their occurrence. A present object causes a word through association. The causing of a word by an absent object is harder to explain, but in general whenever we use a word aloud or inwardly, some sensation or image (either of which may be itself a word) which has frequently occurred in the past together with the word, now through habit causes the word. When we 'understand' a word, the word and the image of what it means are reciprocally associated, so that either may cause the other. Hence we can by speech produce in others 'the images which are in us'.[1] And the word by telescoping can produce the same effect without the intervening image: words, after they have been learnt, tend to work without images.

Images as well as words have meanings, and the meanings of images are more primitive. They are, however, usually vague, since images are very often compromise copies of several prototypes and so approach the general idea in function. This generality is also evident if we consider the causal efficacy of an image. If an image is a copy of a definite object, St. Paul's Cathedral, for example, it shares some effects with its object, especially those which depend on association. This connection between the causal laws of the object and the causal laws of the image extends also to vague images: the vague image of a dog, for instance, has effects connected only with dogs in general. So the meaning of an image must be defined by both (a) its resemblance to its prototype(s) and (b) causal efficacy.

We may extend this analysis to meaning in general. If in mnemic causation the stimulus effect of an image or a word is nearly the same as that of its object would be, then the image or word means the object. If, on the other hand, the mnemic effects are only generic, then the image or word is general. Generality and particularity are thus both a matter of degree. If two particulars differ sufficiently little, their mnemic effects will be the same. In that case no image or word can mean the one as opposed to the other, which sets a bound to particularity of meaning. On the other hand, mnemic effects of sufficiently dissimilar objects will share nothing discoverable: words such as 'entity', which aim at complete generality of meaning, are devoid of mnemic effect and therefore meaningless. In practice, however, 'such words have *verbal* associations, the learning of which constitutes the study of metaphysics.'

The meaning of words which are not onomatopoeic is constituted only by mnemic laws and not by resemblance. Hence the meaning of a word is more precise than that of an image

[1] See *Analysis of Mind*, p. 206. Mr. Russell presumably means similar images.

(though neither is quite precise, and this is not the fault of defective analysis), and the intelligent use of words can, by telescoping, proceed without use of images. Given correct association of words with objects, the theoretical understanding of them can advance merely by correctly associating them with each other, while their practical understanding involves associations with other bodily movements.

Words, as compared with images, have many advantages for thinking. A word can be produced at will. Being concrete, sensible, and not charged with irrelevancies, it enables us to dwell on abstractions. Two instances of a word are so similar that they share all associations, which greatly facilitates generalization. Yet, Mr. Russell warns, to go back and contemplate facts through images is the only way to guard against a false parallelism of facts and sentences.

'I am an Englishman,' said Sir Charles Dilke: 'I have no general ideas.' It is not surprising to find that Mr. Russell, discussing general ideas and thought,[1] in the main accepts the view of Berkeley and Hume that abstract general ideas are a myth, and that a particular image can serve to signify all other particulars. He finds Berkeley to have erred chiefly is not realizing that images are usually vague and have more than one prototype. One can have a vague average image like a composite photograph, but to make it function as a general idea one must also have particular images 'sufficiently clear to be recognized as different, and as instances of the generalized picture',[2] with which it must be possible to contrast them.[3] Vague, particular, and general ideas may be distinguished by the reactions they produce as well as by content. 'Smith', for example, is vague, because it applies to several individuals but to each *qua* individual. 'Man', on the other hand, is general: we say, 'This is Smith', but 'This is *a* man'. 'I am inclined to think', says Mr. Russell, 'that [the difference] consists merely in the knowledge that no one individual is represented, so that what distinguishes a general name from a vague idea is merely the presence of a certain accompanying belief.'[4] This is analogous to the belief which refers a memory image to the past.

Mr. Russell then attempts to clarify his attitude towards

---

[1] See *Analysis of Mind*, Ch. XI.   [2] Ibid., p. 221.
[3] On 'vagueness' see p. 103.   [4] Ibid., p. 222.

'universals'.¹ He points out that on a view such as Brentano's, which gives all mental content an essential reference to an object, we could assert a particular mental content having a universal as opposed to a particular for its object, but not on his own view that a mental content is a particular occurrence related only causally and indirectly to its 'object'. So, says he, we cannot decide what a mental content means by examining its intrinsic character, but 'only by knowing its causal connection in the case of the person concerned'. A horse behaves in much the same way whether he smells a bearskin or a live bear, but he is not therefore conscious of a 'universal'. There is no more reason to suppose a man in the same circumstances conscious of a 'universal'. It is only when the logician comes to reflect on similarities and differences that there is any such consciousness, and then it is never consciousness of a single object in the way in which something perceived appears as a single object. It might, however, Mr. Russell thinks, be logically argued that universals are part of the structure of the world, but 'they are an inferred part, not a part of our data'.²

The history of Mr. Russell's views on universals would not be easy to write. Once, guided by a popular interpretation of Plato, he regarded them as 'subsistent' but not 'existent' real things, some of them, including similarity, known by direct acquaintance.³ From that position he has moved tentatively towards the view that, given the word 'similar' (but not 'similarity'), we need no more by way of a universal to help us describe the world.⁴ The doctrine of general ideas which I have been trying to elicit from *Analysis of Mind*, Chapter XI, is very characteristic. The transition from vague to general is said to come with the negative knowledge (or belief) that no one individual is represented. Yet Mr. Russell accepts from Ribot the view that 'the vague appears [in the progress of intelligence, which is from indefinite to definite] earlier than the particular or the general'.⁵

¹ Ibid., pp. 227 ff.   ² Ibid., p. 228.
³ See *Problems of Philosophy*, 1912, Chapters IX and X.
⁴ Cp. *The Philosophy of Bertrand Russell*, p. 688: 'If it is true, as it seems to be, that the world cannot be described without the use of the word "similar" or some equivalent, that seems to imply something about the world, though I do not know exactly what. This is the sense in which I still believe in universals.' And p. 694: 'I hold that such a sentence as "a is similar to b" may assert a fact, and that this fact cannot be asserted without the use of the word "similar" or some equivalent. But I do not commit myself as to the analysis of this fact, or as to why the word "similar" is necessary but the word "similarity" is not.'   ⁵ *Analysis of Mind*, p. 222.

That, however, suggests that the knowledge that no one individual is represented is far from being a merely negative judgment; rather that it is the extremely positive knowledge of general and particular as intelligible only together and in complementary contrast. But that is too like identity-in-difference and ill suits Mr. Russell's basic contention that particulars are data and universals a matter of dubious inference. Generality, like belief-feeling, slips in unacknowledged from common experience, and Mr. Russell does his best to suppress it in the interests of the bare particular, the ideal indubitable.

The topic of universals is bound to recur when we come to discuss logic and language. Meanwhile we may try to follow Mr. Russell's account of belief in general, which he regards as constituting the central problem in the analysis of mind. It does little, however, to solve the difficulties raised by the emergence of belief-feeling in memory, and I shall pass on to what is subsequently said of truth and knowledge before I pause again to comment in any detail.

Mr. Russell makes five preliminary points which he regards as embodying requisites of any theory of belief.[1]

(1) Words have meaning, and meaning is simple relation to an object. A belief, on the other hand, is either true or false, and so has a dual reference to its 'objective', to the fact, that is, which makes it true or false. This implies that its truth or falsity, being thus dependent on fact which is outside the belief, is not the intrinsic character of a belief.

(2) Belief-feeling, whether in bare assent, memory, or expectation, is the same irrespective not only of truth and falsity but also of the content of the belief.

(3) The belief-feeling and the content must both be present occurrences to the believer.

(4) The gulf between the present content and the 'objective' is often so wide that we feel we cannot know anything of the outer world. This feeling is mistaken.

(5) The reference of a belief to its 'objective' must be somehow derived from all or some of the words or images which make up the content. Yet here emerge two difficulties which any theory must meet. (a) A memory-image seems only to get its meaning through memory-belief, but this would seem to make belief more

[1] *Analysis of Mind*, Chapter XIII.

primitive than the meaning of a memory-image. (*b*) It is odd that meaning which is single should generate objective reference which can be either true or false.[1]

Mr. Russell next analyses the content of belief. What is believed—for example, that x occurred, or that x has a property or a relation—is always complex. Its constituents, which must be related, may be words only or images only; or a mixture of either or both with sensations. Thus one constituent must be a word or an image, and a belief-content cannot contain only mere sensations, although it can consist only of words, which are themselves sensations but are also signs with meanings. The pure sensation in the experience of memory, the noise of the tram, for example, in the belief 'That is a tram', is part not only of the content believed but also of the objective fact which verifies it; but only the meaning and not the noise of the word 'tram' is part of the objective fact. If the content of the belief is words only it is a proposition. It is, that is to say, words which have an objective reference and can be asserted or denied. Such a proposition is determinate and intelligible on first hearing to anyone who knows the meaning of the words and the rules of syntax. But a belief-content of mere images, though relatively primitive and often unconscious, can have the same objective as the verbal proposition in which it is subsequently expressed. We might call it an 'image-proposition', taking a proposition in general to be simply the content of an actual or possible belief and essentially true or false.

Mr. Russell now asks what constitutes believing (not, of course, any 'act' of believing), as opposed to the content believed.[2] Rejecting, though not unsympathetically, the behaviourist view that the *differentia* of belief lies in its causing vital bodily movement, and also the Jamesian theory that we believe every idea we entertain unless it is positively counteracted, he concludes that besides the attitude in which we merely entertain a content without judging, there are three special kinds of belief-feeling, viz. memory, expectation, and bare assent, which are linked to their content and not merely coexistent with it.[3] He confesses

---

[1] With the decay of logical atomism the difference between truth and meaning will, as we shall later see, assume primary importance.

[2] *Analysis of Mind*, p.243.

[3] Though this does not, on Mr. Russell's view, affect the intrinsic nature of the content.

that he cannot analyse the belief-feeling, though he thinks it could be analysed, and he inclines to James's view that believing is akin to emotion, and that a man may believe without knowing what he believes. This occurs in nitrous-oxide intoxication and may be the explanation of claims to mystic insight.

Truth and falsity, Mr. Russell's next topic,[1] are conferred on belief by relation to a fact, which may lie outside the experience of the believer. They are therefore not strictly within the scope of an analysis of mind, which is a psychological study of mental occurrences as they are in themselves and ought to terminate with belief. Yet we cannot, says he, ignore truth and falsehood, because 'the question whether our minds are instruments of knowledge, and if so in what sense, is so vital that any suggested analysis of mind must be examined in relation to this question', and there follows a discussion of knowledge in four parts.[2]

The significance of Mr. Russell's transition from psychology to theory of knowledge is not very clear. He begins his analysis of knowledge by criticizing a behaviourist view, which presumably amounts to a claim by psychology to embrace theory of knowledge: Man's knowledge is just his response to stimuli in so far as it is accurate, in so far, that is, as it differs as and when the stimuli differ relevantly and remains the same when they do not differ relevantly. But accurate response is not the whole of knowledge for two reasons: What is known may, outside sense-knowledge, be quite different from the stimulus, as in knowledge of the future or knowledge of timeless abstractions; and, secondly, appropriateness as well as accuracy of response (in which a calculating machine exceeds a man), is needed for knowledge, and that means suitability to purpose.

At this point we may ask whether truth and falsehood are after all intrinsic to belief and independent of reference to outside fact. If so, there seem to be three possibilities. (a) Is the truth of a true belief its self-evidence? In that case all self-evident beliefs must be mutually consistent, but unhappily the same proposition can appear self-evident to one man and not to another. Self-evidence, therefore, seems useless as a practical criterion of truth. This is confirmed if we examine suggested instances. '$2+2=4$' is not self-evident but a purely logical deduction from definitions; not, that is, from properties of things but from meanings of

[1] *Analysis of Mind*, Chapter XIII.   [2] Ibid., pp. 253 ff.

I

symbols which we assign as we choose, even if this is not the whole truth about mathematical symbols. The impossibility of a thing being in two places at once results not self-evidently from a law of physics but from our definitions of one thing and one place; it represents our decision as to the use of certain words, not any property of things. 'This buttercup is yellow' is, in its simplest form, a judgment of similarity. But it is not self-evident, because such judgments are vague and never quite infallible.

(*b*) Does the truth of true beliefs consist in their mutual coherence? Mr. Russell replies that the coherence theory of truth, which (one wonders why) he regards as entailing the view that the world can be deduced by pure thought, rests on a false view of relations. His treatment here is brief and superficial, and we shall do best to postpone any discussion of the controversy involved.[1] Incidentally, he makes the revealing remark that 'Leibniz's conception of many possible worlds seems to accord much better with modern logic and with the *practical* empiricism which is now universal.'[2]

(*c*) Is verification an infallible test of the truth or falsity of beliefs? No, it can only test their probability, and it is not perfectly easy to see how this occurs. The everyday happening of an expected event provides the typical case of verification. Here the image accompanied by expectation-belief 'means' the sensation-event (what actually happens) and is similar to it. But how can we in fact compare these two terms? Mr. Russell prefers a more external and causal view of the relation between them, meaning presumably a more behaviouristic view. Verification attains its maximum when we first have an expectation which enables us to take action appropriate to the event, and then the event gives us a feeling of expectedness related to memory of the expectation. Scientific hypotheses are thus verified,[3] but the process assumes causal laws, and we have no right to regard the existence and persistence of causal laws as more than a lucky accident. Verification thus merely provides the practical method by which the system of our beliefs grows towards the 'unattainable ideal of impeccable knowledge'.[4]

---

[1] See pp. 165–6 and Part III *passim*.   [2] Ibid., p. 268. My italics.
[3] Professor Ayer's term 'probabilified' might here be more accurate.
[4] One wonders sometimes how ideals, even if unattainable, get into Mr. Russell's philosophy. 'Impeccable knowledge' would presumably be knowledge by acquaintance of all the bare particulars there are—or have been up to date.

The final part of Mr. Russell's discussion of knowledge, which seems so far to have advanced little beyond Hume's virtual replacement of knowledge by belief, is an attempt to reach a formal definition of truth in terms of the reference of a proposition to its objective. The objective reference of a proposition is analogous to the meaning of a word, and is a function of the meanings of the words which compose the proposition. But whereas meanings and facts are single, the reference of a proposition to an objective is dual, because truth and falsehood are a duality. You may, for example, believe 'Today is Tuesday' (*a*) when it is, and (*b*) when it is not. If it is not Tuesday, this negative fact is the objective of your belief; but the relation of your belief to the fact is then different from what it would be were today in fact Tuesday. We may say metaphorically that the true belief points towards the fact while the false one points away from it. Thus to determine the relation of reference we must include the direction of the belief, but to do that we must know the truth or falsehood of the proposition. It is therefore better to define the reference of a proposition hypothetically and say that the meaning of 'Today is Tuesday' consists in pointing to the fact that today is Tuesday, if it is Tuesday, but away from it if it is not. This enables us to speak of the meaning of a proposition without knowing whether it is true or false. To know its meaning is now defined as knowing what would make it true and what would make it false.

In very simple cases of image-propositions we can say that the true proposition resembles its objective as the false proposition does not. A true proposition such as a true memory-belief image, 'Window to left of door', corresponds simply to the objective. A false proposition has a less simple relation to the objective.

This theory of truth as formal correspondence between proposition and objective could not be generalized without a good deal of modification. In the first place, any word-proposition necessarily has more terms than the fact to which it refers, because relations are usually expressed in words which are terms and not themselves relations, though they mean relations. Thus 'Socrates preceded Plato' consists of three terms with a relation of order between them, but the objective which makes it true has only two terms with a relation between them. Secondly, negative propositions and negative facts add a further complication. An image-proposition is necessarily positive only: we can disbelieve 'Window to left of door', but we can form no image of the negative fact that the window is not to the left of the door. Moreover, word-propositions, like image-propositions, are always themselves positive facts. In English the fact that the word 'precedes' occurs between 'Socrates' and 'Plato' symbolizes the fact that Socrates precedes Plato. But we cannot symbolize the fact that Plato does not precede Socrates by omitting 'precedes' between 'Plato' and 'Socrates'. A negative fact is not sensible, but language, being intended for communication, must be sensible, and to say what we mean we have to insert 'does not precede' (three positive facts) between 'Plato' and 'Socrates'.

Mr. Russell nevertheless holds that this formal definition of truth as correspondence of proposition and objective is sound so far as it goes. In the case of a positive 'atomic' proposition (a proposition in which only one word expresses a relation and the word 'not' is absent) the objective is obtained by replacing each word with what it means, the word meaning a relation being replaced with this relation among the meanings of the other words. 'Socrates', for instance, is replaced by Socrates, 'Plato' by Plato, and 'precedes' by the relation of preceding between Socrates and Plato. If the result is a fact the proposition is true; if not, it is false. If the (false) proposition is, for example, 'Socrates does not precede Plato', the conditions of truth and falsehood are exactly reversed. 'More complicated propositions may be dealt with on the same lines.'[1] This formal definition of truth is, however, inadequate because it throws no light on our preference for true beliefs rather than false ones. To explain that we must take account of the causal efficacy of beliefs and the greater appropriateness of responses to true beliefs. But appropriateness depends on purpose, which thus becomes a vital part of the theory of knowledge.

Throughout *The Analysis of Mind* the emphasis lies on the cognitive side of experience. Feeling, for example, we have so far met with only in the shape of belief-feeling. Mr. Russell does, however, devote a short space to emotions (which he does not very clearly differentiate from feelings), desire, and the will. Since we have been told that we prefer true beliefs to false ones

[1] *Analysis of Mind*, p. 278.

because they cause responses more appropriate to purpose, and that purpose is a vital part of the theory of knowledge, a brief account of what he says on these topics may not come amiss, although he starts by confessing that he has no original contribution to make and discusses them only in order to complete his main thesis that all psychical phenomena are built up out of sensations and images alone.

A modern analysis of emotion in terms of physiological causation, which is what Mr. Russell proposes, must start, he considers, from the James-Lange theory, namely from the view that the true causal sequence is not (1) perception of fact, (2) emotion, (3) bodily expression, as men ordinarily suppose, but perception of fact followed by a bodily change which is accompanied by emotion, and this emotion is nothing but the feeling of the bodily change. This revolution Mr. Russell in general accepts, but he prefers to use 'emotion' to mean the whole process, of which perception thus becomes only a cross-section, and in order to reduce the ingredients of emotion to no more than sensations, images, and bodily movements[1] he starts by excluding pleasures and pains and desires. These, he says, are 'dynamic elements' of an emotion but not ingredients.

To explain this we must turn back to what Mr. Russell has said of desire and feeling in *Analysis of Mind*, Chapter III. Human desire is commonly supposed to be an attitude towards something unactual and merely imagined, namely the 'end' of desire, which is also called the 'purpose' of any action resulting from the desire. On this view an image of rain is the identical content of belief when I expect rain, and of hope when I hope for it. The sequence is image, then feeling of desire, then action. This view is false. The first evidence against it is Freud's discovery that we often believe we desire A in cases where observation shows that in fact we desire B, and that this applies also to the means we pursue. B is usually less reputable than A, so Freud holds that in these cases desire for B has been pushed down into the subconscious by 'the censor', and we deceive ourselves. Mr. Russell, however, thinks that a 'censor' is unnecessary and that most desire is unconscious anyhow. He first considers animals. We do not expect animals to be ethical, and they obviously do many useful

---

[1] Aristotle regarded an emotion as a λόγος ἔνυλος, an embodied or 'enmattered' rationale. Mr. Russell discards the rationale and analyses the matter.

things for the first time—nest-building, for example—without prevision. There is no doubt that we can observe what animals desire. Their desires must, therefore, be exhibited in their actions, which are all that we can observe. We observe, for instance, restless hunger-behaviour in a dog, and the vulgar may say that they infer its 'state of mind' and thence deduce its subsequent behaviour, namely a continuance of restless movement until it finds food, then probably, unless fear interrupts, repose and sleep. But the inference is very precarious. It is better to omit mind and say no more than that the dog exhibits hunger-behaviour. Thus we simply identify the hunger desire with the observed restless movements, although Mr. Russell admits that these cyclic movements differ from mechanical movements which, if they intervene, 'teach' the animal and modify the cycle. The obvious absence of prevision in instinctive action, such as the nesting and brooding of birds, shows that the stimulus is an impulsion *a tergo*, an initial discomfort (rather than pain). The so-called 'purpose' is the result which brings the process to an end, normally in quiescence which feels pleasant.

Mr. Russell now turns to human hunger and finds it much the same. Consciousness in the sense of saying to oneself, I am hungry, may supervene, but we may very well before that have been suffering the uncomfortable sensation of hunger, and have been acting to quiet it by eating. When we are absorbed in reading, for example, eating may continue, and stop when we have had enough quite unconsciously. 'Consciousness' seems to be a mere spectator, and to think that we had the final situation in mind all along is pure illusion. Even if we have come to know what satisfies, and the image of it supervenes quickly on the sensation of discomfort, still the latter is the prime mover. Conscious desire is this discomfort added to belief as to what would allay it, belief which may be true but is so frequently false that Freud was led into his wrong view that we deceive ourselves.

Two points are worth noting as we pass. Because it would be something impossible to observe, Mr. Russell cannot admit any element of potentiality in instinct, anything which may develop and change in kind; nor can he use potentiality to explain unconscious desire. It was for a similar reason that he preferred mnemic causation to the engram theory of memory.[1] Yet it is

[1] See p. 93.

hard to see how his own view of habit can fail to imply potentiality. Secondly, Mr. Russell construes the discomfort of desire as not a tension between actual and ideal but a purely negative repulsion of the actual. It seems we only desire, consciously or unconsciously, not to desire, as when we scratch an itch. Juliet, I suppose, only wanted not to go on wanting Romeo—if, of course, one logical construction can want not to go on wanting another.

Mr. Russell remarks on a complicated consequence of his doctrine. A false belief that one desires x may cause one actually to desire x. These secondary desires, if satisfied, leave the primary desire unsatisfied; hence belief in the vanity of human wishes. A particular case of secondary desire is wishing the impossible and then desiring to believe it realized or about to be realized. Hence spring vanity, optimism, and religion. But these complications do not fundamentally alter the character which human desire shares with animal desire.

To the will Mr. Russell devotes only a few rather desultory remarks. Against the behaviourists he repeats the distinction he has drawn between mechanical and vital movement. As compared with the beating of the pulse, action following decision is voluntary, and breathing, which we can neither cause nor go on preventing by our own decision except indirectly by, for instance, the use of drugs, is intermediate between the two. But Mr. Russell accepts James's view that the only distinctive characteristic of a voluntary act is that it tends to be caused by an idea of movement to be performed, an idea which is made up of memory-images of kinaesthetic sensations which we had when the same movement occurred on a previous occasion. Volition, in the emphatic sense, includes also a judgment after deliberation ('I shall do this'), and a sensation of tension during doubt, which changes as decision is reached. Volition includes no more than this, though there must be conflict of desires if it is to be emphatic.

We may now examine this account of desire and will as a commentary on Mr. Russell's contention that purpose is a vital part of the theory of knowledge. We have been told that the end or purpose of desire is a result which terminates in pleasant quiescence a process initiated *a tergo* by discomfort. Consciousness, if present at all, is a mere spectator: it supplies no final cause. The satisfaction of purpose in actual volition does not seem to be anything more than this same termination of discomfort in the presence of a passive consciousness. Mr. Russell says that the cause of voluntary action is an idea of movement *to be performed*. That at first sight makes the idea look like a final cause, an ideal end operating *a fronte*, particularly when Mr. Russell says that emphatic volition includes a judgment after deliberation. But the content of this idea turns out to be nothing but memory-images of kinaesthetic sensations experienced on a previous occasion when the same movement occurred. It seems, then, that deliberation and judgment amount to no more than the spectator's perfectly otiose comment on the process: Mr. Russell is just borrowing the notion of will from common experience and paying nothing back. We have to conclude that the only purpose to which true beliefs contribute through the responses they provoke is the termination of discomfort. The economic character of Mr. Russell's theory of knowledge is clear enough, and his picture of man's unconscious pursuit of (or drift towards?) ἀταραξία is uncommonly dreary.

Of feelings and/or emotions we have learned little save that they are of different kinds, and that belief-feeling does not necessarily entail knowledge of what is believed. Yet Mr. Russell is content to leave ultimate values to feeling.

The goal for which Mr. Russell is heading might be thus expressed. Suppose that some modern Daedalus had constructed not merely a very elaborate electronic 'brain' but a whole electronic 'organism', and that he had made it capable of responding by signals both 'intellectually' and 'emotionally' to a vast range of stimuli. Suppose that someone who was quite unaware that it had a maker went on tapping the keys and recording the responses until he had sufficient data to produce an account of how it worked. Then his account would be very like Mr. Russell's account of mind—provided, of course, that it could (somehow) include a description of the physical parts of the machine as logical constructions of sensa and sensibilia.

I have dwelt, as I threatened, long and, as I fear, tediously on Mr. Russell's *Analysis of Mind*. I have done so because, although it belongs to the most formative (or should I say disintegrative?) phase in the main current of twentieth-century British thinking, it still offers us a system.[1] I do not know how

[1] See pp. 81-2.

to criticize or even present a philosophical position save as itself a systematic attempt to work out a *Weltanschauung*, or else as a position reached through criticism of such a system. One can begin the study of British empiricism in its classical period with Locke and hope to make some sense of the *Essay* by itself, but to explain Hume's *Treatise* entirely without reference to its antecedents is not a possible task. Scepticism is parasitic; it makes no sense at all until you know what is being disbelieved and destroyed. I have lingered, and I must still for a little time continue to linger, over Mr. Russell, because he alone provides the positive background against which more modern philosophizings in this country can be understood.

Mr. Russell's system is of course a dissolving system; it would not be a fair sample of its century if it were not. Indeed one might say that the very nature of it, the very essence of that reductive analysis in which as a method it consists, is self-dissolution. It is none the less still a system as well as a method. It has a metaphysical basis which holds it together somewhat as the canvas holds together the pigments of an oil painting, a basis which would hold it together even if Mr. Russell could really finish his job and reduce all inferred entities and all logical constructions—all the bits of soft patchwork which he would like to get rid of—to hard particulars. For Mr. Russell still believes in a world of facts. The canvas is fabricated of atomic facts, positive and negative, and if Mr. Russell could show us the truth, the whole truth, and nothing but the truth, all logical constructions and inferred entities would have vanished. We should see nothing but a ubiquitous one-one correspondence of atomic facts with atomic propositions, and we ourselves should somehow be a homogeneous part of what we saw.

Just what on the theory of neutral monism facts are, especially negative facts, was never very clear. If truth depends on a relation between propositions and facts, one might expect facts to be postulated on one side only of the relation; yet for Mr. Russell propositions, too, are facts. For any thinker, however, who assumes, consciously or not, that the only world is the object-world of the economic observer, the concept of fact is bound to become unmanageably ambiguous. But we need not spend further time in criticizing Mr. Russell. His own lapses towards phenomenalism from a causal theory of perception, and his resigned attitude towards the threat of solipsism, show that his metaphysical canvas was very flimsy and he knew it. His successors have ripped it away, believing that philosophies are better without metaphysical backings, and he himself has done a great deal to help them in their work. In the next chapter we must consider the logical aspect of Mr. Russell's atomism, and also his attitude to language not as a psychologist but as a logician, which was one source of the next generation's anti-metaphysical campaign.

CHAPTER VII

LOGIC, LANGUAGE, AND THE
DECLINE OF LOGICAL ATOMISM

THROUGHOUT its long history formal deductive logic has fascinated its addicts, but what from century to century they have supposed its purpose to be is not so clear. Its traditional founder conceived logic in general as a propaedeutic to teach men on what terms statements pertaining to various types of enquiry should be accepted as true. Aristotle treats logical forms as differing in status and importance, sometimes according to the nature of the reality which they reflect, sometimes according to the degree of truth with which they reflect it; and it is not easy to decide how far these are alternative views between which he wavers, how far he supposed them to be mutually compatible and complementary. To the formal logic of class inclusion which emerges in the *Prior Analytics* he clearly accorded a secondary status. It was a mode of formulating scientific material preliminary to the construction of strictly universal and necessary demonstrative syllogisms, and it was the proper logical form for ordering the unscientific, or less scientific, arguments of everyday reasoning in terms of mere validity. On the other hand, Aristotle's basic apodeictic syllogism of the inherence of essential accident in substantial *infima species* owes its form to the structure of a reality which it precisely and truly reflects. This conception may represent a mistaken as well as an unfulfilled ideal, but the apodeictic syllogism is as far as it could be from representing a merely valid form of thought. If in modern terminology you called its three terms 'variables', you could not, on Aristotle's view, find values to determine them without rational insight into real connections which are neither particular nor merely general but at once necessary and universal. The separation of validity from material truth, of bare logical form from content, is, on Aristotle's account of the matter, a feature which increases proportionately as the subject-matter becomes less important, more and more contingent and confused. It becomes sharper and sharper as we descend from the logic of science (a term for him including metaphysics) to the logic of everyday thinking. The purpose of formal logic, recognized or not by its professors, is revealed in the late editorial title of *Organon*, which has attached itself for two thousand odd years to the body of Aristotle's logical treatises, though it appropriately qualifies only some of them. If it has a purpose, formal logic is an instrument designed to improve men's thinking by testing its consistency in a sphere where validity and material truth diverge; and that is *par excellence* the sphere of economic thought.

Validity is the ghost of system. In economic thinking the emphasis lies on the particular event in the particular context which is economically relevant. That particular contexts all fall within one system is for the economic observer a presupposition, but a presupposition only sufficiently determinate to operate as a test of whether he has succeeded in avoiding self-contradiction in thinking out the relevant situation. Consistency in his thinking, when he achieves it, is purely hypothetical and adds nothing actual, no material truth, to the content of his thought, to the actual situation as he establishes it. When the economic observer turns empirical psychologist and tries to observe minds for practical purposes, he becomes, if he is consistent, a behaviourist. When he attempts, for the equally practical purpose of improving his own practical thinking, to reflect on that consistency which has seemed to be a necessary though not a sufficient condition of success in his thinking, he becomes a formal logician, and that is to say he does not become a philosopher. He does not try to answer the question, What sort of system is the universe which contains all particular contexts? He does not even ask it, because he is not concerned with the universe save as the bare objective unity which forms the objective aspect of the transcendental unity of apperception.[1] So when he discovers certain principles in which this consistency seems to articulate itself he attaches no metaphysical importance to them. He does not enquire whether they are laws of thought or laws of things. The ghost of system is still accepted without question of its credentials.

It is only when logic begins to interest philosophers that this

[1] See p. 32.

problem of status arises, and it is at once obvious that modern philosophers—by which I mean the logisticians, the logical positivists, the semanticists, the semioticists; the generality of modern thinkers who combine empiricism with a strong interest in formal logic—retain uncriticized the economic observer's attitude and treat the problem as one which does not properly arise at all. The laws, for example, of identity, contradiction, and excluded middle were regarded by Aristotle as ontological, as attributes of being. Later philosophers called them 'the laws of thought', a title which stuck, and to some thinkers they have appeared to be laws at once of thought and things. L. S. Stebbing, in a discussion which, I think, fairly represents the general view held by logical atomists and logical positivists, contends that they are not attributes of being, because they hold independently of whatever is actual or given, and not laws of thought (by which she clearly means psychological laws), because we sometimes fail to think in accordance with them. They and any other strictly logical principles there may be are, says she, pure form, pure in the sense of possessing a 'complete' generality wider than any actual existent or any actual thought. They are, that is to say, 'negative determinations of what is *possible* . . . they in no sense limit the *actual* to be so-and-so'.[1] They are at the same time, she admits, 'principles exemplified in all reasoning'. Thus reasoning is wholly independent of its subject-matter, and its validity, when it is valid, adds nothing whatever to knowledge of the actual. Why or how bare possibility articulates itself into distinct logical forms, which to some misguided philosophers have seemed to exhibit systematic connection, is a question which interests Stebbing as little as it interests the economic observer. These logical bare forms are simply what a certain sort of analysis reveals when pushed as far as modern logicians can push it.

The alliance of formal logic with empiricism is a natural one, but it is not of long standing in this country. Hume had no great interest in the syllogism. J. S. Mill regarded the 'laws of thought' as generalizations from experience. He based all inference on an unanalysed resemblance of particular to particular, and reduced syllogism to the status of a 'collateral security', seeing in its major premiss a mere useful *aide-mémoire* and not any basis for inference. Indeed he carried the attack on formal logic a good deal farther

[1] *A Modern Introduction to Logic*, 1930, p. 471.

than did Hume. His four methods derive from Hume, but his faith in the power of induction to yield certain conclusions would have seemed naïve to his sceptical predecessor. In these days the glory of induction is dimmed, and its claim to be logical inference appears to some as doubtful as it did to Hume. Meanwhile formal logic has risen sharply in status and repute through its union with pure mathematics,[1] which Mill regarded as derived from experience. In this country Mr. Russell was the protagonist of this novel conception of the two sciences.

A layman talking of mathematics soon begins to talk nonsense, but the broad outline of Mr. Russell's doctrine is fairly easy to grasp. It is only puzzling until we understand the sharp distinction between pure mathematics and the familiar mathematics of continuous and discrete quantity. The former aims at being a purely formal structure of rigid deductive reasoning from indemonstrable principles, and every statement of the pure mathematician is to be analytic and *a priori*. The latter are 'interpretations' of this structure in empirical media which become less and less abstract as we descend from pure mathematics. The first step in modern times towards the discovery of a perfectly pure and formal mathematical structure was the successful definition of geometrical entities in terms of number, the arithmetization, that is, of geometry. It was then found that behind the current definition of number itself lies something more abstract. Peano has offered Zero, Number, and Successor as the three primitive concepts necessary and sufficient for deducing the arithmetic of finite cardinal numbers, but it was shown that these concepts can be more abstractly and more accurately defined in terms of Class, Class-membership, and Similar. But class, class-membership, and similar, so runs the argument, are pure logical forms; hence in principle formal logic and pure mathematics coincide, and the principles of consistency in which bare possibility articulates itself turn out to be just precisely the deductive structure of pure mathematics.[2]

---

[1] Or at any rate its close association.

[2] Mr. Russell devoted *Principia Mathematica*, 1912, to working out the identification over large areas of mathematics. I am quite incompetent to indicate just what the order of abstractness among special mathematical disciplines would be. At the bottom Euclidean geometry is presumably as empirical as natural science, because it applies to perceptual space. At the top would seem to come arithmetic with number defined in terms of class, class-membership, and similar. Somewhere between, I suppose, we should find geometries based on denying the axiom of

An analogous process of identification, or at least of close *rappro-chement*, has taken place in modern philosophy between formal logic and language, and again Mr. Russell has played a leading role. Its course has been less clear, but the considerations which led to it appear to have been roughly these. Pure logico-mathematics, like all thinking, requires expression in language. Because it is completely abstract and independent of content, its proper language must consist of symbols. But a logical symbol must in turn be verbally expressible, even if no exact verbal equivalent for it can be found. The further relation of logic to language in modern philosophy rests, I think, on certain assumptions which a few general remarks on the subject of language may serve to elicit.

It is generally accepted that speech[1] is a mode of experience higher than imaging, at least in the sense that it is a further stage in the maturing of human intelligence. Even as inward and un-voiced, a man's words are more under his control than his images, and language has to be taught and learned. The relation of language to thought presents a certain ambiguity. On the one hand, thought succeeds speech as a further stage of development. As we sensate and image, as it were, in order to talk, so we fumble with words, voiced or unvoiced, in order to think: a single content develops through phases. On the other hand, the prior phase does not wholly vanish in its successor. Thought is not mature until it is expressed in words, and that may at first sight suggest that the relation is reversed, and that words in expressing and completing thought succeed it. But that would be a mistake. For the words in which we stumble on our way to thinking as we begin to supersede mere imagery, are not the words in which we finally express our thought; and the words in which we do finally express our thought do not succeed and supersede it. Rather our thought completes *itself* in the words which express it: words and thought are here an organic unity of elements within which thought saturates and dominates, so to say, the words which are its indispensable complement. My phrase is, I confess, full of metaphor, and there is a problem

parallels and topology. One may also ask whether, when Mr. Russell says that physics gives only mathematical truth, this means only formal consistency and not any material truth.

[1] The general nature of language as coincident with all expression may here, I think, be safely ignored, though it is not irrelevant.

here to which I hope later to return.[1] In the meantime I would
stress only that thought and expressive speech are a unity, and if
you break them apart you change their natures. Both as psychologist and as logician the modern philosopher has tended to
ignore the essential unity of thought and its verbal expression.
The behaviourist reduces thought to speech, and speech to muscular movement in the tongue and larynx. The modern logician
sees language only as it exists in dictionaries and grammars,
and language so embalmed is a very obviously economic product.
Neither can there be any doubt as to why or how it is produced.
Men believe it useful for themselves or their children to learn a
foreign language, either an ancient language or the language of a
country in which the learner has no opportunity to reside and pick
it up without systematic instruction. Here is a practical problem,
and someone must observe and map out the situation relevant to
the purpose in hand. Someone must contrive to envisage as an
empirical object a nation's whole experience in its linguistic
expression; turn a living language into a serviceable apparatus, a
readily assimilable set of sounds and signs, with rules for their
use to be faithfully learned and exactly followed. To construct
this desiccated schematic abstract is the strictly economic task of
the lexicographer and the grammarian. When speech and its
meaning, the thought which it expresses, are divorced for this
practical purpose, the orderly movement of actual spoken thought
ossifies into rules of syntax; words and sentences become mere
types, generalizations abstracted from all particular contexts of
application; the actual everywhere shrinks to the possible. A
language taken in this pedagogic sense stands in a quite loose
external relation to the thought which it exists to express, and the
student may very likely present to himself the relation of words to
thoughts as that of garments to the otherwise naked bodies which
they clothe and reclothe, a simile which expresses very fairly well
what a boy does when he translates from one language into
another, but very ill what a man does when he speaks his own
language intelligently.

The modern formal logician accepts this economic product as
the essence of language. He finds in rules of syntax a clue to the

---

[1] The relation between imagery and language is analogous to the relation between
language and thought, and presents a corresponding problem. Both are cases of
that incomplete self-transcendence which I shall argue throughout Part III to be a
distinctive character of human experience.

logico-mathematical principles of consistency. Thus it seems that one may proceed to the principles of formal logic through the purification either of mathematics or of the syntactical structures of languages. The various languages distinguished by the philologist would, I presume, resemble the various mathematical disciplines in that the former, too, would be special 'interpretations' of pure logical principles, owing to logic nothing of their actual content but only their formal consistency. The two ways of approach to logic would meet in a set of symbols: pure language and pure mathematics would equally be symbolic.

This procedure by purification is of course conceived as analysis. We shall perhaps understand it better if we consider again some of the things which we have learnt in this and the last two chapters. Mr. Russell told us that analysis in mathematics starts with ordinary mathematical notions and resolves these crass complexes into their simple constituents; it reaches, that is to say, more abstract, logically simpler, and more general notions in terms of which we can define or deduce what was our starting-point. Fresh lines of deductive advance towards new mathematical subjects now become possible.[1] One of these, when analysis has enabled the redefinition of number in terms of class, class-membership, and similar, is formal logic. It would in fact seem to be the most important of them and in a sense to cover them all, since with this redefinition of number formal logic and the highest, purest mathematics turn out to be identical.[2]

If we now look for the analogue of this dual process in psychology and physics, in the field, that is, covered by neutral monism, we find that the analytic process there signifies a critical separation of the 'hard' elements from the 'soft' in any proposed psychological or physical definition or description; and we are told that an element is 'harder' the nearer it is to the ideal particular to be known by acquaintance in sense-perception, 'softer' the more merely inferential it is. So the discarding of soft elements would correspond to the mathematical analysis which proceeds from more to less empirical levels of mathematics until it reaches and reveals bare form in pure logico-mathematics. Finally, I presume, to the deductive elaboration of logico-mathematics which Mr. Russell undertakes in *Principia Mathematica*, would correspond in

[1] See pp. 85–6.　　　　　　　　[2] See p. 126.

K

the realm of neutral monism the excogitation of logical constructions to replace the soft products of inference.

The second way of approach to formal logic is the analysis of
language, and as you might call the first way either mathematical
or logical, so, I suppose, you might call the second way either
logical or linguistic. It is an analysis of propositions which
elicits formal structure by substitution of symbols, and its main
purpose in Mr. Russell's hands was the construction of a language
really adequate to express the Russellian universe.[1]

Mr. Russell in fact proposes a hierarchy of languages, each of
which will contain all its subordinates.[2] The basic stratum of this
abstract *Stufenleiter* would be a primary language consisting of
'object words' which possessed meaning in isolation and could
be directly learnt without need for any other words to have been
previously learnt by the pupil. Each of these 'object words'
would express knowledge by acquaintance of a particular perceived event, and each would thus be a proper name for a perceived occurrence.[3] Their number would in consequence be
indefinitely large. A word in the object language would be
asserted truly if it corresponded to the perception, falsely if it
did not. But the words 'true' and 'false' would belong not to
the primary object language but only to the languages above it,
each of which would serve the purpose of making statements
about what was said in the lower languages which it contained.[4]
Presumably the highest language would be an ideal syntax of
symbols at once logical and mathematical, which would express
perfectly the pure form of all empirical content.

We may now attempt to set out Mr. Russell's entire atomistic
system as an ideal schema. The governing principle—*O sancta
simplicitas!*—is that the complex everywhere consists of atomic
simples and is precisely their sum and no more than their sum.
This is most clearly seen in the logical aspect. Every complex
proposition is, ideally, the 'truth function' of the atomic propositions which constitute it; is such, that is, that its truth or falsity

---

[1] The suggestion of a sinister resemblance to 'Newspeak' in George Orwell's
1984 would, I suppose, horrify Mr. Russell.

[2] See particularly *Meaning and Truth, passim.*

[3] Compare pp. 105–6. In ordinary language the nearest approach to a proper
name, a name appropriate to a bare particular, is held by Mr. Russell to be a demonstrative such as 'this' or 'that'.

[4] This recalls Mr. Russell's theory of logical types, constructed to solve puzzles
such as the statement of Epimenides the Cretan that all Cretans were liars.

can be determined from the truth or falsity alone of its atomic constituents.[1] Applying the principle of atomicity to all three aspects of the system, empirical, linguistic, and logical, we should get at the basic level a correspondence between bare neutral monist particulars and object words; but there would, I suppose, be no logical correlate at this level, because it is a level below truth and falsity[2]—unless we could fill the gap with class-members taken in abstraction from classes. At the next level there would, I imagine, be co-ordinate correspondence of (1) the simplest and hardest logical constructions, (2) atomic sentences with only one verb, and (3) atomic propositions. Above this there would be a parallel ascent in stages of (1) more complex logical constructions, (2) molecular sentences, and (3) molecular propositions. The metaphysical backing to this system would begin with atomic facts at the level, I think, of atomic sentences and propositions,[3] and rise through levels of gradually more complex facts.

I have no great faith in this harmonizing of the Russellian gospels, but it is perhaps worth asking the question, How nearly, as science and the ideal language make progress hand in hand, can they be expected to approach the logical ideal? How much will escape the twofold slicing of Occam's razor, the two-directional purge towards pure form on the one hand and pure particulars on the other? We might for a moment think that the ideal pursued by logical atomism is the complete union of consistency and material truth by reduction of particulars to nothing but class-members. Since class-membership is a logical concept conferring no actual character on particulars, that would be a sort of formal panlogism, an entirely one-sided reduction of the world to pure logico-mathematical form. But greatly as Mr. Russell is influenced by Leibniz, he has no intention of reducing sense to

---

[1] Mr. Russell, however, often doubts whether it is theoretically possible to construe the general proposition extensionally as the truth function of constituent atomic propositions. For Mr. Russell's wavering doctrine of universals see pp. 110–11.

[2] Mr. Russell seems to waver on this point, too. In *Meaning and Truth* he allows a correspondence relation between an object proposition and its object which involves some sort of truth or falsity, although this truth or falsity can only be expressed upstairs in a second order proposition.

[3] Or do atomic facts begin on the ground-floor, as what I have said in the preceding footnote seems to suggest? The simples on which Mr. Russell's system is based ought to be indisputably clear and distinct. Unhappily in no single instance are they. The atom seems always to be splitting—not that there is in that anything surprising: sheer analysis is bound to disintegrate *ad indefinitum* that on which it works.

confused thought. His particulars are not mere class-members. They have, one might think, been severely docked to fit a logical bed of Procrustes,[1] but they are offered as hard, strictly empirical data, known as individuals by direct acquaintance. Pure forms at one end, and at the other an inexhaustible supply of bare particulars requiring to be given proper names—these remain the opposite poles of the system, and the question is what will survive between them. The answer is not very clear, and perhaps I speculate idly. The differences between the five senses will, I suppose, abide intact, for the physicist's account of sense covers only the conditions of sensation; it cannot, so long at least as Mr. Russell retains neutral monism, completely replace the psychological account. Moreover, according to Mr. Russell, 'physics reveals only certain mathematical characters of the material with which it deals'.[2] This tempts one to ask whether or not mathematical physics is destined under analysis to become a part of logic; whether, that is, the empirical element in physics must always survive, or whether it is a 'soft' residue of dubious inferential objects which will gradually wither away, first into logical constructions and then into mathematical equations. Perhaps the second answer is the right one, but the case of causal laws is harder. On the account of causation which Mr. Russell gives in *Analysis of Mind*[3] they are little more than statistical, but that they exist and persist is, he thinks, only a lucky accident: they are certainly not logical forms. In short, logical form and empirical content remain distinct, but the aim of analysis is to reduce the latter so far as may be to fit the former neatly.

Mr. Russell's logical atomism is thus based on certain assumptions which might be called ontological or epistemological or both: pure logical form and bare particulars, the latter known in principle by direct acquaintance, even if none of us ever met one. But the system is not a static one, since the supply of particular sensations or perceptions is in principle inexhaustible, and logical

---

[1] One may here touch on the opposite side of the picture. Logical form is just as drastically gutted to receive its content as particulars are cut to fit it. Logical classes are constructed solely in extension. Between their intensions there is such perfect disconnection that, although true propositions imply no false ones, yet all true propositions 'imply' one another, and every false proposition 'implies' every true proposition. Validity, poor ghost of system, virtually vanishes in classification, and 'implication' in the sense to which it is wrested is a veritable *lucus a non lucendo*.

[2] *Analysis of Matter*, p. 10.

[3] See p. 87. But Mr. Russell's conception of causation is apt to vary.

classes can accordingly be infinite. Moreover, Mr. Russell's constant hesitation to decide whether his assumptions are in fact ontological or merely epistemological makes it clear that in his philosophy, even as early as *The Analysis of Mind*, system was beginning to vanish into mere method.[1] He starts with a causal theory of perception, and he gives his picture of the world at least a quasi-metaphysical backing of facts. But he soon shaves down causation as nearly as he dares to *de facto* sequence, and his attitude is as often as not phenomenalist. He is also a mathematician, and whether mathematics is a systematic account of certain abstracted characters of material things, or a way of thinking about them which is independent of their actual characters, a sheer method, that is (or, as H. A. Prichard called it, a 'dodge'), became a possible question to ask as soon as Plato pointed out that geometry was not derived empirically from land survey. Mr. Russell's identification of mathematics with formal logic was already a clear indication of the trend from system to method in contemporary British philosophy.

Mr. Russell's effort to reduce the world to logical form and bare empirical particulars is in the end self-defeating. The formal and the empirical elements will not remain apart on Mr. Russell's terms. His bare empirical particular we saw long ago to be a myth.[2] His docking and trimming destroy its empirical character. It becomes after all and against his intention virtually nothing but a class-member, and particulars which are nothing but class-members are themselves an element of logical form. We need not, however, press this point, for the fate which awaits logical atomism is perfectly plain. The study of pure logic becomes the function of the mathematician, and what we used to call Nature is reduced to logical constructions which are at once philosophical and scientific. In other words, as natural science progresses philosophy must go on vanishing into it, until it becomes obvious that the analytical philosopher has argued himself out of a job. Equally in this progress the mind of a man, be he a Plato or an Einstein, a Shakespeare or a Mozart, a Napoleon or a Jesus of Nazareth, becomes a logical construction of particular events which are really the concern of nobody but the empirical psycho-

[1] The time was coming when candidates for Fellowships in philosophy at Oxford (and Cambridge, too, I suppose) would almost invariably be recommended by their sponsors as possessing 'powerful logical techniques'.
[2] See pp. 95–8.

logist. This whole astonishing industry is an effort to remap the universe as an object for the economic observer. But on its own hypothesis it is otiose: this useful work is being quite happily done in the departments. It needs no unprofessional assistance from outside.[1]

After logical atomism[2] the philosophy of analysis steadily contracts its scope. We have seen that the unpretentious metaphysical backing of Mr. Russell's picture was evanescent. Now it disappears altogether. Metaphysical speculation of any sort is rejected as meaningless nonsense: it is not simply, in the manner of the classical empiricists, condemned as idle on the ground that metaphysical statements, though intelligible, cannot be tested, and that therefore metaphysical truth cannot be reached.[3]

Before anything is said of the logical positivism into which logical atomism declined, it is important to note what this uncompromising dismissal of metaphysics entails. On the assumptions of analytical philosophy, once the general principle of truth by correspondence is eliminated as metaphysical, material truth, the truth of all true empirical propositions, is bound to vanish, too, and there remains only formal truth. But it is absurd on the basis of any kind of logic to suppose that formal truth can subsist by itself. The logical atomists held formal truths to be true because their denial involved self-contradiction. On this view formal truths are known by intuition or inference, independently of material truth; for formal truths are tautologous, and to the analytic philosopher tautology suggests something safe and indisputable, though to everybody else something vacuous and abortive. In the sphere of economic observation the remote alliance of formal and material truth works tolerably well, but it only works at all because it is an alliance of complementaries. Form, however pure, is the form of its content. If the definition and

[1] In 'The Philosophy of Logical Analysis', *The Monist*, 1918–19, Mr. Russell himself said, 'The only difference between science and philosophy is that science is what you more or less know, and philosophy is what you do not know.'

[2] For the sake of convenient exposition I have more or less equated logical atomism and Mr. Russell, but 'after logical atomism' is not intended to imply that Mr. Russell is not sometimes to be found keeping company with thinkers who have rejected logical atomism. Historical order is not my main concern, and in any case it could not, of course, be established definitively among philosophers many of whom are still alive.

[3] Mr. J. O. Urmson in *Philosophical Analysis*, 1956, p. 102, makes this point very well. In this chapter I have borrowed largely but gratefully from Part II of his book in respect both of material and emphasis.

criterion of material truth is put away, another partner for the widowed truth of tautology has got to be found. But what is it to be? On the correspondence theory material truth is correctness, and a proposition possesses it by virtue of exact correspondence to a fact. But the fact must be metaphysical. A physical fact may correspond to another physical fact, as the height of a column of mercury, for example, may correspond with a degree of atmospheric pressure, or the flesh of a finger with a finger print; but the correspondence which is alleged to make a proposition correct can be no more than the analogue of a correspondence between physical facts, and the analogy is dangerously misleading.[1] The successors of the logical atomists, as we shall see, rightly rejected the analogy, but when they had ruled it out, how were they to define material truth? We shall find that they never seriously met the challenge. They virtually abandoned material truth and tried to work instead with the concept of meaning. Meaning necessarily implies truth, but for that they cared little, and after making some play with the notion of 'verification', they set to work to bury their heads in the sand of a sort of second-degree, linguistic phenomenalism.

The collapse of Russellian metaphysics was already prophesied as early as 1919 in the *Tractatus Logico-philosophicus* of Mr. Russell's pupil Wittgenstein. The beginning and main content of this work is an exposition of logical atomism even more confidently and uncompromisingly atomistic than his master's teaching. It does not otherwise differ from its model in any respect which need here concern us. But this rather fascinating discourse, at once epigrammatic and dreamily reflective (or so I feel it), and wholly refreshing in the brevity of its German sentences, has not reached the halfway mark before the reader notes an intermittent outcrop of sceptical remarks, and the *Tractatus* ends with what sounds like a complete palinode. The position from which the collapse begins is this. 'The totality of true propositions,' says Wittgenstein, 'is the total natural science (or the totality of the natural sciences)' (4.11), and he has already told us that a proposition is, in a broad and loose sense, a picture which represents a fact. But the attempt to make this relation of correspondence precise lands Wittgenstein in the difficulties which recur monotonously with every recrudescence of empiricism. On the picture side, Wittgenstein

[1] Cp. Joachim, *Logical Studies*, 1948, Part III, especially pp. 230-41.

takes as given the empirical content on which an empirical proposition is based, and he states (4.064) that every proposition
must already have a meaning before it is asserted, because the
meaning is what the proposition asserts.[1] Here Wittgenstein,
like Mr. Russell and most of our linguisticians, is clearly thinking
of meanings as typified and stored in dictionaries, where they
presuppose the assertions in which they were begotten and from
which lexicographers collected them. Wittgenstein, however,
does warn us that a proposition pictures facts only in so far as it is
logically articulated (4.032), and that although propositions can
represent the whole of reality they cannot represent what they
must have in common with reality in order to represent it, namely
logical form. To make them do that we should have to put ourselves and our propositions outside logic, that is, outside the world
(4.12). We are told that this logical form 'mirrors itself' in the
proposition and 'expresses itself *in*' language, and that is why the
proposition cannot represent it, and why we cannot express it '*by*'
language: the proposition 'shows' the form of reality (4.121).

This confession of philosophical aphasia means that for logical
atomism a real world—even a real world modestly defined as all
that happens to be the case but might be otherwise—has turned
out to be a quite indefensible postulate. Had Wittgenstein, whom
I can never feel to have been a natural empiricist, been more
fortunate in his philosophical education, it might have struck him
that one can and must put oneself and one's propositions outside
the world—such a logic and such a world—if one proposes to
philosophize. But Wittgenstein follows the now inescapable path
towards solipsism. It seems he will encounter darkness like
a bride: 'What solipsism *intends* is quite correct, only it cannot be
said: it shows itself' (5.62). He continues, 'That the world is *my*
world shows itself in the fact that the limits of language (*the*
language, which I alone understand) mean the limits of *my* world.
The world and life are one. I am my world. (The microcosm.)'
But he recognizes at once that solipsism destroys itself: 'The
thinking, presenting subject; there is no such thing. . . . Solipsism
strictly carried out coincides with pure realism. The *ego* of solipsism shrinks to an extensionless point, and there remains the
reality coordinated with it' (5.64).

Here, in a tantalizing section (5.641), Wittgenstein adds a

[1] Cp. p. 115.

corollary which he does not develop, a recollection of Kant perhaps: 'There is, therefore, really a sense in which in philosophy we can talk of the *ego* not psychologically. The *ego* occurs in philosophy through the fact that "the world is my world". The philosophical *ego* is not the man, not the human body or human soul of which psychology treats, but the metaphysical subject, the limit—not a part of the world.' Is this a reprieve for metaphysics? Is Wittgenstein on the edge of saying with Hegel that to recognize a limit is to have overstepped it? There are other *dicta*, too, which suggest that it might be so: 'The solution of the riddle of life in space and time lies *outside* space and time' (6.4312). But no; there is no solution because there is no riddle: 'The solution of the problem of life is seen in the vanishing of this problem' (6.521). Metaphysics must go. Philosophy is not a theory but an activity of elucidation. Then comes the final paradox: if the philosopher utters propositions, they are bound to be senseless. The notorious penultimate section of the *Tractatus* reads: 'My propositions are elucidatory in this way: he who understands me finally recognizes them as meaningless, when he has climbed out through them, on them, over them. (He must, so to speak, throw away the ladder after he has climbed up on it.)'

This climax has a fine appearance of uncompromising logic. We seem to have watched the quarry ruthlessly pursued and killed. But the fox has only gone to ground. For if Wittgenstein's elucidatory propositions are senseless, not less senseless are the words in which he discards them. The last sentence of the *Tractatus* is, 'Concerning what one cannot speak of one must be silent,' but the author does not add, 'Sorry I spoke.'

Here once again, one would have said, empiricism is shown to refute itself, and not metaphysics only but logical atomism *in toto* has perished. The vacuum-cleaner has swallowed its latest over-inquisitive owner, despite the virtuosity of his acrobatics on the brink. The critics of logical atomism, however, preferred to accept the annihilation of metaphysics and attempt to reconstruct empiricism without it. I shall try to offer some representative samples of doctrine, again without strict observance of historical order.

If you deny metaphysics and the correspondence of true empirical propositions to facts which they in some sense picture; if at the same time you retain the originally Russellian theory of sense-data; then you will very likely place your hopes in the principle of verification as a substitute theory of material truth and a less ambiguous way of exploding metaphysics than Wittgenstein's. Perhaps you will start by saying, 'The meaning of a statement is the meaning of its verification.' This at any rate quickly disposes of metaphysics, because metaphysical statements, being neither tautologous nor verifiable by any conceivable method, must be meaningless. The onus now lies on you to explain what actual verification is, and you must, I think, be prepared to maintain that we do sometimes have absolutely veridical and indisputable sense-data which can either fully confirm empirical statements or at least make them probable. You may have an uneasy feeling that your notion of material truth is still rather ambiguous, but you have at any rate rid yourself of metaphysics. If you still find it convenient to talk of 'facts', you will not meaninglessly mean facts beyond experience to which propositions unverifiably correspond. So for the moment you may forget possible holes in your position and proceed to consider what will now be the function of philosophical analysis, the only sort of philosophizing which has ever come within your ken. Here you will have to make an important change. You can still work with symbolic logic as your tool, substituting one verbal form for another as its equivalent by a logico-mathematical equation, with the purpose of clarifying the structure of language. You will not, however, be able to claim, as the logical atomists claimed, that the further purpose of this analysis is to elucidate the structure and relationship of facts beyond experience. Your linguistical analysis may, nevertheless, seem to be exposing enough metaphysical nonsense to keep you happily occupied, and you may even hope to expand it into a clarification of the whole language of science conceived as covering in principle all empirical statement. To that end you may set about building a fabric of higher- and higher-order tautologies after the model of Mr. Russell's *Principia Mathematica*; but facts in the old sense you must eschew.

I have tried to describe in rough and general terms the initial position of logical positivism. In England it arose through criticism of Mr. Russell and Wittgenstein, but under strong influence from the Vienna circle, especially from Carnap. But in modern British philosophy cross-breeding is quick and frequent, and there would be little profit in genealogical research.

The effort to clarify scientific language made small progress, and there does not seem to be evidence that the scientists took much notice of it. The difficulties of the new position soon became apparent, and the conflicts which arose are revealing. Some held a 'strong' theory of verification, contending that empirical statements are significant if and only if they can in principle be verified conclusively. This suits the still retained view that beyond simple atomic propositions there are only complex propositions which are strict truth-functions of their constituent atoms. Even Mr. Russell, however, though not yet Wittgenstein, had sometimes wondered whether one could reasonably treat general propositions as no more than truth-functions of all their indefinitely numerous constituents, and this doubt persisted.[1] Others preferred their verification 'weak', taking the *prima facie* more prudent view that no atomic propositions—no 'protocol statements', as they were called—however simple a matter of fact they record, are perfectly certain. They held that an empirical proposition is significant if there is some evidence of its truth or falsity, some observation which would be relevant to the establishing or refuting of it. But this introduction of degrees of meaning created obvious difficulties: how are we, for example, to understand the meaning of a partly unverifiable statement in so far as it is not verifiable? Moreover, either formulation of the verification principle seems to require the occurrence of some indisputably veridical sense-data. Meaning begins to slip back into truth, and truth again to depend metaphysically upon correspondence to fact.

The struggle of the logical positivists to keep verification and discard fact was often ingenious but never convincing. They had designed themselves a pure logico-linguistic asylum, and they wanted to organize its syntactical structure and select the words of its vocabulary free from any external interference. At all costs they must avoid building any extra-linguistic element into its foundations. So, if they were asked what was the relation between sense-data and material things, they would say that, as it stood, that was a senseless question, and they would transform it into a sensible one by introducing a severality of languages. You may, they would tell you, at your convenience describe what you experience either in terms of sense-data or alternatively in terms of material things. You have an equal chance of speaking the truth in either case, but if you do not wish to be misunderstood and

[1] For Mr. Russell's own cautious view of verification see p. 114.

accused of contradiction, you must define your terms, explain
what usage you are adopting, say which language you are talking.
It was not meant that you could avoid contradiction by perfectly
arbitrary definitions of the meanings of words. The idea was that
salvation lay in not confusing the established usages of words. To
accept the sense-data theory appeared to Professor Ayer in 1940 to
involve 'nothing more than a decision to use a technical language.'[1]

Carnap banged the door on metaphysics yet more brusquely.
He distinguished between a material mode of speech in which
ordinary men talk about facts and things, and a formal mode in
which nothing but words is spoken of. The difference can be
indicated in print by the use of inverted commas, and anything
said in the material mode can in principle, and by philosophers
must, be translated into the formal mode. For example, 'A rose
is a thing' becomes ' "Rose" is a substantive'. This struggle to
remain inside the safe limits of significant language—it is like a
Freudian baby trying to shirk the trauma of birth into a real world
of truth and falsity—reached its climax when Carnap asked himself on what principle the basic 'protocol statements' of language
are to be determined. It was usual to say that they are such reports
of direct experience as we take to be accurate, but for Carnap's
uncompromising positivism a report of direct experience was
taboo. Such a thing could only be expressed in the material mode
—'Here, now, blue', for example, or 'There red'—and it had got
to be translated into the formal mode before it could become a
constituent of Carnapian language. But the translation yields
only, ' "Here, now, blue" and "There red" are protocol statements.' Here Carnap throws over the verification principle as
metaphysical. He maintains that the meaning of a word is only
given by translation or definition, even in the case of so-called
'ostensive definitions', alleged communications of meaning
achieved by pointing to an object. But once translated into the
formal mode in order to qualify for admission into the linguistic
asylum, a direct report of experience or ostensive definition has
quite obviously not gained but lost meaning. It has vanished
into the bare form of 'protocol sentence'. The Carnapian language, in other words, cannot procure itself a vocabulary. We
have seen how in Mr. Russell's system the empirical begins to
disappear into the formal.[2] Now, when the metaphysical backing

---

[1] *Foundations of Empirical Knowledge*, p. 57. Cp. p. 100, note.   [2] See pp. 131–4.

is completely torn from the picture, it evaporates without trace.

Carnap's conclusion was too uncompromising for his British friends—it virtually destroys empiricism—and he himself later recanted. If all philosophical statements are tautological equivalences, as the logical positivists maintained, it is hardly possible to refute Carnap's position, but most British analysts were content for a time to take refuge from metaphysics in quite uncritical phenomenalism. There was after all still plenty of fun to be had out of the analytical tracing of particular metaphysical chimeras to linguistic confusion. If one could assume that the metaphysicians had accepted the general authority of grammar and syntax in their talking and writing, and if one could further assume that the way in which one talks and writes moulds one's thinking rather than vice versa, then, always provided that one is sure that one has a much truer idea of grammar and syntax than the metaphysicians were blessed with, it seems easy to show that most of what they said is nonsense. If one is asked what this true grammar and syntax is, and who or what sets it in authority over philosophic thinking, the answer is plain so long as one accepts mathematical logic as, subject to quite minor modifications, indisputable because tautologous: the true grammar and syntax is ordinary everyday grammar and syntax reduced by analysis to a perfectly logical structure.

Thus the real basis of this anti-metaphysical confidence was still the union of mathematics with formal logic, which seemed to be fully attested by *Principia Mathematica*. Mr. Russell had married mathematics to logic, and the twain really did seem to be one flesh—or one skeleton. He had applied reductive analysis in the fields of psychology and physics, and nobody really modern had protested. The scientists were busy. They may not, if they read Mr. Russell, have learned much from him that helped them in their work, but he was their declared friend. It was when his disciples turned their attention to more concrete subject-matters that their faith was shaken. The effort to analyse material objects into logical constructions of sense-data might produce difficulties,[1] but the attempt to analyse nations as if they related truth-functionally to the acts of singular individual men produced nothing at all but pretty clear evidence that linguistic equivalences simply will not work in political theory as equations work in

[1] See pp. 151–2. Cp. also p. 100 and footnote, and Urmson, op. cit., pp. 154–8.

mathematics and mathematical physics. The declaration of faith
that Napoleon was just a logical construction could hardly be
tested in detail, and it might perhaps be accepted as true 'in
principle', but try to tackle the old examination question, Whose
act is an act of state? by reductive analysis, and the method
patently fails. Occam's razor lies blunted past all stropping.[1]

There seemed to be only two ways out of this impasse. One
could remain with Carnap unshakably loyal to the old logic, put
the blame on ordinary language as hopelessly clumsy and incoherent, and continue to labour towards the construction, or
towards a plan for the construction, of an ideally perfect language.
But Carnap's distinctions between mode and mode and language
and language were blatantly superficial. They pointed rather to
a different way out, serving only to reveal the true and terrifying
inference which must be drawn from the breakdown: what we
must have is not new languages but new logics extracted from
old language. Ordinary speech that was our Caliban to be cuffed
and reformed, or if found intractable banished quite from polite
philosophical circles, must now become our revered master.
We must examine tenderly—may we still say 'analyse'?—the
use and wont of vulgar talk, the idioms and constructions of the
common man. We must not castigate them for their superficial
confusion but welcome in them the accumulated insight of robust
common sense. We must coin fresh phrases to celebrate our new
linguistic liberalism: 'emotive significance', 'verbal recommenda-
tions', 'persuasive definitions'. We may even have to be polite
to the metaphysicians. Mr. Urmson cites two contemporary
slogans as rough labels for the new revelation: 'Don't ask for the
meaning, ask for the use', and 'Every statement has its own logic'.[2]

The significance of this staggering outbreak of logical anarchy
must be considered again before Part II of this book is ended,
but in the following chapter I shall first try to present the decline
and fall of logical atomism a little more concretely. I shall not
offer a series of supporting quotations but try, as I did in the case
of Mr. Russell, to exhibit one or two important figures of the
period actually at work. I shall of course not pretend that all
they say exactly fits the historical outline which I have sketched,
and for that reason I shall not refrain from any direct criticism
which may seem apposite.

[1] See Urmson, op. cit., pp. 150 ff.   [2] Op. cit., p. 179.

CHAPTER VIII

ANALYSTS IN RETREAT

IN the early nineteen-thirties Professor Ryle, to judge from his published work, had lost interest in logical atomism. He was busy torturing common speech, pointing out the traps it lays for innocent philosophers, and reducing to nonsense by linguistic manipulation the problems and theories of metaphysically tainted thinkers. It was, however, well in the Russellian tradition to bait the more pretentious metaphysicians at any rate, and Professor Ryle's main weapon was Mr. Russell's theory of descriptions. It is further worth remark that Professor Ryle shares, or at that time shared, with Mr. Russell a certain regret that the scope of modern philosophy should be as narrow as they both supposed it inevitably to be. Mr. Russell belongs to the liberal and rationalist tradition. He hates tyranny no less sincerely than he loves mathematics, and he does not gladly relegate values to feeling.[1] His often repeated statement that there is no logical reason for believing cruelty to be morally wrong is the constant return of the tongue to the aching tooth. Professor Ryle, too, was not quite happy in his job. In an article entitled *Systematically Misleading Expressions*, which his editor calls his 'first plain, powerful manifesto',[2] he wrote, 'I would rather allot to philosophy a sublimer task than the detection of the sources in linguistic idioms of recurrent misconstructions and absurd theories.'

The 'plain, powerful manifesto' is a document of interest.[3]

[1] See p. 81.
[2] See the Introduction to *Logic and Language*, First Series, edited by A. G. N. Flew, 1952. The article was originally published in 1932. My references will be to the paging of *Logic and Language*.
[3] Was Professor Ryle at this time a logical positivist? In the article he doubts Wittgenstein's view that there is a real and non-conventional relation of picturing between an expression and the fact it expresses (p.34), but he speaks of 'the form of the facts into which philosophy is the inquiry' (p.36). I suspect, however, that these 'facts' are already conceived by Professor Ryle as purely linguistic and without metaphysical implication. See p. 146.

I will take an example or two from each of Professor Ryle's types of misleading expression.[1] 'Carnivorous cows do not exist' is a true and idiomatically correct statement in the mouth of the ordinary man,[2] but it may, says Professor Ryle, mislead a philosopher into believing that it denies a predicate of a proper logical subject, as does, for example, 'I am not sleepy'. It may then make him contradict himself by asserting non-existence, and at the same time implying existence, of the same subject. Logically, 'carnivorous cows' is not a subject-term but a concealed predicative expression. The deceived philosopher is the victim of a systematically misleading quasi-ontological statement, of which the logically correct expression is, 'Nothing is both a cow and carnivorous'. The same snare lurks in existential statements of which the grammatical subject is mythological or fictitious— unicorns, Satan, Mr. Pickwick—and even if so genuine a person as Professor Ryle himself is stated to be, or to be real, or to be an actual entity,[3] the same logical error occurs. For if it were false that Professor Ryle exists there would be no one for the statement to be about. In all these quasi-ontological statements the grammatical predicate misleadingly suggests possession by the subject, not of a specified character but of a specified status.[4] The truth which, if true, they record can, and should by philosophers, be re-stated without such ontological predicates. Philosophers should say, not 'Ryle exists', but 'There is a philosopher and his name is Ryle', just as, for example, 'Mr. Pickwick is a fiction'

---

[1] In what follows I have substituted names of living men where Professor Ryle's nominees have since died, following the example of Professor E. E. Harris, who has aptly criticized this article in his own article, 'Misleading Analyses', *Philosophical Quarterly*, October 1953.

[2] Whether the statements here discussed are actually true or false is irrelevant to the argument.

[3] Professor Ryle's actual lists of bogus ontological predicates (see op. cit., p.17) run as follows:

Mr. Baldwin—	Mr. Pickwick—
is a being.	is a nonentity.
is real, or a reality.	is unreal or an unreality, or an appearance.
is a genuine entity.	is a bogus or sham entity.
is a substance.	is not a substance.
is an actual object or entity.	is an unreal object or entity.
is objective.	is not objective or is subjective.
is a concrete reality.	is a fiction or figment.
is an object.	is an imaginary object.
is.	is not.
	is a mere idea.
	is an abstraction.
	is a logical construction.

[4] Ibid., p. 18. The reference to status is the important point.

should be replaced by 'There was a story-teller called Dickens, and he coined the pseudo-proper name Pickwick'.

Professor Ryle next tears the mask off 'statements seemingly about universals, quasi-Platonic statements'. 'Unpunctuality is reprehensible' should be replaced by 'Whoever is unpunctual merits reproof', 'Virtue is its own reward' by 'Whoever is good gains something thereby', 'Colour involves extension' by 'Whatever is coloured is extended', etc. Professor Ryle expresses, but does not here defend, the Russellian view that general terms are never proper names and therefore never really the names of subjects of attributes.

The axe then falls on certain quasi-descriptive phrases of the form 'The so-and-so', which are such that the world contains nothing or nobody which or whom they could describe. For example, 'Mendès-France is not the King of France'[1] seems formally analogous to 'Mary Jones is not the Queen of England'. But it is not; for if the latter is true, then its converse, 'The Queen of England is not Mary Jones', is also true, whereas it is neither true nor false to say, 'The King of France is not Mendès-France'. Therefore 'Mendès-France is not the King of France' should be restated as (1) 'Someone is called Mendès-France', and (2) 'Mendès-France has not the rank, being King of France', the implication that there is a King of France being thus avoided. Similarly, 'The top of the tree' does not refer to a thing; it merely signifies an attribute which a thing may have, viz. being in a certain relative position. Professor Ryle suggests that Descartes and Newton made blunders about space and time by hypostases such as 'region', 'path', 'date', etc. Again, 'Jones hates the thought of going to hospital', or 'The idea of having a holiday', may falsely suggest that there are entities called 'thoughts' and 'ideas'. They should be re-stated as 'Jones is distressed when he thinks of going to hospital', and 'I have been thinking that I might have a holiday'.

Certain points emerge. (1) Professor Ryle, though less interested in science than Mr. Russell, is presupposing something fairly like the Russellian world. He is assuming that the only proper logical subjects are particulars standing in external relations and possessing particular qualities or characters by virtue

---

[1] That Professor Ryle is inspired by Mr. Russell's theory of descriptions here becomes obvious.

of which they are similar or dissimilar to one another: his world excludes universals. But Professor Ryle's particulars are not, I think, the bare atomic particulars which alone are, on Mr. Russell's view, strictly entitled to proper names, but just such 'things' as would survive in ordinary discourse purged of logical misbehaviour.

(2) If I do not misunderstand Professor Ryle, any ascription of logical status to these particulars which are true logical subjects would be nonsense. A risky argument *ex silentio* from Professor Ryle's lists of bogus ontological predicates might lead one to conclude that Professor Ryle himself was at least a logical construction. But I think one would be wrong, and I feel sure that in 'There is a philosopher and his name is Ryle' one must not take 'There is' as an assertion of *Dasein*. Not only are all high-flown metaphysical entities annihilated but even the humblest existent of common sense. Professor Ryle's interpretation of Kant's *dictum* that existence is not a predicate seems to be not merely that the 'is' of predication must be clearly distinguished from the 'is' of existence, but that the former is to be substituted *in toto* for the latter. In other words, the metaphysical backing to the Russellian picture has disappeared. Formal logic takes the place of metaphysics, and particulars alone can be logical subjects of predication, not because they are 'real' or 'substantive' or anything else of that bogus metaphysical sort, but because, in Professor Ryle's later terminology, they occupy a certain region in what 'logical geography' maps. Professor Ryle thus modestly reduces himself to a phrase—though I do not forget that 'the sound of a breath may shake the world'. What logical geography maps seems to be just the world (or 'set-up', if 'world' sounds too concrete) of significant human discourse taken as having no reference beyond itself to anything which determines it to significance. Professor Ryle has almost reached a sort of linguistic phenomenalism analogous to common phenomenalism based on sense-perception. His particulars are not really things but names.

By 1948, when he wrote *The Concept of Mind*, Professor Ryle had, I think, fully accepted linguistic phenomenalism. In the Introduction to that work we learn that 'logical geography' maps the knowledge which we already possess, and that to misuse a logical category comes of mistaking the set of ways in which it is legitimate to use a certain concept. The mistake leads to paralo-

gisms and antinomies. Analysis following abstraction and generalization will show us that propositions naturally consequential on,
for instance, 'Mr. Pickwick is a fictitious person' and 'The equator
circles the globe', propositions, that is, such as 'Mr. Pickwick
was born in such and such a year' and 'The equator is of such and
such a thickness', are not merely materially false but in contradiction with something in their apparent logical antecedents. We see
at that point that fictitious persons cannot have actual birthdays,
and that the equator is not a girdle in the sense of a ring or ribbon.

Thus in *The Concept of Mind* Professor Ryle's categories are in
no sense ontological. They do not, like Aristotle's, exhibit the
structure of Being as reflected in discourse, but only the structure
of discourse. An intermediate article by Professor Ryle entitled
Categories[1] already maintains the same view, but perhaps with a
little hesitation. It teaches that categories are types of 'proposition-factors'; that 'proposition-factors' are partial expressions
which can enter propositions otherwise dissimilar but cannot
exist by themselves;[2] that they are what remains when 'sentence-
factors' are stripped of all such (non-logical) differences as the
difference between one language and another. 'Proposition-
factors' are by no means confined to the 'terms' of singular
propositions, and there is no ground for believing that there is
any particular finite number of categories. Categories control and
are controlled by the logical form of the proposition into which
they enter; indeed, to know the form of a proposition is to know
the categoreal types of its factors. Contradictions such as seem to
arise when I state (*a*) the cause and (*b*) the motive of an action,
or when I say I see the bent stick which I know to be straight,
are resolved when we realize that the forms of the propositions
expressing the contradiction, or the categories involved, are not
what we supposed them to be. And that is so because it is only in
virtue of their form, or the form of their category-types, that one
proposition implies another proposition or the negative of it.

In one or two passages Professor Ryle's argument might seem
to imply that categories do have ontological significance. He
holds it 'prudent' to use the 'semantic' idiom, in order to make it
clear that the question always is how expressions, not how what

[1] See *Logic and Language*, Second Series, chapter IV, ed. A. G. N. Flew, 1953.
The article was originally published in 1938.
[2] That is to say a proposition-factor is, in another terminology, whatever can be
a variable in a propositional function.

they signify, can or cannot be coupled without contradiction and absurdity.[1] That, he argues, always is the question, because only expressions can be affirmed or denied to be absurd: Nature provides no absurdities. One might have supposed that it was just because the categories were grounded in Nature that expressions could absurdly violate the order which categories impose on speech that is correct. But Nature is clearly for Professor Ryle merely a part of human discourse, not anything beyond it. Again, in the last paragraph of the article he says that the fact that absurdity can only be asserted or denied of collocated symbols does not imply that propositions about categories can say nothing about 'the nature of things'. He continues, 'If a child's perplexity why the equator can be crossed but not seen, or why the Cheshire cat could not leave its grin behind it,[2] is perplexity about 'the nature of things', then certain category-propositions will give the required information about the nature of things.' But this for Professor Ryle only means that the child will be rid of the discomfort of self-contradiction.

We shall not be far from the truth, then, if we charge Professor Ryle with linguistic phenomenalism in both these articles. Moreover, Professor Ryle's linguistical world is a highly artificial one despite the camouflage of robust common sense in his writings. He forbids us (assuming us to be philosophers) to state that anything exists, lest we attribute to it a specified status and start miscreating ontological monsters. This presumably means that things do not have being either as (a) specified status, which would imply that things can differ in status, or as (b) a general status, which would differentiate them from not being.[3] For according to him it is equally absurd for philosophers to predicate non-existence of carnivorous cows, existence, or being-as-a-real-man, of a living historical figure, being-as-a-fiction of Mr. Pickwick, and being-as-a-quasi-Platonic-Form of unpunctuality; and it is absurd, not for a different reason in each case but for the single reason in all the cases that 'ontological status' is nonsensical: there is (*may* I say 'is'?) only position assigned by logical

---

[1] See op. cit., pp. 76–7. Later, p. 81, he says that only collocations of symbols can be asserted to be absurd.

[2] Was Professor Ryle really such a precocious child that he wondered why it couldn't and not why it could?

[3] Professor Ryle, that is, would regard it as equally false to say with Aristotle τὸ ὂν λέγεται πολλαχῶς and to say τὸ ὂν λέγεται.

geography. Professor Ryle quite often asserts that philosophy is not lexicography, but plainly what he does when he leaves the common man to frame his sentences as he will and confines the philosopher within a pale of logically accurate discourse is precisely to abandon living speech for the lexicon and the grammar, though he would doubtless have his own contributions to make to fresh editions of such works. He forgets, as formal logicians have always tended to forget, that you cannot make up an example of a proposition and argue about its logical form, its consistency or inconsistency with other propositions, and so forth, unless it states something that a rational human being could assert or deny in some context and on some grounds whether adequate or not. In logic that condition must be fulfilled on pain of talking nonsense; in grammar it need not be. Words taken in their dictionary meanings can be strung together to make a sentence which is logically nonsensical but grammatically correct. 'If Homer nods, equities will boom' is a perfectly good example of a conditional sentence, but as a proposition allegedly expressing a hypothetical judgment it is not false but nonsensical. 'Mendès-France is not the King of France' is, according to Professor Ryle, neither true nor false, but has a meaning which could be expressed in a better logical form. But a sentence can have a meaning only if it is either (a) what could be stated by a rational man in some context and on some grounds, or (b) a grammatically formed sentence of words taken as possessing their dictionary meanings. If it is (a), it is either true or false; if it is (b), it is no more a proposition than a mirage is an oasis, and it is not amenable to any logical analysis at all. The question whether existence can be a predicate depends on whether there can be contexts in which something can be stated truly and relevantly to exist or to be. Certainly it is plausible—on the principle that 'if everybody's somebody then no one's anybody'—to deny that existence or being can be a predicate, if you also deny that there are degrees or kinds of being. That was what Aristotle meant when he said that Being was not a kind. But, except on the assumption of linguistic phenomenalism, I can find no grounds whatever for denying that there are kinds or degrees of being; nor, I imagine, could Aristotle when he said that Being is 'declined' through the categories.[1]

[1] If we reject the lexicographical assumption, and say with Aristotle that Being is

The Concept of Mind is devoted to further and more concrete explanation of discourse. The book is offered as philosophical psychology, and the author wields the sword of logic in one hand and the club of common sense in the other.[1] The main monster he sets out to slay is called 'the ghost in the machine'. It is the conception of a mind 'inside' a body, which performs operations hidden from the observation of other minds and knowable to them only by precarious inference from 'external' bodily behaviour. In the course of his crusade he attacks and rather effectively damages some minor monsters bred, or at least brought up, by his own positivisitic friends.

Professor Ryle's argument is based largely on common sense, and he appeals constantly to common linguistic usage.[1] We all habitually observe other men behaving thoughtfully, casually, purposefully, stupidly, skilfully and so forth, and we observe 'retrospectively', but *not* 'introspectively', that we ourselves have behaved, or are behaving, in similar ways. In neither case is there any evidence of two parallel processes, the one 'internal' and the other 'external'. These intelligent operations are each a single process, although each admits of and requires different kinds of explanatory description from, for example, the physicist, the physiologist, the logician, etc. A main source of the 'ghost in the machine' error is a misinterpretation of self-consciousness. We do *not* have privileged access to a view of our own mental operations which gives us a better knowledge of ourselves than others can have and a basis from which to infer to their mental operations. We have to learn about ourselves exactly as we have to learn about other people, and they often succeed in knowing more about us than we know ourselves: 'Would some God. . . .' Thus Professor Ryle, while scouting such fictions as detachable immortal souls, has comfort for the man who fears that successful description of human conduct in physical terms by the radical behaviourist has reduced men to mere material mechanisms. He confesses himself a sort of behaviourist, but he thinks that human behaviour may just as legitimately be called intelligent,

not a kind but is declined through the categories and predicated in many senses, then the veto is lifted from ontological expeditions beyond the linguistic iron curtain. Then it becomes reasonable to question each of Professor Ryle's types of misleading expression on its own merits. We might argue that fictions have their own kind and degree of reality, and that Plato did not in fact just reify adjectives to make his Forms. [1] See p. 152, footnote 1.

or romantic, or honest, or artistic as it may be described in terms of mechanical response to stimulus.

Clearly this criticism of 'the ghost in the machine' threatens death to introspection, to any theory of an 'inner' sense working parallel with an 'outer' sense, and it is illuminating in this context to examine Professor Ryle's onslaught on the sense-data theory. This doctrine is an attempt to explain sense-perception and to solve by the way the problem of illusions. It has varied in detail, but its chief contention is that the immediate object of sensation is not a common object of perception, not a tree or a house or a mountain, as the ordinary man takes for granted that it is, but privately owned sense-data: colour-patches, sound-elements, scent-whiffs, touch-feelings and so on. If all the increment of imagination and all the interpretation which thought contributes are removed from the perceived common object, then there remain, according to the sense-data theorists, indisputably sensated or intuited sense-data. On this account a mirage is not a miraculous non-entity which 'isn't there', but 'wild' sense-data erroneously constructed into an oasis by supra-sensuous activity of the mind; and the elliptical look of a tilted coin, or the two candle flames observed by a drunken man seeing double, are genuine objects of sensation actually observed, and they are made of exactly the same stuff, so to say, as the sense-data which enter into normal perception of common objects. As to the precise relation of sense-data to common objects there has been some disagreement. The old empiricist dilemma of choice between realism and phenomenalism, and the old empiricist bogy of solipsism, have not vanished before the dawn of sense-data. Some champions of the theory have held that sense-data can be an actual part of a 'physical' object, some have not. Some— it was inevitable—have suggested that there are two equally good languages, a sense-data language and a physical object language; that the common object of perception can be alternatively described in terms of either without self-contradiction, and that each language has its usefulness in certain contexts.[1]

Professor Ryle retorts, if I follow him, that sensation is not perception nor observation nor any sort of cognition, and it therefore has no object. Nor can a sensation be itself an observed

---

[1] For this doctrine see pp. 139–40. It is the very acme of economic linguistic phenomenalism.

object: it can only be 'had' and attended to, and nothing is then observed or ascertained. Professor Ryle concedes that perceiving an object implies having at least one sensation, but he argues, very much as has been argued against older theories of mental images, that if sensation is taken to be observation of an object an indefinite regress ensues. He appeals for support to the linguistic fact that we do not ordinarily speak of sensations 'neat', but in naming them refer to perceived objects. We do not, for example, talk of a green look (unless we do not know what it is that looks green) but of something looking green.[1]

Professor Ryle solves the problems of illusions, elliptical looks of pennies, etc., by means of the logical distinction between hypothetical and categorical statements. 'That penny looks elliptical' is really a 'mongrel-categorical' statement. It contains the concealed hypothetical statement that the penny looks as an untilted disk would look in that place. The distinction between categorical and hypothetical is, indeed, of major importance to Professor Ryle. He uses it to explain the nature of all dispositions and potentialities in men and things. Statements asserting them can, we are told, all be 'unpacked' into hypothetical propositions, and this fact supplies, it would seem, an adequate solution of any problems which may arise as to their nature.[2]

This doctrine, which foreshadows very clearly the contemporary shrinkage of truth into mere meaning, is worth a word of comment. You can, doubtless, explain a mirage as what a real oasis would look like, and you can explain the dispositions of tiltable disks, dormant explosives, or bad-tempered men in terms of what they would do or suffer in certain conditions. Moreover, such an expression of the situation is often quite adequate for purposes of communication and action. But when the ordinary man says, 'It'll blow up if you aren't careful', he quite certainly implies, and expects to be taken as implying, much more than that. He means that the bomb is other than it would be if his hypothetical statement were not true, and that it is this character in the bomb which makes his statement true. He takes the nature

---

[1] The reader will note that in the sixteen years elapsed since *Systematically Misleading Statements* Professor Ryle had become vastly more sympathetic to ordinary language. He and his colleagues were now prepared to look for guidance to its usages. It might be thought that he was now moving to join the logical anarchists with their slogan, 'Every statement has its own logic'. It seems more likely, however, that as a logical geographer he still believed that there was only one world to map. [2] See *The Concept of Mind*, pp. 84–5.

of the bomb, that is, as including both its present and its possible future. Thus Professor Ryle's theory gains no support from common sense, and as a piece of logical geography it still rests on the old doctrine of external relations. The inseparability and mutual implication of categorical and hypothetical judgment is not a new philosophical problem, and it is not dissolved by baldly stating that they are mutually exclusive. That fact and necessary connection never perfectly coincide in human experience, and that it is often inevitable in practice to state the one and leave the other tacitly implied, is no ground for denying that there is any logical implication (in the serious sense) between the two.

Professor Ryle's exorcism of the ghost in the machine and the sense-data theory is more successful. It is based on an appeal to common sense against the scientific attempt to turn everything into an object of cognition, and on the rejection of the Russellian hard particular. To that extent it might be called an episode of fratricidal strife within modern philosophy.[1] Professor Ryle argues that both theories erroneously split one integral process into two separate elements and make the second into an object, which in the case of the ghost theory is a process of privately introspectable consciousness, in the case of the sense-data theory a sensum which is certainly a cognized object, whatever its precise status may be. Professor Ryle is right in holding that both these theories mistake the nature of self-consciousness, but it is less clear what positive doctrine he would substitute. One would like to know just how retrospection is possible though introspection is not, and just how it is that our single intelligent operations admit of and require more than one explanatory description.[2] But at this point Professor Ryle seems just to sink back on the support of such ordinary common-sense people as never thought of sense-data and do not happen to believe in ghosts in machines.

In this connection I may perhaps be forgiven for repeating, because I do not know how to improve, what I have said elsewhere: In a philosophical court the place for common sense is in the dock, or on occasion the witness-box, never the bench. Nor is there any gain of magisterial dignity when English common-sense usage is first arbitrarily disciplined and then set up as at

---

[1] On the other hand, it is not very clear who, besides Descartes, are supposed to be the champions of the ghost. Realists, I suppose; some pre-behaviourist psychologists, and all believers in personal survival, perhaps. Certainly not the idealists.

[2] See p. 150.

once the guide and the field of research for all good philosophers.[1] By 'usage' some linguisticians seem to mean 'standard English',[2] and 'standard English' is, I suppose, the vocabulary, idiom, grammar, and syntax accepted by the best lexicographers and grammarians as those now used in common by 'educated' Englishmen; and it would exclude technical terms adapted or invented *ad hoc* by philosophers and scientists. That 'standard English' is an arbitrary and fluctuating concept, based on the social approval of a group and incapable of yielding absolute rules, is among the points made effectively (and in excellent and tolerably standard English) by Mr. Heath; yet if the lexicographers and grammarians are not entirely wasting their time, their standard English must possess some authority. Here we may ask how this standard, vague, local, and transitory as it may be, was actually reached. Clearly it is the gradual outcome of successful expression and communication of thought, emotion, and will by a group sufficiently influential to capture the writers of grammars and dictionaries, from whom, as has been already noticed, our philosophical linguisticians have learned their schoolboy conception of language. Neither is it hard to see what the nature of this gradual process has been, and roughly where it has got to. If we consider those mental acts and operations which modern philosophers still constantly discuss, it is a commonplace that the words for them in standard English started life as elements in the description of physical process or of purely sensuous experience. Some of them did not succeed in entirely discarding their past when they rose to a higher social plane. 'Inference' and 'deduction' once meant, I presume, nothing but a physical carrying into and a material drawing from. 'Intuition' was first a mere ocular looking, but at some time or other it was found to be the best word available to express ('squeeze out') a philosophic or a feminine apprehension ('grasping with the hand') of the invisible. Yet still I may see a rainbow, and I may 'see' that you are right. There is no need to multiply examples of a familiar fact to which the whole texture of standard English—and for that matter most

---

[1] There has been a good deal of wobbling between the disciplinary and the submissive attitude. One might have guessed that this would come when Professor Ryle's plain, powerful manifesto graciously permitted the man in the street to go on talking what it pronounced to be philosophically nonsense; see p. 144.

[2] See *The Appeal to Ordinary Language*, by P. L. Heath, *Philosophical Quarterly*, January 1952, a very good article. For this identification of usage and standard English the author cites Mr. Flew's Introduction to *Logic and Language*.

sorts of English—bears witness; and it testifies no less clearly that it was almost wholly constructed by practical men dealing with practical situations and having need to talk about them. It is the language of common sense. So indeed were standard Latin and standard Saxon, in the making of which had already occurred some of the verbal promotions which I instanced; and so, I suppose, is the standard usage of words the whole world over. It is the fact, reflected in standard usage, that mankind moves, always has moved, and always will move most habitually and readily at levels of sense and practical action that makes standard English rather less vague, parochial, and transient than to anyone but a modern linguistician it might at first sight appear to be.

It does not, however, follow that standard English should be allowed to prescribe any sort of authoritative rule for philosophers, even for English philosophers. The error springs in general from the very nature of empiricism and positivism, but in particular from forgetting how language develops, even the language of common sense which pedagogues for a secondary practical purpose dissect and fix as 'standard'. Words work their way up through metaphor to the full possession of new meanings because men have something new to say, and modern philosophers, who have not anything very new to say, can easily enough take words and phrases *au pied de la lettre* and charge their less infantile predecessors with creating metaphysical monstrosities. Language is not the content of grammars and dictionaries but an activity, and it might be said that when a man's mind is really active, whether he is philosophizing, exercising his will, or creating a poem, he never uses a word in precisely the same sense as it was ever used before. That only sounds paradoxical because men's minds are so seldom really active.[1] It is just as true as, and usually more important than, the fact that man's creative utterance shows recognizable conformity with the vocabulary and rules of standard usage pressed in the pages of a pedagogic *hortus siccus*. Obviously in all self-expression in all media of the mind the new springs from the old, *pensiero pensante* from *pensiero pensato*, and yet more obviously communication would be everywhere impossible without recognition of an already classified identity which the fresh

---

[1] Also because much of our speech, like much of our other activities, has got to become habitual and automatic if we are to get on with the business of life: we have not time to be always thinking what we say.

growth of thought or imagination differentiates. But to say that is little more than to expand Aristotle's remark that all learning and teaching by way of argument proceeds from pre-existent knowledge. Provided that a philosopher can make his hearers think with him, he has no duty whatever to treat current usage as a boundary which he must not overstep, and to suppose that he must treat it as his philosophic counsellor and guide is preposterous nonsense. It is nowadays our poets rather than our philosophers who need to be reminded of standard English.[1] There is, moreover, no little irony in the fact that common-sense usage has given no support at all to many philosophical doctrines now fashionable. The man in the street talks and always has talked, not as a phenomenalist but as a naïve realist; not as a determinist but as a moderate libertarian; not as a subjectivist but as a man convinced of objective distinctions both ethical and aesthetic.[2] The modern linguistician alternately bullies and flatters common-sense usage; he is either at its throat or its feet.

On the whole he is at present inclined to flatter. The most important document attesting the retreat of the analysts from ideal language to the supposedly safer ground of common-sense talk is Wittgenstein's *Philosophical Investigations*.[3]

Mr. P. F. Strawson called Wittgenstein 'the first philosopher of the age'.[4] One might think him at any rate a good one-eyed king among the blind. His work was not the product of any broad and liberal education in philosophy, and its scope is fashionably narrow; yet within limits which strike one as unhappily accidental rather than natively inherent his mind moves subtly, flexibly, and unaggressively until the rigid atomism of the *Tractatus* is quite dissolved. On the other hand, the fertility of his thought makes it often elusive. Reading the *Investigations*, I have a vision of an inland sea, tideless and with no very distant horizon. It pushes gentle wavelets up the shore, often depositing a treasure which the next wave covers and sucks back before one can see clearly what it is. But sometimes a later wave will wash it up again, and with patience one can often net a catch worth having. Witt-

[1] Cp. my *Study of Hegel's Logic*, 1950, pp. 16–27.
[2] Mr. J. D. Mabbott makes this point admirably in *Contemporary British Philosophy*, Third Series, 1956, pp. 304–9.
[3] Published posthumously in 1953. It contains (*a*) the author's reflections between 1929 and 1945, and (*b*) additional material put together between 1947 and 1949.   [4] See *Mind*, January 1954, p. 78.

genstein's reveries defy abridgment. I shall merely select from what seem main elements in his thought, and they may well be themes rather than conclusions. His speculative method is decidedly un-English (though he once refers to Lewis Carroll), and I do not know where it would have led him if he had lived longer.

Wittgenstein in the *Investigations* rejects explicitly any metaphysical background of fact which might give meaning to words and guarantee truth, provided they correspond, to propositions. The nature of truth, at all events as a specific problem, drops away,[1] and the dominant theme is the constantly reiterated assertion that the meaning of words is only to be discovered in their actual use. The function of philosophy is to present linguistic usages clearly and give us what we really need, namely that insight into connections which our grammar fails to yield: 'Hence the importance of finding and inventing intermediate links' (p. 49, § 122). 'The concept of perspicuous presentation,' Wittgenstein continues, 'is of fundamental significance for us. It marks the form of our presentation, the way we look at things. (Is this a "Weltanschauung"?)'[2] The next three sections read as follows: 'A philosophical problem has the form: "I don't know my way about". Philosophy may in no way interfere with the actual use of language; it can in the end only describe it. For it cannot provide any ground for it. It leaves everything as it is. It leaves mathematics, too, as it is, and no mathematical discovery can advance it. A "leading problem of mathematical logic" is for us a problem of mathematics like any other mathematical problem. It is not the business of philosophy to resolve a contradiction by means of a mathematical or logico-mathematical discovery, but to enable us to get a clearer view of the state of mathematics which troubles us: the state of affairs *before* the contradiction is resolved.'

Wittgenstein has already in an earlier section proclaimed his revolt from mathematical logic and its analytic application. He speaks (p. 46, §107) of the intolerable conflict between actual language and the 'crystalline purity' of logic, 'which was of course not a result of investigation but a requirement.' We have to get off this slippery ice on to rough ground which we can walk on. 'We see that what we call "proposition" (*Satz*) and "language"'

---

[1] Cp. p. 135.   [2] A most pertinent question.

are not the formal unities I imagined they were, but are families of more or less kindred structures. But what becomes of logic now? Its rigour seems to be coming unstuck here. But in that case doesn't logic completely disappear? For how can logic lose its rigour? Of course not by our abating some of its rigour. The *preconceived idea* (*Vorurteil*) of crystalline purity can only be removed by turning round our whole treatment of the subject.' Thus the gist of the Wittgensteinian revolution would seem to be this. We must abandon formal logic and ideal language because they nowhere give us what we really want. The symbolic procedures of mathematics as well as the usages of ordinary language are to be examined by the new method of perspicuous presentation, which will be a purely descriptive and non-normative discipline. Wittgenstein remains a positivist.

To exhibit the use of words perspicuously is, according to Wittgenstein, to exhibit them at work in their actual contexts. 'Philosophical problems arise,' he says, 'when language goes on holiday.'[1] This notion of words significant not in isolated idleness but as they work in a context[2] is a healthy reaction from the lexicographical view which has so much obsessed our linguisticians,[3] and it is a welcome relief from the atomistic principle, the naïve conception of absolute simples and purely additive composites upon which depended all the main doctrines of logical atomism: logical constructions, sheerly external relations, truth-functional complex propositions and the rest. He will have nothing more to do with all that. 'We use,' he says,[4] 'the word "composite" (and therefore the word "simple") in countless different and differently related ways. . . . To the philosophical question, "Is the visual image of this tree composite (*zusammengesetzt*), and what are its component parts?" the correct answer is: "That depends on what you understand by 'composite'." (And that is of course not an answer but a rejection of the question.)' It is, however, important to examine closely this reaction from the dictatorial unity of formal logic and the single ideal language. Wittgenstein sees the types of working

---

[1] p. 19, §38. He clearly means problems raised by philosophers with whom he is no longer in sympathy.

[2] *Zusammenhang.* He will speak also of the *Umgebung* or the *Feld* of a word or phrase.

[3] It is not really a view so much as the naïve assumption of academic persons that languages were made for philologists.   [4] p. 22, §47 *ad fin.*

contexts as 'language-games', a phrase by which he intends to indicate that speech is always a part of an activity or a form of life. Each of these games has its own set of rules agreed upon by the players, and it is always the endless multiplicity of language-games which impresses Wittgenstein, not any systematic totality which they might constitute.[1] Although we know well enough what language-games are, we cannot, he thinks, even name a characteristic common to them all. If one observes ordinary games (which are presumably fewer than language-games) one sees a complicated network of similarities overlapping and criss-crossing; sometimes overall similarities, sometimes similarities of detail. The best name for these is 'family likenesses' (pp. 31–2, §§ 66–7). It is true that he compares a language to 'an ancient city: a maze of little streets and squares, of old and new houses, and of houses with additions from various periods; and this is surrounded by a multitude of new suburbs with straight, regular streets and uniform houses' (p. 8, § 16). The complicated network of overlapping and criss-crossing similarities is a very long way from Mr. Russell's contention that, given the word 'similar', we need no more by way of a universal to help us describe the world,[2] but for all Wittgenstein's stress on the need to find and invent intermediate links,[3] it is sheer sprawling diversity rather than unity in difference which his picturesque simile of the ancient city seems intended to express. He has not got very far beyond the notion of unanalysed resemblance.

[1] Compare p. 11, §23: 'Review the multiplicity of language-games in the following examples and others:

> Giving orders and obeying them—
> Describing the appearance of an object, or giving its measurements—
> Constructing an object from a description (a drawing)—
> Reporting an event—
> Speculating about an event—
> Forming and testing a hypothesis—
> Presenting the results of an experiment in tables and diagrams—
> Making up a story; and reading it—
> Singing catches—
> Guessing riddles—
> Making a joke; telling it—
> Solving a problem in practical arithmetic—
> Translating from one language into another—
> Asking, thanking, cursing, greeting, praying.

'It is interesting to compare the multiplicity of the tools in language and of the ways in which they are used, with what logicians have said about the structure of language. (Including the author of the *Tractatus Logico-Philosophicus*.)'

[2] See 110.   [3] See p. 157.

He has done much to break down the barrier separating formal logic from its material content, but he cannot discover (or rediscover) the concrete logic which springs from their union. He does not actually assert the nightmarishly irrational doctrine of many logics, but although he is aware of the danger he never fairly meets the threat of anarchy which follows the dethroning of formal logic. He has grasped in part, but in part only, the truth that the demand of reason is not for formal logic but for concrete system. He does not see that all rational language-games are played under the presupposition of an embracing unity of thought, which the philosophical logician must explicitly posit if he is to show the possibility of rational thinking, notwithstanding the fact that most of us play most of our language-games unreflectively. The philosopher, on Wittgenstein's view, can only watch a language-game from the touchline, so to say. He may not interfere during the game nor even after it. He can ascertain by observation what the rules agreed by the players are, and he can describe them; but he can discover no rational ground of which a particular set of rules might be the interconnected consequence, and far less any connection deeper than family likeness between the rules which govern different games. If, then, the philosopher can offer no interpretation of a language-game, one might suppose that his description of it, his allegedly needful perspicuous presentation of it, could be a means to the subsequent improvement of the rules, or at least to the better playing of the game within the current rules. But apparently it could not. A language-game is just a given form of life which has to be accepted *wie es geht und steht*.[1] The philosopher on the touchline seems simply otiose; or is he still, like Professor Ryle, occupied merely in presenting perspicuously the meaninglessness of metaphysics?[2]

What is the answer, then, if one asks what truth, having ceased to depend on correspondence, has now become? One observes a language-game in progress and discovers the rules which give meaning to the words and phrases used. One at least finds out how the players communicate. Perhaps one can discover the purposes, over and above communication, for which the

---

[1] See *Investigations*, p. 226.

[2] What about philosophy itself as a language-game? Is its perspicuous presentation of connections which grammar fails to yield any real advance on the aphasia which overcame it at the end of the *Tractatus*?

players talk, but if one hears them making statements which claim to be true (and surely one does), can one find out by listening what conditions would make their statements true, or even what conditions they themselves believe would make their statements true? Or must the philosopher ignore all question of material truth and its criterion, confining himself to an underworld, a Platonic cave, of meaning, and not daring to ask whether any statements could signify unless some statements were true?

On the whole we must accept the latter alternative. Wittgenstein remains a positivist. The close of the *Tractatus* was not mystical, as at first sight one might have thought it, but a confession that the author had reached a hopeless impasse. In the *Investigations* he takes refuge in linguistic phenomenalism. Except for certain, I hope pregnant, doubts to which I shall return,[1] he substitutes language for thought much as Hume substituted imagination.[2] Our reply to his question must be that his concept of perspicuous presentation is very certainly not a *Weltanschauung*.[3] Presumably some language-games might concern values, though Wittgenstein's examples[4] scarcely suggest it, and presumably the philosopher might discover the linguistic rules in accordance with which men express and communicate their emotions and opinions about various forms of good and bad. But could this, on Wittgenstein's view, help him to construct any theory of value, even a subjectivist one? I suppose that Wittgenstein would have consigned value to feeling as readily as does Mr. Russell.

The Wittgensteinian revolution has, nevertheless, implications which might be developed towards a very different philosophy, a way of thinking which has roots as old as Plato and still, as I believe, has not yielded all its fruit. Philosophy must develop from within and under its own self-criticism, and I shall have no particularly new form of objective idealism to offer; but our modern philosophy carries, I fancy, the bar sinister on its escutcheon, and at this point it may be worth our while to look back at the last legitimate offspring (in this country) of a sounder stock. If, to vary the metaphor, one has lost one's way, one can either try a short cut across country, or one can return to where the road forked and read the signpost more intelligently. The first

---

[1] See p. 163, footnote 2. [2] See p. 66.
[3] See p. 157. [4] Quoted p. 159, footnote 1.

M

method may save time, or it may lead one completely astray. It is at least courageous, and very likely modern thinkers will choose to pursue it, but I prefer to go back and look at the sign-post.

In Wittgenstein's remarks on usage and working context one is tempted to see the coherence theory of truth returning. Many of them take one's mind back to Bernard Bosanquet's *Logic*. Consider these sentences from the Introduction to that work, which was probably unknown to Wittgenstein, but is long over-due for re-reading by English philosophers: 'Except in the in-stance of a logical textbook, the utterance of a single word always implies a sentence, and usually a judgment' (p. 9). 'A name is a sign which rouses the mind to a set of activities having an identical element' (p. 12). 'That which the name signifies *is*, for us at all events, an identical character exhibited by different contexts, or different contexts united by a common character' (p. 13). Bosanquet's conception of context, however, differs greatly from Wittgenstein's. It is the notion of an all-pervading identity in difference, whereas for Wittgenstein the various con-texts in which a word works, the various language-games in which it is used, do not, as we saw, appear to constitute any system even in principle. His notion of context is only a local co-herence within each language-game. He sets out to seek insight into connections and to discover intermediate links, but he halts, appalled by the *prima facie* endless criss-cross of similarities which one would have thought it his business to interpret systematically if he hoped to contribute anything to philosophy by the study of language. He cannot fully grasp the demand of reason for co-herent identity in difference, because he lacks the main principle of Bosanquet's thinking. 'For logic,' says Bosanquet, 'it is a postulate that "truth is the whole" ' (p. 2), and later he observes, 'the truth, the fact, the reality, may be considered, in relation to the human intelligence, as the content of a single persistent and all-embracing judgment, by which every individual intelli-gence affirms the ideas which form its knowledge to be true of the world which is brought home to it as real by sense-perception (p. 3).

Bosanquet, like F. H. Bradley though less sharply, drew a questionable distinction between logic and metaphysics:[1] for

[1] See p. 188.

logic it is only a postulate that the truth is the whole. But this postulate is barely intelligible without reference to the metaphysics which Bosanquet's logical theory at once depends upon and develops. To put it briefly and crudely, Bosanquet is conceiving the single persistent all-embracing judgment as at once and in one (*a*) a self-affirming activity of absolute mind, and (*b*) the judging activity of the individual human mind. (*a*) is thus not something perfect in self-sufficient exclusion like an Epicurean god, not something separate and independent like a Platonic Form popularly conceived. (*a*) affirms and constitutes itself, essentially and by no supererogatory act of grace, in and as (*b*), and (*b*) is, for that reason, a self-transcending activity, a man's progressive self-realization as thinker and knower. Thus not only is truth the whole and the movement of human thought always in terms of the universal, but also, as Bosanquet somewhere puts it, 'truth lies always ahead.' Therefore every phase in the progress of human thinking and knowing finds and realizes its truth, its true nature, in the phase which succeeds it—thinking *is* development—and the phases of human experience which human thinking and knowing presuppose realize their truth each in its successor and all in the explicit thinking and knowing in which they culminate. Sensation, perception, imagination, language, thinking—each phase, though not without residue, absorbs and develops its predecessor,[1] and in thought itself the lift from level to level continues. In modern British philosophy truth lies always behind. Thinking dwindles into talking, truth into meaning, imagery into strings of sense-data, and in the bulldozing days of logical atomism all complex intellectual content—even, though with occasional qualms, that awkward intruder in a world of utter simples, the universal—was reduced to the mere aggregated truth-function of atomic constituents.[2]

[1] Cp. p. 29.

[2] It must be gratefully acknowledged that in the latter part of *Investigations* Wittgenstein is beginning to be worried by the difficulty of relating one level of cognitive experience to another. He is mainly concerned with puzzles such as the sudden change from seeing a drawing as the head of a rabbit to seeing it as the head of a duck, but his 'duck-rabbit' sets him reflecting on the function of interpretation in sense experience, and he begins to drop remarks like these:

'I meet someone whom I have not seen for years; I see him clearly but fail to know him, I see the old face in the altered one. I believe that I should do a different portrait of him now if I could paint.

'Now when I know my acquaintance in a crowd, perhaps after looking in his direction for quite a while,—is this a special sort of seeing? Is it a case of both

The distinction which Bosanquet conceives between (*a*) the self-affirming activity of absolute mind, and (*b*) the judging activity of the individual human mind, is of course a distinction *for* the human thinker. It is a distinction between reality and appearance, and the reality is the absolute whole within which must fall the appearances of reality and both sides of any distinction which man makes between truth and reality or truth and fact. But since the distinction of (*a*) and (*b*) is a distinction *for* the individual human thinker, reality as opposed to its own appearance is for him always and necessarily an ideal inadequately realized. It is not a mere empty ideal, not a purely regulative and non-constitutive Kantian ideal, any more than appearance is sheer illusion. Because it constitutes him in constituting itself in and as his thinking activity, man can possess a partial but expansible knowledge of it, which is, on the one side, self-knowledge. But man's knowing is not absolute but, *whatever its scope and content*, an always uncompleted thinking, the truth of which is a matter of degree:[1] and human thinking and knowing is always in a measure a subjective believing.[2] Reality and appearance, and all such other antitheses as totality and fragment, or subject and object, remain for man only intelligible if grasped together in synthesis, and then only intelligible in degree. It follows that this whole metaphysical position is itself logically defensible only in a degree, only in so far as it can be developed against other

---

seeing and thinking? Or an amalgam (*Verschmelzung*) of the two, as I should almost like to say?' (p. 197).

A little later he observes, 'The concept of the presentation (*Darstellung*) of what is seen, like that of the copy of it, is very elastic, and so *together with it* is the concept of what is seen. The two are intimately connected. (Which is not to say that they are alike.)'

The suggestion that modes of experiencing are terms in developing series might have interested him, but he nowhere makes it. He just remains puzzled: 'But how is it possible to *see* an object according to an *interpretation*? The question represents it as a queer fact, as if something were being forced into a form it did not really fit. But no squeezing, no forcing, took place here' (p.200). And again: 'When I see the picture of a galloping horse, do I merely *know* that this is the kind of movement meant? Is it a superstition to think I *see* the horse galloping in the picture?—And does my visual impression gallop, too?' (p. 202).

What Wittgenstein entirely fails to 'see' is that, quite apart from the specially striking case of ambiguous drawings, the act of sense-perception is always and as such an interpretative development of a more primitive content more primitively apprehended. If it were not so, pictures of galloping horses, which if effective are never quite naturalistic ('Movement,' says Sir Kenneth Clark, 'cannot be realized in art without some degree of distortion'), would make singularly little sense.

[1] Not, however, degree of correctness; see pp. 134–5 and pp. 185–6.

[2] If it were not, meaning would not be distinct from truth, and there would be no such thing as error.

philosophical positions to show that nothing else makes sense of human experience in general, nor in particular explains mankind's universal conviction both of its knowledge and of its illimitable ignorance and error.

Empiricists, before they abandoned truth for meaning and metaphysics for phenomenalism, used sometimes to criticize the coherence theory of truth as if coherence were no more than consistency and therefore far less than truth. A coherent body of theory, so ran their objection, might be unassailable on internal evidence and yet in fact quite false. They conceived such a body of coherent theory under the image of a pattern on a horizontal plane, which floats quite unattached, unsuspended from above and unsupported from below. Even, they said, if you combine coherence with comprehensiveness, as the idealists did, it provides no criterion of truth; it offers no more than a content which expands indefinitely *in vacuo* and out of all contact with fact or reality. I have perhaps already said enough to show that this criticism is based on a mere caricature, but I will try to meet it point by point. To begin with, coherent thinking, on the idealist view, is not a flat pattern but self-developing inference which lifts from level to level. Doubtless when we abstract for discussion what we take as a finished piece of reasoning—a famous scientific discovery, for example, such as Harvey's proof of the circulation of the blood—we are apt to see it as a closed and static system of logically connected elements. In fact not merely is this reasoning dependent on a wider context which operates in it by implication,[1] but also it is a lifting, a self-transcending, movement. It is a passing of premises into a conclusion which is their development.

Secondly, if true thinking is the coherence not of a static self-enclosed pattern but of ascending phases, equally it is not a rope-trick jugglery, an unsuspended climbing in mid-air. It can only seem to be either so long as we suppose that human thinking is no more than the adjective of a singular finite mind. On the view that an activity of mind, which we must by contrast call 'absolute', constitutes itself in and as human thinking, the problem is at once transformed. The wider context which all reasoning implies

---

[1] This context can never be fully specified, and the reasoning remains so far hypothetical. When, however, we abstract a proof of this sort to make a textbook specimen of inference, we fail to specify the context at all.

but can never include is then no longer a limitless field passively awaiting our efforts to cover it: it is *operant* in our inference. That is why the concrete universal, which is neither a truth-functional collection of particulars nor a mere abstract general class intension, is present in all human thinking. That is why in logic, except for ultimately economic special purposes, form and content cannot be held totally apart.

In the third place, true and coherent thinking does not develop upwards unsupported from below. The idealist position is here best explained by contrast with the assumptions of empiricism. The empiricist begins as a naïve realist—if all realism be not naïve. He accepts without qualm the common-sensical economic observer's view that singular individual minds confront an indifferent and independent real world, and he takes for granted that this is the situation in which the philosophical problem of knowledge must begin and end. He then finds himself with two questions to answer: (1) How do these presupposed singular minds get to know the public world which is assumed to be objective and real in independence of them? (2) How do they get to know and communicate with each other? At this stage his topics of discourse are such as 'The cognitive situation', 'Other minds', 'Intersubjective intercourse', and the like. He discovers that however he tries to answer the first question he begs it: any cognitive relation he posits between minds and the objective world turns out to presuppose a prior knowledge of both terms on the part of the minds. So he falls back on the seemingly prudent view that the ideas which arise in men's minds are doubtless in some sense appearances of something real and independent, but unhappily we can know nothing but appearances. These we must therefore take precisely as they are given to sense without enquiring into their credentials. But it gradually dawns on him that to talk about the appearance of a totally unknown reality is still question-begging, and he is forced to retreat further and confess that the sensuous imagery which arises in us (or, indeed, the speech which we find ourselves uttering) is not the appearance of any ulterior reality but just—appearance. He becomes a fully fledged (or fully plucked) phenomenalist. Meanwhile, having started to answer the second question by saying that we get to know other minds by inference from our own, he comes first to admit with a shrug that solipsism cannot be logically refuted, and then to eliminate the subject altogether by saying, after Hume, that he cannot find any such thing in his phenomenal object.

The tale of the empiricist's disappearance into his own vacuum-cleaner has been twice told in this book, once in an eighteenth-century setting, once as re-enacted in modern dress. I repeat it here only to point out that this *reductio ad absurdum* is quite inevitable if we accept the initial realist presuppositions, and it is these which we must first flatly reject if we are to escape the fiasco of phenomenalism; for phenomenalism is nothing but realism without a real.

We can now consider an alternative. If a total or absolute activity constitutes itself in constituting human intelligence, the scope of this activity cannot be confined to thought: it must cover the whole of human experience and, within it, sense-perception. The distinction of subject and object, even manifested as the distinction of percipient and *perceptum*, only arises within that constitutive act, and the distinction is therefore not an absolute mutual independence to be taken for granted in the theory of knowledge; it is a correlation of opposites on a basis of identity. Asked what are the antecedents of an act of sense-perception in which a subject distinguishes himself from an object, we might—and perhaps without exciting suspicion in the realist—reply that it arises out of mere sensation in which this distinction was not yet present. This, it might seem, is a plain temporal transition which we can recognize on reflection as happening every day. So indeed it is, when the necessary abstraction has been made; but before the abstraction has been made it is a great deal more than that. For until the distinction of subject and object arises in sense-perception, there is no subject and there is no object. This does not mean that we and our object come to be in each percipient act and are then annihilated until the next one. It means that the transition from sensation to sense-perception is logical or metaphysical, and that only under an abstraction is it a temporal process of events. It is, one might say, the logical genesis of the individual mind as subject together with its object. And that is no mystery unless we cling to the abstraction and forget the concrete from which it is abstracted; unless, that is, we deny that in all human experience a mind which is total or absolute constitutes itself in and as the subject and object of percipience arising from sheer sensation. Truth lies ahead. It is the transcendent totality towards which coherent thinking strives. But

truth is also immanent in coherent thinking, and it is immanent
ab initio. For when we affirm our ideas as true of the world
brought home to us as real by sense-perception, we are not
applying them *ab extra*: they are the ideality of that real world without which it would not be real. The expanding coherence which
is truth has its roots in the same reality towards which it strives.

The fruits of revolution and anarchy are hard to predict, but
one remembers that Wittgenstein prefaced the manuscript of
Investigations with a quotation from Nestroy: '*Uberhaupt hat der
Fortschritt das an sich, dass er viel grösser erscheint, als er wirklich ist.*
It has, I think, become obvious that Wittgenstein's notion of a
context conferring significance and his puzzles about the relation
of levels in cognitive experience are still but distantly analogous
to the coherence theory of truth.[1]

In order to show this I have briefly developed an idealist theory
of knowledge from its root in sense-perception. I have, however,
in speaking of coherence said nothing of value. In Part III I shall
make a fresh start. I shall offer a tentative and perhaps rather
eclectic sketch of objective idealism as a philosophy of value (for
that is what objective idealism primarily is), and so pass from
coherence as mere system to coherence as intrinsic value. I shall
begin to make this transition by treating philosophy as itself a
form of value-experience,[2] and if at first we have to re-traverse
ground already covered I can only beg the reader's indulgence.

[1] In a paper called *Language Strata*, written in 1946 and published in *Logic and
Language*, Second Series, Dr. F. Waismann takes a view of language very similar
to Wittgenstein's. He suggests that languages (if Wittgenstein's *Investigations* had
appeared by then, he might perhaps have called them 'language-games') could
profitably be ordered in layers. He means, if I understand him, that they constitute
some sort of *Stufenleiter*, so that statements about an object which seem to conflict
if taken as made on the same level, can be seen to complement one another when
assigned to different levels. An action, for example, can on this hypothesis intelligibly be said to have both a cause and a reason. I do not know that Dr. Waismann
would hold that all languages (or language-games) could in principle be ordered on
one *Stufenleiter*—he often in fact seems nearer than Wittgenstein to the view that
every statement has its own logic—but there seems to be a definite hint here that
thought might be self-developing or even dialectical in its movement. At any rate
Dr. Waismann is thinking in terms not of an ideal scientific language but of all
language. His concept clearly has a Russellian root, but his *Stufenleiter* would at
least be more concretely systematic than Mr. Russell's ideal hierarchy of languages
and meta-languages, that almost vanished ghost of dialectic in a mathematical world.
     In a later article, *How I see Philosophy* (*Contemporary British Philosophy*, Third
Series, 1956), Dr. Waismann struggles to find a position from which philosophy can
be defended as rational and argumentative, though not consisting in logical proofs
from premises. Since his model for inference is formal deduction, he is not unnaturally driven towards a one-sided intuitionist view of philosophy which faintly
recalls the Bergsonian dichotomy. Yet on the way to it he says much that suggests
he may be also on the way to discovering several old truths.   [2] See pp. 183 ff.

PART III

Value

CHAPTER IX

VALUE IN GENERAL

THE objects which constitute the world of the economic observer are not good or bad *per se*, but only, when the economic agent, as it were, considers the report of the economic observer, judged good or bad as means or hindrances to practical ends. Why knowledge of them, save for practical ends or as a prelude to knowledge of intrinsic value, should be thought worth pursuing I cannot say, but the type of thinker whom we have been discussing believes that it is. In his view, if I rightly interpret it, knowledge of logical principles, formal rules of valid thinking, is possible, but there is no knowledge of material truth save knowledge of the detached world which confronts the economic observer. If anything concrete is to be known it must belong to that world, or it must be forced into it. If we would know mind or any element of it, we must forget that an object implies a subject which cannot be divorced from it, and envisage all the actions and passions of the mind as parts of the economic observer's object-world.

On this account, value cannot be known. It must be denied existence or relegated to feeling; and not to feeling turned into a more or less cognizable object (on Mr. Russell's view a logical construction), since that would *ex hypothesi* convert it into something devoid of value, but to feeling as the purely subjective satisfaction of singular minds. This will apply to all values, and among them, a degree paradoxically, to the intrinsic value which true knowledge is still held to possess. Thus a value-feeling will be non-rational, devoid of logical ground, both in the sense that it is not any sort of cognizable object, however knowingly philosophers may talk about it, and also in the sense that it is not itself a cognition of any character belonging to an object. It is usually no doubt a direct or indirect response to a cognition,[1] but the

---

[1] One can, on Mr. Russell's view, both desire and believe one knows not what; cp. p. 113 and pp. 119-20.

object of *that* cognition is *ex hypothesi* free of value, and when the uninstructed man says, 'A is good', or 'B is bad', he is wrong if on reflection he supposes he has made an objective judgment. He was really not judging but ejaculating. The modern philosopher, having a paramount interest in linguistic form, usually approaches the problem of value through a criticism of the judgment of value, which he holds to be merely an expression of felt satisfaction or dissatisfaction misleadingly couched in the grammatical form proper to statements of fact.

It is both interesting and important to note that some modern thinkers who consign value to non-rational subjective feeling then attempt a partial retreat from their position, desiring, it would seem, to have it both ways. Often the feeling expressed in the pseudo-judgment of value is said to be one of approval or disapproval, and Mr. Russell is prepared to concede a certain universality to such expressions. He would interpret 'A is good' in an ethical context as meaning 'Would that all men desired A'.[1] But these death-bed repentances, whether they spring from fear of too much flouting common moral notions or from a belated perception of the theoretical ruin to which consistency would lead, win no remission of logical sins. If the feeling expressed is one of approval, the speaker is not simply ejaculating; he is very obviously claiming to refer to something beyond his own feeling and to judge it by some objective standard.[2] If there is nothing in his claim, why call his feeling approval and not sheer liking? Equally any sane man who said, 'Would that all men desired A', would have some sort of logical ground to offer if asked why; whereas Mr. Russell's only logical answer would be 'Because I do'. These efforts to smuggle a respectable touch of objectivity into what is first taken as purely subjective either are disingenuous or spring from a complete failure to understand what feeling is. On the subjectivist theory, the feeling wrongly couched in the form of a judgment can only be a singular individual's like or dislike. Our modern empiricists, being practical men, have been mainly concerned to dispose of ethical values, but their position

---

[1] Cp. *Philosophy of Bertrand Russell*, p. 722. In Chapter VI we watched Mr. Russell depress feeling, emotion and desire to an almost purely physiological level. I wonder if, when he is attacking Government policy on nuclear weapons, he ever wavers in his conviction that there is nothing rational in a sense of values.

[2] The point is well made in Prof. E. E. Harris's inaugural lecture, *Objectivity and Reason*, Witwatersrand University Press, 1955.

holds generally for all values. We are offered very little beyond this meagre core of positive doctrine except linguistical refutation of more ambitious theories of value. The study of ethical language has proved an effective safeguard against any genuinely objective treatment of moral conduct. The degree of dull remoteness which can be achieved by discussing the language of a subject instead of the subject itself is remarkable.[1]

I have contended that philosophy is concerned primarily with instrinsic value and is itself a form of intrinsic value. I shall oppose the denial of rationality to value with a position which makes no pretence to novelty, and I shall here outline it barely and with no attempt to differentiate kinds of intrinsic value with precision. The preliminary points of it may be roughly stated as follows:

(1) No form of intrinsic goodness is a character of any object of economic observation.

(2) Intrinsic goodness is not one among several characters of anything. It may perhaps be called a 'toti-resultant' character,[2] provided that be taken to mean, not an additional character of which other characters are merely causes or conditions, but a character of totality which is also a totality of character. For whatever has intrinsic goodness—or, we had better now say, any intrinsic good—is as such a totality, a whole. In so far as it does not fail in intrinsic goodness its goodness is its whole nature, not its adjective.

(3) An intrinsic good is, nevertheless, not simple and atomic. Its unity is the individuality of coherent system. If it is analysed, a diversity of 'parts', or 'characters', or 'aspects' will indubitably emerge. But none of these will, outside the totality of their synthesis, reveal intrinsic value. Analysis pushed far enough will even exhibit purely economic characters. If you analyse moral conduct (assuming it to be an intrinsic good) you will in the last resort find bodily movements in a physical environment. Analysis of an aesthetic experience may lead down through proportion and harmony to patches of pigment, which may be in turn dissolved into their chemical constituents. To a purely analytic thinker it must remain a sheer mystery that these products of

---

[1] See, for example, Charles L. Stevenson, *Ethics and Language*, R. M. Hare, *The Language of Morals*, T. D. Weldon, *The Vocabulary of Politics*.
[2] Cp. Sir David Ross, *The Right and the Good*, 1930, p. 122.

analysis should have anything at all to do with intrinsic value. What can he do but deny that they have and consign value to feeling?

The mystery remains until it is seen that *pure* analysis does not lead towards the essential nature of the intrinsically good (or of anything else), but away from it and towards some fragmentary abstraction. Analysis is a moment in all thinking, but philosophical thinking is at once an intuition and a dual movement in which analysis and synthesis are inseparable. Analysis of the intrinsically good may lead us to economically observable facts, and since the lack of value in the economically observed world is a privation and not a sheer absence, we may even say that value is 'founded on' empirical fact. But that metaphor will prove ruinous, unless we remember that foundations exist for the sake of what is built upon them, and that value makes sense of fact (so far as that is possible in human experience), not fact of value.

(4) It follows that the criterion of value for whatever is an intrinsic good is immanent in it. That might seem tautologous and already contained in the meaning of the word 'intrinsic', but it can be forgotten and its implications can be misunderstood. It implies a certain autonomy in the forms of value-experience, a certain right to ignore alien criteria, but it does not, as we have already seen in (3), mean that we are aware of an intrinsic good as a simple content which we either intuite (or feel) fully and certainly or else simply miss altogether. We can judge value rationally, because the intrinsic good has an intelligible structure. It is true that the man in the street often makes snap judgments of good and bad which are not much more than mere expressions of taste or prejudice, but human life would be an even sorrier muddle than it is if he did not quite often succeed to some extent in eliciting the intelligible structure in the intrinsically good, or the perversion of this structure in the bad, and so contrive to pass judgments not wholly devoid of rational ground. In all genuine judgment of value, even the humblest, what is judged good (or bad) is assigned (or denied) a place in the totality which is the criterion of judgment.

(5) The only intrinsic value, or good *per se*, is a mind's self-conscious activity which is in some sense total; nothing else fulfils the four conditions already stated. Hence value and consciousness of value are in a sense identical.

(6) From (4) and (5) it follows that in order to think out the general structure of the intrinsic good, and to differentiate and relate the kinds of it, if it has kinds, the philosopher must reflect on the whole human adventure in pursuit, creation, and enjoyment of values, and that in the course of that reflection he may have to modify considerably the vulgar notion of minds as singular individual minds.

I have sketched this rough initial outline of a theory in opposition to the subjectivist doctrine, but there is a kinship between the two. Only when this is made clear can either of them be properly understood, but to make it clear may need a little time.

The subjectivist theory of value, whenever it has appeared in the history of philosophy, has met with a charge of hedonism, which it has never quite succeeded in evading. We discussed this charge in connection with Hume, and it was then suggested that the likeliest means to a coherent hedonism is to take as man's end the economic pleasures, the pleasurable activities distinctive of the purely selfish economic agent.[1] The crudest of these are plain sensual satisfactions. The wants so satisfied are conditions of a human being's very existence, not in the sense that without them he would perish—in that sense they are rather symptoms of his perishability—but in the sense that without them there would be no human being to perish when they were not satisfied, or to survive when they were. It is as constitutive elements of himself that a man experiences thirst, hunger, sexual appetite and their satisfaction, and also that which fulfils the want and satisfies. His consciousness of them is feeling. He cannot doubt them—although he can only be said (as he commonly is said) to be certain of them in a proleptic sense of certainty —because without them there is no self to doubt or be certain of anything. When, for example, a man is violently hungry to the exclusion of any sophisticating reflection on his hunger, and he then eats and is satisfied, he cannot doubt his want, nor his satisfaction, nor the food which he consumes into himself; for he is compact of these elements, and he is not unless they are. Here one is apt to be misled. When one thinks of a man satisfying his hunger by eating a steak, one thinks of it in a certain context. One imagines the hungry man and the steak as two things which were apart and came together, and as each of them, together with

[1] See p. 68.

the environment, susceptible of long and complicated scientific analysis. One thinks of all this scientifically analysable world as a sort of theatre in which the event occurred, and as presupposed by the occurrence. But in so thinking and imagining one has turned economic observer, and economic observation is not a primitive experience. In a much more fundamental sense this scientifically analysable world, within which, and as a part of which, we observe hungry men eating, presupposes primitive experience such as I have illustrated by hunger. These elementary wants and their fillings, and these satisfactions, comprise a sort of embryo of immediately and unbrokenly felt differences, which then develops into a subject who can distinguish from himself what he had felt as an element of himself; indeed, into a man whose life can also manifest intrinsic values which he is capable of judging. But with this development we are not yet concerned.

The satisfaction, then, of a primitive want is immediate feeling; and it is pleasant. The pleasure is not an ingredient of the experience but the whole experience in a certain form, and the pleasure is the feeling.[1] In short, the whole content of the experience has pleasurable feeling for its form. The distinction of a subject from what he feels, or from a particular object recognized as giving satisfaction, or from an objective environment, arises only as primitive experience is mediated and developed, and the same is true of any distinction of form from content within the experience. In elementary sensuous experience such distinctions are merely implicit, mere felt differences which cannot be named and described except proleptically.

Thus sheer feeling is a phase—*not* a stratum—of experience, which we can only verify by contrast as we 'come to ourselves' in passing out of it. 'Verify' is even, perhaps, too precise a word; sheer feeling is a presupposition which we must make in order to understand our present experience, a memory, but a memory rather of the direction in which we have come than of an actual starting-point. Our everyday satisfaction of bodily wants is not quite primitive, for in it the consciousness of an individual self has already emerged, and the distinguishing of subject and object has begun; but feeling has not vanished. It is still present, not as an ingredient of the experience—that it never is—but as a not fully superseded form of the experience as a whole.[2] The pleasure

[1] See pp. 63–6.   [2] Cp. pp. 65–6.

of satisfying a physical need is still self-feeling in an object which is not strictly an object, not fully distinct from the self. It is subjective in the sense that it is private, but not in any sense which would quite exclude the object from the pleased self. On reflection we may say, 'I felt pleasure', and 'It gave me pleasure', and, again, 'My pleasure was indubitable'. But in the experience to which we so refer, especially if it was intense, the difference between 'I' and 'it' was barely explicit, and the certainty, though not to be questioned, was not yet affirmation.

The subjectivist school finds the archetype of value-experience in the common sensuous satisfactions, whether or not it overtly accepts hedonism. When the common man (as he commonly does) goes from 'It (the object, that is, which satisfied him) was pleasant' to 'It was good', the subjectivists tell him that he was expressing his feelings. That is true. But they add that he is making no sort of objective judgment, and that is not true. In fact the common man has characterized an object, though he has characterized it as something barely more than an element of himself.[1] Doubtless his judgment is not much more than private subjective feeling, and the 'object' of it does not yet belong to the detached world of the economic observer, where all is fact and nothing is value. But the fully fledged cognizable objects which confront the economic observer do not come from nowhere. They develop out of feeling, and man *qua* economic agent plays a vital part in their development.

Thinkers who deny any advance when the common man passes from 'pleasant' to 'good' seem to stand convicted of a very crude psychological hedonism. If, however, we look again at the alternative doctrine which I sketched, we shall find a considerable *prima facie* resemblance between five of its six points and the subjectivist view. The pleasure of primitive satisfactions is not a quality of any object of economic observation (1). A satisfaction of this kind is felt as a whole, and as owing its pleasantness neither to anything beyond it nor to any isolable element within it (2). It is complex, and analysis of it will yield elements in which value (here equivalent to pleasure) is absent (3). The pleasure of it is very obviously immanent in it: *if* pleasure is value it is very

---

[1] It must be remembered that a man is always in process of construction, which is in part self-construction. He does not come to experience as a ready-made singular individual mind. There is at least that much truth in Professor Ryle's tirade against 'the ghost in the machine'.

N

certainly intrinsic value (4). One cannot make a difference between pleasure and the feeling of pleasure (5).

The degree of coincidence between the two views is remarkable. What, then, is the objection to regarding the pleasure of these elementary satisfactions as good *per se*? Why should we not take it as the archetype of all intrinsic values? The answer to these questions is old and plain. These pleasures, considered in abstraction as the pleasures of the economic agent, are neither good nor bad. They can be good or bad only as transformed within moral experience.[1] Therefore they cannot provide the archetype or the essence of intrinsic value. On the other hand, the resemblance between the two views is not simply superficial. These economic pleasures, as I have called them, are the source, the potentiality and promise, of intrinsic value. In themselves they are merely pleasant and not good, but they are the basis from which all value develops. To regard them as the essential archetype and pattern of value is an inversion typical of the sheerly analytic view.

Between the economic pleasures and the traditional modes of value-experience lies this main difference. The former are selfish, self-contained and without reference beyond themselves;[2] but in the latter, though differently in each, the singular individual is transcended. We may consider them in turn.

In respect of moral action the mere fact of contrast hardly needs to be argued. To the puritan moralist it is so sharp that he is apt to see it as the sheer mutual exclusion of opposites, but it is not so simple as that. I have maintained as the fifth point of a barely sketched theory of value that there is no good or bad *per se* but a mind's self-conscious activity, and that consequently value and the consciousness of it are in some sense identical. If, then, moral action contrasts as unselfish with the economic pleasures, it can only be because in moral action the will of the singular individual is actively identified with a will which is beyond him as well as within him, with a will, that is, which at once constitutes the individual as a moral agent and constitutes itself in and as the

[1] Or perhaps, *mutatis mutandis*, within aesthetic experience. The relation of economic pleasures to morality is much more obvious and familiar, but it seems to me possible that all art may contain a transcended sensual element.

[2] For the converse reason, the activity of the economic observer is not self-transcending. Scientific and mathematical thinking are not self-consciousness: in them the 'detached' object develops but not the merely presupposed constant subject.

individual. That is a hard saying, perhaps, though not a new one; yet to ascribe moral value to anything which is less than this self-transcendence leads in the end, so far as I can see, to absurdity. The will of the bare individual self cannot be *per se* good or bad; it is impulse rather than truly will, and its exercise can only be pleasant or painful. Nor can it be *intrinsically* good by virtue of mere conformity to a command, the command, for example, of a despot, a state, or a god. And even if there were any sense in saying that conformity could confer intrinsic goodness, what could, on the other side, make the source of command intrinsically good as such? What relevant goodness could belong to a despot, a state, or a god thus externally related to an obedient servant? Surely none which human morality could be supposed to take as its pattern. I think we cannot on reflection make any sense philosophically of morality unless we take it as an experience in which an individual realizes his own nature in a will which was beyond him as a mere particular individual, and equally as an experience in which that will is self-constitutive. To say that a state is nothing apart from its citizens has, after all, been a commonplace since Plato, but a god, too, whose nature utterly transcends his worshippers is little more than a cipher, an imaginative severance and personification of a will which man in moral activity finds at once in him and beyond him.[1] If the will of the bare individual is no more than morally indifferent, equally the will which thus appears to the individual as both beyond him and in him becomes a mere ideal abstraction hypostasized when it is taken to be, *qua* beyond him and independent of him, self-subsistent. Certainly in the process of moral self-transcendence the individual takes his relation to the will with which he strives to identify himself as in various ways external. He may take it as obedience to a master, to a state or some other community, to an abstract moral law or to a god, and where morality approaches religion obedience may be felt as worship. This sense of externality is not illusory but integral to the process of moral experience. Indeed, all the phenomena of the moral life, normal and perverse, familiar and strange, are bound up with this partial externality and vary with the degree to which it is suffered or overcome, remains rigid or is transcended. But only to the two terms taken

---

[1] This criticism would apply in various forms to the gods of Aristotle, Epicurus, and Spinoza, and perhaps of some Christian theologians.

together, only to the particular and the universal in so far as they are one and not two, does it make sense to ascribe the intrinsic good which is the good will.

Aesthetic vision, whether in the artist or the contemplator, is never the enjoyment of a merely private and particular good, and it can only be made to appear so if, trading on the fact that the medium of aesthetic experience is sensuous, we obliterate the distinction between the sensuous and the sensual. On the contrary, the *maximum visible*, the whole possible content, of aesthetic vision does not fall short of the whole universe, and the experience of it is so far universal and objective. On the other hand, the aesthetic object is not fact related to will. The universe does not present itself in aesthetic experience as the whole possible economic object; it is not the *maximum observabile* inviting the economic agent to explore and exploit it. Rather it is a universal activity, at once sentient and rational, which constitutes itself in human aesthetic experience, and in which, conversely, the aesthetic experient realizes his own nature. Nothing less than this integral unity of the two sides has intrinsic value, is the aesthetic good *per se*. The dual self-constitution is not on either side the *nisus* of will—it is a seeing and not a doing—but if you subject it to analysis it falls apart, much as moral experience falls apart, into separate elements. None of these has value save, as it were, in a light reflected from the unity out of which it has been abstracted, and some of them have in themselves no value at all. We sometimes talk of beauty as if it were a character of 'detached' economic objects, a 'tertiary quality', perhaps. The spectator, we say, contemplates it with appropriate aesthetic feelings, and he may, if he is an artist, attempt to copy it or, if that seems too crude, to 'represent' it. We regard the beauty in things as an intrinsic value in them, but we also incline to ascribe intrinsic value to the feelings of the spectator, and even more to the artist's 'representation'. And then, perhaps, even 'representation' strikes us as too humble a notion to express the artist's activity: is he not a 'creator'? At least, if he does choose to represent what the vulgar seem to recognize as a common object, the value of his work surely lies in the expression of himself which it manifests. Thus we oscillate with interludes of compromise between an objective and a subjective account of aesthetic value, always tending to interpret object and subject as the economic agent understands the terms. Sometimes we push the subjective account so far as to insist that if an artist is a very pure artist he will try to shake off altogether the shackles of representation. His work, we admit, must be visible or audible, but it will not, so it seems to us in this mood, be truly creative until in the patterns and shapes which it presents no original is represented. And then, by a strange quirk, this abstractive trend, this repudiation of the common object, ceases to be in any obvious sense subjective. It becomes remote and impersonal and is quite possibly lauded for those very qualities.

All these attitudes, like the roughly analogous attitudes of the moral life, are genuine phenomena of aesthetic experience. As theories they reflect truly enough phases in the artist's self-critical struggle to find out what his activity is, but when they pretend to be more than that they wither under philosophic criticism. The beautiful detached object, the copy, the representation, the abstract work of art, the feelings of the artist or the spectator, even if these latter are not blind likings but full of insight as well as personally expressive—none of them, and still less the practical technique which is a means to artistic expression, has value save in a borrowed light. To call any of them good *per se* provokes an unanswerable Why? Set them in order, on the other hand, synthesize the isolated products of analysis, and together they begin to make some sense. Only to a partial union of man with an activity which he feels as his but as also beyond him, only to a co-operation or a conspiracy which can be called 'creative' not because it is practical but because human nature moves on in the phases of it, can aesthetic value be attributed with any pretence of philosophic intelligibility.

I have tried so far to show that moral and aesthetic experience involve self-transcendence, and are not, as the subjectivist doctrine implies, identical with the economic pleasures. I have now to argue the same view in respect of philosophical truth.

It will be well to clear up a preliminary point. If philosophical truth is truth of values and itself a value, there is on a view like Mr. Russell's no such thing at all as philosophical truth.[1] Philosophy for Mr. Russell is nothing but immature science, and there is therefore for him no difference between the essence of truth

---

[1] Mr. Russell figures so prominently in the following discussion of truth because his phenomenalist successors have, as we saw, virtually abandoned truth for meaning.

in philosophy and the essence of truth in science. To value he
allows no rational criterion at all. The awkward consequence
of this position is that if any man believes that the pursuit and
attainment of scientific truth have intrinsic as well as practical
value—and I suppose that Mr. Russell does believe that—this
belief has no more logical ground than the belief that cruelty
is wrong. Mr. Russell never conceals his regret that morality has
no logical basis, but he seems not even to notice that he has
denied all logical justification to his own professional pursuits.
To press this point here, however, might obscure the main issue.
Mr. Russell has given us his own account of truth in the world of
science and mathematics, and I propose that we should recall it in
the hope that it may make us a stepping-stone to our own view of
philosophical truth.

Material truth, with which we shall do best to begin, is conceived by Mr. Russell, as we saw in Chapter VII, as a property
conferred on a proposition by a relation of correspondence to fact,
positive fact if the true proposition is positive, negative if it is
negative. Since all facts are atomic facts or aggregates of atomic
facts, the simplest case of material truth, to which all material
truth can in principle be reduced, is correspondence of an atomic
proposition to an atomic fact. The simplest case of falsity is the
failure of correspondence which occurs when an atomic proposition 'refers to' an atomic fact, sometimes called by Mr. Russell
its 'verifier', by pointing away from it. The true proposition is
thus true because it corresponds to fact, but the relation, like all
Mr. Russell's relations, is external, as is also the relation of the
proposition to the individual subject asserting it. It is neither
the external fact—the proposition itself, according to Mr. Russell,
is a fact—nor the knowing or believing of a mind which
is properly to be called true, but the bare proposition. This
account[1] certainly preserves one character which any sort of
truth must possess: it saves truth from simple Protagorean
dependence on the individual thinker. But the individual thinker
is not transcended; he is ignored. If he happens by a belief-feeling
to attach himself to a true proposition, so much the better, I
suppose, for him; but the attachment is quite external and makes
no difference to the proposition, the truth of which depends on

[1] For various inconsistent views of truth in Mr. Russell's writings see Joachim,
Logical Studies, p. 230, footnote 3.

nothing but a one-one relation of correspondence to its 'verifier'.

If its implications are pursued, this doctrine may seem crude, but it belongs to a world in which awkward epistemological questions are not relevant. It fits very fairly well the conception of truth with which the economic observer works when he verifies and classifies the particular facts in which he is interested. Indeed, one would be hard put to it to persuade him that when so engaged he is using any criterion of truth but correspondence. This theory of truth, in short, adequately reflects one element or aspect of the world of science. On the other hand, it neglects very completely another aspect or element of that world, namely system. For that there may seem to be an excuse. System, on the view I took at the beginning of this chapter, is intimately connected with value; for if intrinsic value is rational, immanent, and total, system must at any rate be a general character of it. But science is not concerned with intrinsic value. It would, on the other hand, seem a wild paradox to exclude system from science. We must try to solve this dilemma.

I have contended in Chapter II that science is the privation and not the mere absence of value. Science progresses towards its useful end by abstractive analysis, by attenuation of the systems which give it its hypotheses. It moves by the steady analytical reduction of those systems from concrete identity in difference towards something more abstract, towards some sort of class structure. Thus in a certain sense system is something which science perpetually destroys as it advances.[1] On the other hand, a world of atomic facts and wholly external relations is a sufficiently remote scientific ideal, which can never be completely fulfilled, not because the human mind is too weak but because the world of science is the privation and not the sheer absence of value. Whether the light of value visibly illuminates the world of science depends on the direction in which you look. If you turn your

---

[1] It is sometimes convenient but always dangerous to assign provinces to the special sciences, and to think of each as abiding within the limits set by the definition of its subject-matter, as progressing on a uniform level without reconstituting the field in which it works. The conception is Aristotelian, there is truth in it, and the emphasis was appropriate at a time when the need to distinguish one science from another was urgent. But scientific advance, at least from the days of Descartes, has made it clear that a science is not so much an ordered body of ascertained knowledge to be added to without changing it in kind, as a method which steadily modifies its subject-matter by simplification.

gaze back towards the full concrete world from which science
sprang by abstraction, you will still see in the systems of science
the persisting trace of value upon which science itself turns its
back; but if you look forward with the scientist to the goal at
which he aims, you will see system, not as connoting value but
as an ever more abstract hypothesis controlling and directing
observation. Thus Mr. Russell's view of material truth makes
sense in one part of science, in what I might perhaps call the
business end of scientific procedure, and occasionally—on occasions when he recalls that there is system as well as analysis in
science—he even allows that coherence may have something to
do with truth. But he does not associate system and coherence
with value. He is not even prepared to recognize that in system,
even scientific system, the cohering elements are not mere intensions of classes but universals, and that here connections of
content are necessary and no relation is purely external.[1] For in
his view we need in the way of universals no more than the word
'similar' to help us describe the world,[2] and the world to be
described is in the end a contingent aggregate of atoms. His
doctrine of formal truth or validity complements his view of
material truth.[3] Pure logical, or logico-mathematical, propositions are analytic and tautologous. They are, even more obviously
than true empirical propositions, independent of the individual
thinker, but they are not exhibited by Mr. Russell and other
modern logicians as systematically connected.[4] I have called
validity the ghost of system, but Mr. Russell has forgotten altogether its ghostly nature and its consequent though remote
connection with value.

Thus the connection of system or coherence with value begins
to emerge when we examine the systems of science without
scientific spectacles. In the first instance, we begin then to see
that in order to save truth from Protagorean dependence on the
singular individual thinker we need some other criterion of truth
than static correspondence of a proposition with external fact.
Once relations are no longer taken as external to their terms and
system is accepted as connection of universals, truth must consist
not in correspondence but in coherence. The truth of the system,
that is to say, must be immanent in the system and not a character

[1] Cp. pp. 26–7.   [2] Cp. p. 110.
[3] Cp. pp. 130–1.   [4] Cp. p. 125.

which propositions acquire by corresponding to it as to an external 'verifier'. But it now becomes clear that our conception of system must undergo a change. At present the reader may well object that system, as I have described it, is no more than scientific system with its internal coherence taken seriously; and he may add that system, for all I have said, is still as remotely and externally related to the mind supposed to grasp its truth as was the Russellian proposition.

Let us confine ourselves at present to the second objection. It is certain that system cannot stand, as the economic observer takes his object to stand, in an external relation to the thinking mind. We must reply to the objection that system in some sense actually constitutes the mind which in common parlance 'grasps' it; that the universal is now to be conceived not as any static external 'verifier' but as a self-developing activity of thought which *is* the individual thinker; that this self-development is, consequently, to be construed as the development equally of subject and object.

To stop at this point, however, would be to court a further and fatal objection which the believer in correspondence would be quick to raise. If the coherence of universals, he would say, actually constitutes, actually is, the singular individual mind, then knowledge is no more than belief and coherence no more than internal consistency of subjective ideas.[1] Our position, he would say, has in fact become worse than Protagorean, since now not merely do truth, knowledge, and coherence vanish from the scene but also belief and consistency; for belief means nothing save by constrast with knowledge, and consistency without objective coherence is a notion null and void.

We must, then, take a further step. We are in fact already committed to it. A system of cohering universals is not a bundle of empiricist particular ideas. It obviously cannot exhaust its nature in constituting a particular finite thinker, if only because it can be possessed by, or can possess, several finite thinkers. But fragmentation and partition of the universal such as that suggests is patently absurd, unless we say that in true thinking the finite mind transcends itself and is not simply singular. And with that, if the term 'self-transcendence' is not to be left hopelessly vague, we must amplify our statement that the universal

[1] Cp. p. 165.

is a self-developing activity of thought which *is* the individual thinker. We must say that it is a self-developing activity of thought which constitutes not merely the individual thinker but also and *eo ipso* itself.[1]

This conception of philosophic truth brings it formally into line with the other forms of intrinsic value which we have considered, and its suggestion of an essential duality in human thinking may promise a better defence against Protagoreanism, and a less crude account of the relation between belief and knowledge, than Mr. Russell has to offer. It cannot, however, for a reason which will become obvious if we contrast it with those notions of truth with which this discussion started, be quickly justified. Material truth in science depends, if Mr. Russell is right, on correspondence. It is, I suppose, most simply exemplified when a proposition expressing a calculated measurement is verified as corresponding exactly with fact. Truth so defined might well be renamed 'correctness'. Philosophic truth, as I have described it, is not external correspondence but immanent coherence. It is the real nature of a system manifesting itself in and as concrete thinking, constituting and maintaining itself in finite thinking, which for that reason is self-transcending. 'Genuineness' might serve as another name for it, and this implication is present no less in Plato's ἀλήθεια than in Hegel's *Wahrheit*, from which the instructed reader will readily perceive that I have taken it. He will also see that, if truth is held to be the genuineness, the immanent reality, of concrete thinking, then only his own active elaboration of a philosophic system, only the actual development of philosophical thought in himself, can reasonably convince a man that this theory of truth is itself true. That is the reason why such a theory cannot be quickly justified. Meanwhile the notion of philosophic truth which I have so briefly sketched contrasts not only with material truth by correspondence but also with the validity or formal consistency which governs scientific inference irrespective of its special content—the truth, that is, of formal logic and, ideally at least, if Mr. Russell is right, of mathematics. *Prima facie* the uncritical acceptance of validity as self-evident and the conception of propositions in logic and mathematics as tautologous and yet significant sound like a confession of bankruptcy. A significant tautology seems as odd

[1] Cp. p. 163.

a paradox as the sheerly particular datum which, on Mr. Russell's view, would be the hard currency of a perfected science. But this cold and distant co-operation of formal and material truth, assisted in fact, perhaps, by a little unacknowledged compromise, works well enough in the economic sphere to which it belongs. Here two philosophical nonsenses make a practical sense. On the other hand, if philosophic truth is coherence, formal and material truth cannot within it maintain this chilly separation.

A third contrast, too, here claims attention, namely that between philosophic truth and scientific system. The reader may well again complain that I have associated, even perhaps seemed to identify, value with coherence and system, but have still done nothing to show that system in science, when viewed philosophically as a coherent whole of internally and necessarily connected universals, exhibits value; that I have instead exalted coherence into a mysterious activity which is alleged somehow to be the truth at once of the finite experient and of a non-finite activity which he experiences, or which experiences itself in him; that this may or may not eventually solve the problem of intrinsic value, but that it does little to explain in what sense the recognition of coherent system in science is a recognition of value.

I must at any rate defend this shift—which I freely admit—in the meaning of 'coherence'. If philosophical thinking is what I take it to be it must develop by expanding the concepts which it criticizes, not by substituting forcibly and *ab extra*, concepts of its own. For it has no concepts, in that sense, of its own. It is the mutual externality of elements in a scientific or mathematical system which suggests, or rather expands itself into, the notion of a coherent system within which the elements of the universal mutually determine one another to difference within the identity of a significant concrete whole. To the scientist as such the suggestion does not occur, because his purpose, avowed or not, is to break down system in order to enable action. But to the philosopher, provided that he is not making the misguided effort to philosophize at the level of science, the increasing mutual externality of terms in the successive systems which mark the analytic progress of science must suggest that these are privations of coherence, abstractions which are not philosophically intelligible save in terms of coherence, because coherence is the concrete from which they are for a special non-philosophical purpose abstracted.

But coherence emerging at this level is still itself only a privation of value, a mere promise which must seem remote until it can develop into a fuller and more concrete concept which is only still to be called 'coherence' if it is thought necessary to mark the identity which persists in the development.

In the chapters which follow I shall make some attempt to expand the notion of value which I have so far meagrely sketched. In the meantime it may be helpful to end this chapter by looking back for a moment on the controversy about the nature of truth in which Mr. Russell and F. H. Bradley were protagonists. For it centred—more nearly, indeed, than either of them realized— on the relation of value and system in the world of science and common sense.

Bradley held the test of truth to be, anywhere and everywhere, two inseparable aspects of system, namely coherence and comprehensiveness. The 'coherence theory', as it came to be called, implies the connection, if not the coincidence, of coherence or system with value, but Bradley's position was obscured from the start by the distinction which he drew between logic and metaphysics but did not always strictly observe.[1] On the one hand, although he repudiated everywhere the sharp severance which all formal logic makes between material and formal truth, he regarded logic as a special discipline not to be raised too far above the level of common sense, and limited by certain assumptions which do not bind the metaphysician. On the other hand, even in the *Principles of Logic* he develops the view that perfected individuality (for which 'infinite totality' and 'perfected activity' appear as synonyms) is the ideal completion demanded both by intellectual analysis and synthesis and also by other forms of value experience: 'In this identity of analysis and synthesis we recognize an appearance of our soul's ideal, which in other shapes and in other spheres has perplexed and gladdened us; but which, however it appears, in Metaphysics or Ethics or Religion or Aesthetic, is at bottom the notion of a perfected individuality.'[2]

When Bradley developed the coherence doctrine in polemic directed largely in his latter years against Mr. Russell, the issue was confused both by Bradley's not perfectly firm distinction of

---

[1] I have discussed this distinction with reference to Bradley in my *Introduction to Hegel*, pp. 149 ff., and also in an article entitled 'The Marriage of Universals', *Journal of Philosophical Studies*, Vol. III, Nos. 11 and 12, 1928.

[2] See *Principles of Logic*, Second edn., pp. 466–91, and for the quotation p. 490.

logic from metaphysics and by two further interrelated factors as well. In the first place, neither side recognized the purely economic nature of natural science and mathematics and the consequent character of merely scientific truth. In the second place, Bradley, even when he spoke explicitly as a metaphysician, held that thought is essentially discursive and relational, and that for thought to realize its ideal perfection would entail its metamorphosis into an absolute experience which could not bear the name of thought. Hence when Bradley argued the coherence theory as a logician, as he frequently did, thought still on the whole appeared as no more than the activity of a finite singular mind, and coherence as the connection of universals which form somehow the ideal content of such finite thinking rather than signify the presence of any more than finite thinking activity. The finite particular subject remained over against the object, as it does for the economic observer, and coherence in an ever-expanding ideal content seemed to offer no real criterion of truth as opposed to mere consistency. If thought is envisaged as merely adjectival to a singular finite mind it cannot readily be distinguished from mere belief, and at that point a correspondence theory of truth becomes almost inevitable. Bradley was in fact relying on a metaphysical doctrine which he had excluded from logic.

The main battlefield was provided by the problem of relations,[1] and that meant in effect that fighting took place chiefly in the sphere of everyday common sense and scientific thinking.[2] Bradley argued that all relations are internal and express the nature of their terms. To Mr. Russell and his friends that seemed to blur everything with everything else. That Bradley held all relations to be also external they forgot or ignored, because they could see no sense in his theory that, though all thinking is discursive and relational, yet terms in relation present a contradiction which shows them to be appearance and not reality. It was a metaphysical theory and quite incompatible with their own instinctive economic assumption of a world of facts which may be contingent but are quite indisputably the case, a world in which the

---

[1] It is worth note that the problem of terms and relations never appears *totidem verbis* in Hegel, from whose logic of Essence the British idealists drew their doctrine of identity in difference. In Kant and Hegel the word *Verhältnis* usually means, so far as I can judge, not 'relation' as opposed to 'term' but 'terms-in-relation'.

[2] It is to be remembered that Bradley had originally developed his views against the empiricism of J. S. Mill and Bain, so that this was his familiar field of controversy long before Mr. Russell wrote.

difference between real and apparent is merely subjective. When Bradley talked of data transcending themselves it seemed quite nonsensical to his opponents. If the parties to the dispute had been clearly aware that they were looking at things from quite different points of view, a good deal might have been settled out of court. As it was, the atomists were entirely unconvinced and all the more loudly proclaimed the externality of all relations and the purely analytical character of philosophical method. On the other side, Bradley and his idealist supporters gave the impression of preaching that scientists would do better to work with the notions of internal relations and identity in difference; or at any rate they never succeeded in explaining why science, which ought to know its own business, continually works away from these concepts. Neither did they in polemical discussion bear clearly in mind what is after all the implication of their own metaphysical views, namely that to see objects of common sense and science in terms of coherence is to see them, not as the scientist sees them, not as any one of us sees them when we are economically preoccupied, but with a reference, however distant, to intrinsic value.

It is worth observing in this context that in Hegel's logic the concept of identity in difference, which Bradley borrowed and used ubiquitously, belongs to the logic of Essence (*Wesen*), and that Hegel's logic of Essence is a philosophical critique of the concepts of the Understanding (*Verstand*) which underlie common sense and science. To Hegel identity in difference did not seem a conception adequate to express value. Only in the Hegelian categories of the Notion (*Begriff*) does *Wahrheit* become explicit. But on Bradley's view thought remains relational even for the metaphysician, a position which virtually entails the rejection of the Hegelian conception of Reason (*Vernunft*) and of the categories of the Notion. The philosopher, Bradley held, can show that the concepts of common sense and science break down in self-contradiction and transcend themselves towards the notion of a perfect individuality, an absolute totality; but Bradley's metaphysical absolute totality is a whole of immediate (re-immediated) feeling in which thought itself holds no primacy over, for example, aesthetic and moral experience, but is together with them, and co-ordinately with them, transcended. Hence the philosopher can, over and above his criticism of the concepts of common sense and science, only argue that *somehow* the self-contradiction which these evince is overcome and made good in the Absolute: the very nature of thought prevents him from exhibiting intellectually any detailed process of their self-transcendence. Bradley was still too much of an empiricist to trust dialectical system. In consequence he selects and uses concepts which appear among Hegel's categories of Essence, but rejects the logic of the Notion save in so far as his conception of the concrete universal is based on the initial category of Hegel's Notion, *Der Begriff als solche*, which is the thought of the universal particularizing, or specifying, itself to concrete individuality.[1]

---

[1] As opposed to the genus of species which characterize an indefinite plurality of logically indiscriminable singulars, and to the mere abstract class of particulars.

CHAPTER X

VALUE AND THE DUALITY
OF EXPERIENCE

FOR the dualism of the correspondence theory of truth I have substituted a duality in the heart of human experience, attempting to replace the static antithesis of proposition and fact by the self-transcendence of finite into infinite activity. I have professed to find a like duality and a like self-transcendence in other forms of value-experience, too. The confirmed empiricist will find this whole conception quite rebarbative, particularly at its summit. An 'infinite activity' will seem to him an antiquated and disreputable relic of metaphysical superstition from which a careful study of standard English or a course of positivistic psychotherapy should long ago have purged me. Neither can I suppose that my brief and abrupt statement of this ancient doctrine could convince anyone to whom it was not already familiar and attractive. If it is to be developed, the notion of a finite mind must be examined without economic prejudice, but also without a too speedy appeal to infinity in any shape. I shall still not closely differentiate between one form of value-experience and another. I shall work in terms belonging to logic—universal, particular, singular and so forth—and this may suggest that if I am dealing with value it must be value in the specific form of truth with which I am concerned. That will in a sense be so, but I shall ask the reader to assume that it is so only in the sense that my concern at present is with the rationality in all forms of value-experience. Here is a problem which I cannot yet discuss, but if value as philosophical truth be genuineness, then value in other forms can only be rational in so far as it shares this character with truth. It may be hard on this view to avoid blurring the forms of value, confounding their difference in their common rationality, but that is a difficulty which I must beg leave to postpone, though not to forget.

To pursue our project we must cast back. In discussing the subjectivist view of value, I observed that a man feels the primitive sensual appetites and what satisfied them as constitutive elements of himself, and that for that reason he cannot doubt them.[1] I put forward the view that to the economic observer the satisfaction of hunger appeared as an event in which a man and his food came together in an assumed environment which had previously contained the two in separation; that in a more fundamental sense, however, this whole world which is assumed by the economic observer presupposes primitive experience; that the primitive wants and what satisfies them comprise an embryo of felt differences, which develops into a finite subject distinguishing himself from what he had felt as an element of himself, and ultimately into a man whose life can have intrinsic value which he is capable of judging. In short, this genesis and development of the finite subject in self-distinction from a world is fundamentally logical. It may be partially reflected as a process of events in a description offered by an empirical psychologist, but events only happen to observable objects, and the original, or we might better say 'originative', distinction cannot be called an event until the story is retold in terms of economic observation.[2] In its essential nature it falls outside any temporal process, and we can only say that something logically presupposed by our experience distinguishes itself, but not temporally, into ourselves and our world. I have called this genesis 'logical' because we have reached it, as Descartes reached his *cogito ergo sum*, not by tracing back any temporal process but as the result of asking why a man cannot in the last resort doubt himself and his world.[3] What a philosopher can legitimately say of this something which originates the finite subject and his world is strictly limited to what human experience of value leads us on reflection to presuppose. We cannot even name it until we have examined more closely what is begotten in this logical genesis.

That self-consciousness and consciousness of objects depend

---

[1] See pp. 175–6.   [2] Cp. p. 167.

[3] As a man develops this basic initial assurance he is, of course, plentifully liable to error, but this original unity and distinction of himself and his world guarantees that his error is always in a degree and not absolute. The empiricist's search for an atomic particular datum, conducted on the naïve assumption that the mind is a watcher waiting for a speck to appear on a perfectly blank screen, is fruitless outside the economic world, and even there, as we saw, the impenetrably hard particular is a will-o'-the-wisp ideal; cp. p. 98.

O

upon one another, and that this distinction of inseparables is 'original' in the sense that it is the fundamental presupposition of human experience behind which we cannot go, is a familiar, and was a respectable, doctrine. But both the terms of the distinction require analysis, for they do not constitute a perfectly simple duality. Self-consciousness means, I suppose, consciousness of oneself as an identical individual subject in all one's experience, in all its diversity of modes and content. But it does not merely mean consciousness of oneself as the bare identical subject taken apart from this diversity, for such a subject would not be 'I' as opposed to 'you' or 'he'; it would be no more than a bare abstract universal 'I' quite unparticularized. Self-consciousness means, further, the consciousness of a subject particularized in this diverse experience, consciousness of a concrete individual self, a person. Actual self-consciousness is always somewhere on a scale between these two poles. It could not, *ex vi termini*, exist at either extreme, for self-consciousness is essentially identity in distinction—it is the very archetype of that notion which so much puzzles the empiricist—and at either extreme distinction would vanish. But within these limits and without touching them, it fluctuates considerably. In a casual act of sense-perception one may be aware of oneself as hardly more than a bare subject formally implicated in the act, almost an unnoticed bystander, so to say. But in deeper and more complex phases of experience, more especially, perhaps, where will is dominant, one is explicitly conscious of one's individual self as fully implicated in this experience, and of finding in it one's own concrete content as a person.

Consciousness of objects means strictly, I suppose, consciousness of what one distinguishes as definitely not oneself, in fact consciousness of the 'detached' external objects of economic observation. But we have already seen that so far as the self is a bodily self the distinction between it and external objects is not in actual experience rigid. Parts of my body which I habitually experience as parts of myself may, we found, become external objects to me, and 'things', when I use them, I may experience as elements extending my body within the limits of myself.[1] Nor, if self-consciousness and consciousness of objects are mutually dependent and inseparable, can even the sharpest extrusion and repudiation of an object as not-self, for a philosophical as opposed

[1] Cp. p. 30.

to an economic view, completely sever the bond of identity. Moreover, my experience of not-self is not confined to 'things', for I also experience other people. Their bodies may be detached objects for me, but I am also aware of them as, like me, both subjects and selves. The distinction which I make between myself and them is, consequently, not on all fours with the distinction which I draw between myself and external objects, but it, too, is an 'original' distinction which emerges in the logical genesis of human experience. If I could not without consciousness of objects be conscious of myself, equally my self-consciousness depends upon my consciousness of other human beings from whom I distinguish myself. Here again the distinction fluctuates. In every man a sense of identity with other men alternates with a sense of difference from them.

Thus the product of what I have called 'logical genesis' soon turns out to be far wider and more complex than was suggested by the distinction with which I first illustrated it, the distinction, namely, of a finite subject from the objects of his primitive desires and satisfactions. The position which now begins to emerge is something like this. Subject and object in all forms or phases of experience are correlatives devoid of significance in separation, not merely names appropriate to independent entities on intermittent occasions when these entities enter into a symmetrical but external relation. Within this framework correlation varies in degree and kind. The subject as a finite subject has consciousness of itself as subject, but also and further of itself as a concrete individual self, a person. It could have consciousness of neither without the other, but in actual experience the emphasis is now on the one and now on the other. Consciousness of an individual self is at once distinct from and impossible without (a) consciousness of objects and (b) consciousness of other persons both as subjects and selves, and in both cases the boundary on which the distinction rests is not rigid but fluctuating.

We may now continue the discussion in more precisely logical terms. A particular finite person, a finite subject particularized as a concrete individual self, presents a striking contrast to a Russellian atomic particular. Mr. Russell's hard atom is a singular individual standing in no greater intimacy of connection to any one thing than to any other, because all its relations are sheerly external and do not determine its nature. If it is a blue patch and there are other blue patches, it is similar to them, but we must not, on Mr. Russell's view, even say, as a less sternly atomic empiricist might allow us to say, that all these blue patches share a universal (in the sense of general) character, namely blueness. 'Being similar' is all the universality there is, and each particular, I suppose we must say, is a particular blue rather than a blue particular. In short, the atomic particular is individual purely by exclusion, and its 'what' does not outrun its 'that'. It is to be noted in respect of terminology that on this view what is fully particular is *eo ipso* singular individual. The particular and the singular individual are synonymous for Mr. Russell, as on the whole they were for Bradley.

A finite person, on the other hand, is individual in a different sense. What individuates him in so far as he is individual is primarily the unity which he possesses as the totality of his own experience in all its modes and phases and in all the detail of its content. He is not singular but single. And it is vital to observe that, because he is subject and not object, this totality is not a whole of parts, nor a bundle of operant faculties, nor a logical construction of actual and possible particulars, nor even any such systematic unity as science finds in its object-world and submits to analysis. A person is *totus in toto et totus in qualibet parte.* He enters as a whole person into every act or passion which can be fairly called his. This is no mystic assertion but a familiar fact of human life. It leaps from the pages of any autobiography, any good play or novel. To be sure of it we have only to think about the more markedly individual of our friends and acquaintances, and it is the reason why we find schizophrenia such a horrifying abnormality.

But a finite person differs from a Russellian particular, not merely because he contains internal diversity but also because he is not essentially individuated by exclusion. However widely you bound him, his relations to what lies beyond this limit are never purely external. At every point he draws his nature from a context wider still. Puzzling as it may sound to the empiricist, he appropriates in varying degrees of intimacy what is other than he as the stuff of which he constitutes his individual self. Any man who so desires can readily put this to the test. He has only to suppose the annihilation of any large elements of the world which he experiences—even such elements of it as he is in the habit of distinguishing quite sharply as other than himself—in order to discover that large elements of himself have vanished too. Destroy the whole circle of men and women with whose minds and personalities, through actual acquaintance or through written record, you have some intimacy (I do not mean imagine them dead, for many of them already are dead; I mean make the logical experiment of excluding them from existence); abolish in the same sense the subject-matter of a science of which you know something; wipe out the whole factual basis of a period of history which you have studied deeply—do all or any of this, and is your mind thereby merely altered and not substantially changed? Is not rather half the stuff of it gone? And could you not easily complete the theoretical wrecking of your world and so efface your mind altogether? In so doing you would be merely reversing in imagination the logical genesis and development of yourself as a finite person.

To the empiricist a finite person is a paradox, even an irresoluble contradiction. For a finite person is individual because he is the totality of his internal content, entering whole into every phase of it and stamping every jot of it as his own. But he is not a closed system. The content of his every act of experience is not only *his* content but at the same time an element in a contextual world which in some degree lies beyond him. We might almost, using a crude and partial figure, say that in every phase of his experience the possession of a world is in dispute. He perceives, for instance, a blue patch in a context (blue patches are not otherwise perceptible), and both are actual elements of himself *qua* percipient; but in perceiving the blue patch he *distinguishes* himself from it. Hence the world to which patch and context belong is at the same time not he, and as the context expands beyond the field of his actual content of perception, that world is less and less he. He can no longer claim it save as the world of his *possible* perception. It is now no more than a cross-section of Kant's objective world of possible experience.[1] Spreading stage by stage *ad indefinitum*, it eludes his grasp and denies his allegiance. It becomes more and more the world of *any* finite subject's possible experience, less and less personal. Yet it cannot reach complete self-sufficiency, for it is the object twinned with the subject at one logical birth.

[1] *Erfahrung.* See p. 32.

An act of sense-perception, especially an act of sense-perception conceived abstractly as what might be called a merely economico-cognitive act—and that is how I have been conceiving it—manifests personality less than other kinds of act, because there is a passive element in it which makes us look on it as in some measure reactive rather than active. But if we start instead with an act of philosophic or historical thinking, or again with a moral action or an act of aesthetic creation, we shall find in it the same expansion of the self in appropriation of what lay beyond it. In other words, the identity which binds together in one the internal differences of a person runs outward also to bind him in one with the world beyond him. The tie with the beyond holds in very varying degrees of intimacy, but it is always constitutive, and the stronger it is—here perhaps is the paradox—the more truly and genuinely is he an individual person. A finite person is individuated far more by inclusion than by exclusion. He is always in some degree a world, although the degree varies and fluctuates, because to be a person is to be not accidentally but essentially self-transcending.

The logical doctrine which this conception of a finite person involves may be stated thus. The universal is not the general quality or relation, it is not the class concept, and even less is it 'being similar': it is the subject. The universal is what every man who says 'I' asserts himself to be. Here it is vital to grasp two points. Even if the universal as subject is taken quite abstractly it is still not an adjective but a unity. It is not subjectivity as a character which particular subjects instantiate as blue patches instantiate blueness, but an all-embracing unity of possible experience. It is in fact, taken abstractly, Kant's transcendental unity of apperception. But secondly, just because it is a unity of experience and not an adjective, the universal is *eo ipso* individual. Abstract the universal as subject as sharply as you please from all the diversified content of which it is the unity, conceive it as no more than the bare self-identity which Kant expresses as 'I=I', and it is still universal-individual, concrete universal, not mere generality. If you must have an abstract noun to express it, you may call it wholeness or totality, but truly it is *the* whole. And inasmuch as it is particularized in finite persons, they thereby participate in its dual nature of universal-individual or concrete universal. It is quite false to say that logically we do not reach the individual until we reach the particular or singular individual. If the universal is subject, the distinction between universal and individual is not the same as it is if the universal is taken as an adjectival quality. If the universal is subject it is also as such individual, and the finite individual is also universal.

I shall perhaps here be accused of blurring all distinction between the finite person and the universal in which he participates. There is another side to the picture, to which I must point at the close of this chapter, but my accuser would probably be assuming, consciously or not, that a person is a closed system immutably self-identical, and that is surely implausible in itself as well as quite impossible if the universal as subject is—as I must now openly maintain it to be—activity. If a finite person owes his nature to participation in a universal which is activity, then his nature, the individuality in which he consists, is not a static self-identity but something which he achieves only in this participation. A finite person is *as such* self-transcending: he *is*, in Bosanquet's phrase, 'a *nisus* towards totality'. His individuality is half-possessed, an ideal not fully realized, but so far as he does attain it he is neither diluted nor merely enlarged: he is intensified and heightened, and so far no longer merely finite. It is in human experience enlarged, intensified, and heightened that system, in itself no more than mere unity in diversity, becomes explicit as intrinsic value.[1] For no enlargement of a finite person's experience could give it intrinsic value if this enlargement were mere expansion without self-transcendence, if it were not, to express it conversely, the communication to him of an infinite activity. Mere humanism provides no better basis for a theory of intrinsic value than does the hedonism on which the subjectivist doctrine of value turns out ultimately to be based. *Ein ganzer Mensch*, if he is nothing but an untranscended self, is no more good *per se* than is the crudest voluptuary. Experience of value involves duality; it is, as Bosanquet puts it, 'dual-centred'.

[1] Compare pp. 187–8. Coherence or system becomes explicit as intrinsic value only when it is seen as an activity of self-synthesis which is, furthermore, self-transcendence. System taken to reside in the object abstracted from the subject, as science inevitably takes it, is philosophically ambiguous and provisional. The presence in it of mind (without which nothing is identical in difference, coherent, systematic) is bound to create trouble when scientists, or philosophers who ape them, attempt to philosophize about science without transcending the scientific level. The concrete universal without the subject is a mere equivocal reflection of value, to the serious philosopher a prefiguration, to the scientist a scaffolding necessary at first but to be dismantled when done with.

If I seem still not to have met the charge of blurring, let it be remembered that for the finite subject this duality is as much a separation which he suffers as a union which he enjoys. That is attested in all human experience. And if the accusation is renewed in the form of a charge that I seem to have set up a perfect and absolute infinite, absorbing without trace the finite in which it constitutes itself, let me again repeat that of any infinite immanent in the finite a philosopher has no right to say anything for which he does not find the ground in human experience. In that sense humanism is all that human philosophy can attain to.

In Chapter VIII I contended that only a mind's self-conscious activity which is in some sense total is good *per se*, and that in the experience of value the individual experient transcends himself. By identifying the universal with the subject and with activity, I have now expressed the same doctrine in terms of logic.[1] If I am right, the divorce of the universal from the subject cancels its active nature. Hence, as it seems to me, come all those incomplete conceptions of the universal which the history of thought has made so tiresomely familiar. As the life ebbs from it, the universal becomes a plurality of universals. If any touch of wholeness or individuality remains in these, they may be thought of as timeless, real, and intelligible patterns (some of them value patterns, some not) in which the temporal, imperfectly real particulars of sense somehow derivatively partake. If this seems to make them mere counterparts of mind with a reality of their own too remote to account for any communication of their nature to the allegedly partaking particular, a swing of philosophic taste may bring them down to earth to become merely the adjectives, the qualities and relations, of the particulars which had been held to draw a derivative reality from them by participation. Or they may become 'mental concepts', gathered mysteriously into the mind by generalization from particulars, nominal rather than real. Gradually, as the razor of Occam the nominalist does its work, the relation of original and derivative is turned upside down, and finally nothing real is left but atomic particulars, singular individuals in which wholeness and individuality are contracted to a point. These neither partake in universals nor,

---

[1] The reader will note that in this doctrine value is 'subjective' because it is universal, whereas on the 'subjectivist' view value is 'subjective' because it resides in the feeling of the subject *qua* singular individual. It is vital to relate and distinguish clearly the two senses of 'subjective'.

as it were, 'give off' universals for the generalizing mind to gather. They are similar or dissimilar, but the mutual relations which these words indicate are perfectly external to their terms. Because they are similar and dissimilar, they can be classified in accordance with the principles of a formal logic, but this ghost of system, as I have called it, this form quite external and indifferent to its content, is all that survives of the universal as active subject, single and concrete in the diversity of its content. If value is the primary concern of philosophy, this *dégringolade* is a *reductio ad absurdum*. If, however, the essence of thought is analysis in the interest of economic action, and value can be safely assigned to feeling, like a lunatic certified and segregated from rational society in an asylum, then this *ersatz* philosophy may be defensible. It can, however, serve no genuinely philosophical purpose save to display by contrast the privation of value in the economic world.

I have tried to interpret the general structure of the intrinsically good in terms of the universal as subject, and our next task should be to make some attempt to differentiate the kinds of it. But when we ask, as first we must, how this is to be done, our difficulties quickly multiply. Only one thing is certain: we must not, in seeking precision, lapse into trying to set out a universe of value as if it were an object-world of economic observation. For we are concerned with the subject, and with objects only in explicit relation to the subject. We cannot, like the economic observer, presuppose the subject and then forget it. We are seeking value in and through human experience, and we cannot stand back with him in detached contemplation of an external world which is subjectless and quite devoid of intrinsic value. The scientist thinks his impersonal thoughts in terms of hard data and abstract universals, and it makes no difference to the propositions of science who in particular enunciates them for the first time. But the philosopher struggles towards his conclusions in the medium of self-conscious personality, and for fear I may have seemed hitherto to glorify his function overmuch, I will now instead stress some few of his limitations.

A man comes to philosophize (as he comes to any form of value-experience) by self-transcendence, and the process, though in one sense temporal, is in another and more fundamental sense logical. He comes constituted, made what he is, by lower forms of experience. These could fairly easily be set out in a rough series descending to sensation or some sort of barely differentiated feeling, and any sort of philosopher would find this series tolerably familiar in its general character. But we shall not have succeeded completely in discarding our economic spectacles until we see that this series does not come to a final stop with sensation or primitive feeling: it descends below that into Nature. Sensation or primitive feeling presupposes life, and life presupposes a spatio-temporal world organized once again in descending levels. I shall not try to articulate this extension of the series, this sub-terranean root, so to say, of human personality, because the philosophy of Nature is not our direct concern. But it must be made clear that the descending series of man's modes of experience does not end with the disappearance of his explicit consciousness, and that these lower stages of his logical genesis must not be simply identified with the external world of conscious economic obser-vation, with Nature as the natural scientist views it.[1] That world would in fact not be a possible object of observation if man were not himself natural, and natural science must make its start with the sensible qualities of things (which pose the unanswerable question whether they are 'subjective' or 'objective'), however resolutely it may then pursue its path towards mathematical abstraction. So far as concerns the view of value which I have been maintaining, it would be nonsense to hold that subject and object are inseparable, and that man participates in an infinite activity which constitutes him, without at the same time insisting that man is natural at all levels of Nature, and that none of these is in the last resort quite irrelevant to his personality.

It is the business of the philosopher, I believe, to heighten and expand human self-consciousness by articulating this series, its higher levels as experience of value, its lower levels as the priva-tion, the significant absence, though at the same time the pre-figuration, of value. But every phase of it, or at any rate every conscious phase, sets him a problem which at first sight may well seem to defy solution. He is by nature not static and self-contained but self-transcending, and the truth of him lies always ahead. But there is no lower form of his experience which he can com-pletely transcend. The fact, as we saw in Chapter II,[2] is familiar

---

[1] In my *Introduction to Hegel*, chapter VIII, the position which I am here maintain-ing is set out, perhaps more clearly, in relation to Aristotle and Hegel, though I did not then fully realize the economic nature of natural science.

[2] P. 29.   See also my *Study of Hegel's Logic*, pp. 309-12.

enough in the experience of every day. To sensate, to image, to perceive a sensible object, and to judge that and what the object is, are successive acts. Each, from the second onwards, is a movement to determine and develop its predecessor by absorbing it without residue, not simply to add something to it. Each is a *nisus* to expand an identical content into what it truly is by an act which shall consummate and supersede the preceding act as such. But apart from such difficulties as the selection and omission which each successive act involves, the content and act which, as such, we aim at superseding do not in fact vanish without trace. An unabsorbed residue of each stage or phase persists together with its successor, simultaneous with it, distinguishable from it, indispensably subserving it. At every level there is uneasy and unequal partnership where there should be full integration of the lower in the higher. Robert Bridges's line, 'Man's Reason is in such deep insolvency to sense', aptly expresses the dilemma in its most familiar form.

In the rough series which I took we might interpolate another term, one which confronts the philosopher with an especially acute problem. Speech, I suppose, supervenes upon the co-operation of imagery and perception.[1] We come to thinking through talking, but language persists with thought to subserve it by giving it expression, and thought can never fully supersede it. The language through which we come to think has matured a great deal by the time it becomes the language which expresses thought, but it never ripens fully, and its course, as it continues to develop *pari passu* with thinking, is deceptive and difficult to follow. With the transition from imagery to the verbal expression of everyday common sense a fairly stable linguistic apparatus is established. When the philosopher develops this to express a different kind of thinking, the enterprise is hazardous. The scientist needs only symbols and abbreviations, because his thought remains on one level or descends towards greater abstraction. He can safely coin and define new technical terms for his own purposes. But if the philosopher follows the practice of the scientist, it severs him so sharply from common experience, which it is his business not to side-track but to transcend, that he becomes, like A. N. Whitehead, almost impossible to follow with certainty.[2] He has to rely very largely on pushing metaphor and

[1] Cp. pp. 127–8.
[2] Cp. R. G. Collingwood, *Philosophical Method*, 1933, Chapter X.

simile further than common-sense usage pushes them.[1] He may
easily mislead his hearers, and he is always at the mercy of an
opponent who insists upon attempting to philosophize *au pied de
la lettre*.

However far upwards we extend the developing series of
human experience, the same ambiguity of imperfect self-transcendence will persist. If we follow it downwards, what we find as
we sink into our natural selves will seem more and more alien
and unabsorbed as we try to concentrate our attention on it;
but we shall find nothing that does not somehow subserve our
conscious being, nothing that is not presupposed by it. For man
is the prolongation of a *nisus* to self-transcendence which begins
blindly in Nature. To say that a man achieves his true nature by
self-transcendence and participation in an infinite activity may seem
at first sight to make his physical basis supremely unimportant.
Certainly there are times when a man is bound to feel the natural
element in him a mere clog, a mere alien 'weight of becoming',
but to base a philosophy on this feeling is ruinous. A disembodied
human personality is a confused and contradictory notion. To
maintain it is to divorce physical Nature from the object which is
inseparable from the subject within infinite activity, as well as to
ignore the trace of corporeal feeling which survives, not quite
irrelevantly, in any experience however spiritually exalted. The
effort to glorify man by cutting him from his natural roots can
in the end only make of him a purely finite and worthless thing.

Thus the duality in man of finite and infinite riddles all his
experience with every shape of ambiguity and defect. He draws
his nature at any level not only from what is above him but also
from the world which at that level environs him. Between that
world and himself persists a fluctuating boundary which he can
never fully cancel. In so far as that is so contingency infects both
him and his environing world. The brute empirical shock of the
event, 'external' or 'internal', is for him indubitable, because it is
within the experience of which he consists. But this fact which
happens comes to him as in the last resort the result of chance,
which is to say that it does not come as a result at all. For even if it

[1] See pp. 154-5. The metaphorical and the literal meanings of word or phrase
very well illustrate respectively the dominant phase and the phase which persists,
imperfectly transcended, to subserve it, at every level of experience. I would ask the
reader to examine in this light my use of the terms 'coherence' and 'system' in this
and the previous chapter.

seem proximately necessitated, yet the full necessitating conditions, which he demands to know because infinity is in him, are never present, and he rests unsatisfied. Correspondingly, he appears to himself to be in his own nature contingent, to be situated midway between a wide open future and an entirely indefinite past; and even within that stretch of time which he can establish with some confidence he seems to himself to owe what he is to a series of accidents from his conception and birth onwards, all of which might have happened otherwise or not happened at all. No doubt this sense of contingency in oneself, frightening to lonely men, is never more than partial, but it is not an illusion, and in so far as it is present and really experienced a man is (after all) individual not by inclusion but by exclusion and repulsion; to that extent his individuality is diminished to idiosyncrasy.

This ineliminable factor of contingency and idiosyncrasy becomes especially acute and baffling to the philosopher in the explicit experience of value. Without it there could be no self-transcendence, and it is in fact at each level of experience the unabsorbed residue of lower levels persisting to subserve—and confuse. It is the sensation which survives in the image, the image which still accompanies the word, and the word without which we cannot think. It is the lust which survives in mature sexual passion, the physical thrill of mere colours and shapes in the creating painter, the composer's exultation in mere tone and timbre. In the poet it is these and more, and it is in the great philosophers—those in whom intellectualism has not numbed it—a certain unspecialized fullness of life. Everywhere it is indispensable, yet everywhere it signifies a shortcoming. It is that which dates and places a man in the spatio-temporal show, bounds him with the limit of his own epoch, marks him as falling short of his full nature, subjects him to outward contingency and inward caprice. And since it means defect, caprice, and immaturity, it means also that a man's experience of value is never in its form quite beyond that undeveloped immediacy of feeling which the subjectivist theory misconstrues as the essence of value-experience; it means that human experience never quite succeeds in becoming the fully rational self-conscious activity with which a 'clarified' feeling coincides[1] because such an activity is immediate above and not below mediation.

[1] See p. 65.

This multiform defect in self-transcendence, moreover, is not mere defect: it is also the inexhaustible spring of perversion; of error, evil, and ugliness; of any contrary which attaches to any human value. There is no experience of value which does not consist in the overcoming of such a contrary, and none in which that contrary is completely overcome. The lower level indisputably subserves the higher, but the price of this complementary service is not only a lack in the total activity of the person but also a moment of perversion which in contrast with mere lack is relatively positive. In man's best success there is failure, and no honest man sees his own failures as quite free of disgrace.

I may be thought to have conceded all that I claimed. From crying, 'What a piece of work is a man!' I have turned, it may seem, to echo a more cynical poet:

> Good Lord, what is man! for as simple he looks,
> Do but try to develop his hooks and his crooks,
> With his depths and his shallows, his good and his evil,
> All in all, he's a problem must puzzle the devil.

I cannot deny the *prima facie* contradiction, and in the face of it a philosopher may be tempted to reject self-transcendence altogether, put his faith in a blind sensuous contact with the real, and think out his universe at the lowest possible intellectual level of experience, so proceeding until he becomes as nearly a pure empiricist as the never quite totally pervertible rationality in him permits. Or he may (though it is nowadays unlikely) forget his own finitude, forget that the infinite activity which constitutes him is also beyond him, and that although it is his own real nature and his criterion of truth, it does not give him truth in any final form. Then he will confound appearance with illusion and produce a purely transcendent metaphysic, a fabulous theodicy, or an Absolute in which all cows are black. If, however, he refuses the peaceful asylum from genuine thinking which is offered by either of these cardinal errors, he has in the end no alternative but to anchor his conception of human personality on the shifting sands of self-transcendence. He must accept the disheartening doctrine that truth has degrees and that appearance will always fall short of a reality which is none the less never to be discovered outside it. He must build his whole philosophy on the basis of contradiction, because contradiction makes him what he is.

These are sobering reflections. In the next chapter I shall at length turn to consider intrinsic value according to its kinds, but my contribution to the subject will not be ambitious. If my general description of human experience as self-transcending bears any relation to the truth, the philosopher is bound to treat any subject-matter as some kind of developing series. It follows also, I think, that if main forms of intrinsic value can be distinguished they should reveal their distinctness by themselves falling into a definite order in some such series. Hegel's dialectical system is the most determined attempt by any philosopher since Aristotle to order values on a scale, but I do not find his (nor any other thinker's) ordered articulation sufficiently convincing to accept as it stands, nor have I any detailed and systematic construction of my own to offer in its place. I propose that we shall largely concern ourselves with the transition to a form of value from a level of experience which is not experience of value. That may be a humbler task, but at least we shall be examining the source of most philosophical errors, and there is no philosophical approach to truth except through error. Something I shall say of the relation of value to value, but the reader may expect that any such discussion will leave a wide open question. I shall not pretend to work with any precise and predetermined method. I have learned, mainly from Hegel, that in philosophy method and content are inseparable aspects of the same thing, and I am sure that if I had never struggled to follow and re-think the Hegelian dialectic my notion of method in philosophy would be even dimmer than it is. But my vision of human experience is far too limited and broken to let me suppose that I could present it as any such regularly ordered march of self-development. Most probably our progress will have to consist in following one path so far as it leads us and breaking off, when we can trace it no farther, to start afresh and follow another. I can only hope that I may keep some sense of direction.

CHAPTER XI

MORALITY

M Y general criticism of modern philosophical attitudes has rested on a contention which may be shortly summarized as follows. Economic action, which as such is amoral and self-centred, is presupposed by moral action, which transcends the self-centred character of economic action; whereas economic action does not presuppose moral conduct: they are successive terms in a logically developing series.[1] I have already offered some criticism of Humian and utilitarian ethics from this point of view, urging that they arise inevitably from the denial of transcendence and from accepting the economic agent's world as the only world.[2] We have seen, too, that the modern subjectivist notion of moral value as a matter of private feeling results equally with the utilitarian doctrine in egoistic hedonism.[3] The only significant difference between these is that, while the utilitarians, having made pleasure the good, none the less continued to dwell on the familiar topics of ethical discussion—duty, motive, consequences, and so forth—struggling vainly but honestly to make hedonism ethical, the modern subjectivist has usually been more consistent. His interest in conduct flags—on a hedonistic assumption it is a dull subject—and only his linguistical studies languidly revive it. He turns from thinking about moral actions to analysing ethical sentences.[4]

There is another twentieth-century ethical theory which shares in many respects the economic error against which this book protests. But it is sternly opposed to hedonism, and its contrast with doctrines we have discussed is illuminating. It has for us a further advantage in that its author elaborated it largely through criticism of the kind of ethical view to which our own premisses lead. H. A. Prichard was a dogmatic and aggressive disputant.

[1] See pp. 21-3.
[3] See p. 177.

[2] See pp. 58-63.
[4] Cp. p. 173.

His habit of prefacing his own opinions with the words 'of course' was deeply ingrained. He sought everywhere stark distinctions, uniquely characterized entities, and a bedrock of self-evident truths to bear the weight of inference; nor did he doubt that he had found enough of these to establish unshakably his general philosophical position, which was rigidly realist. Within its narrow pale, beyond which he saw little and that without sympathy,[1] he was meticulous, self-critical, even self-torturing, but those who questioned his basic principles were wrong of course. In his quite unsynoptic vision, his inability to recognize identity in difference, and his relentless pursuit of the hard datum he resembled the logical atomists, but his conception of moral values was poles apart from theirs. It was protestant, even puritan, a clearly stamped product of the Reformation, although not theistic. It owed much to Kant's categorical imperative, but nothing at all to his kingdom of ends.

Prichard held that an obligatory action is not obligatory because it is intrinsically good, nor because it is such as to be a cause of good, and in consequence that not goodness nor the good but duty is the fundamental principle of morality and the primary notion with which ethics is concerned. Moreover, between the adjectival and the substantival usage of 'good' the difference of meaning is, according to Prichard, so complete as to make the term equivocal. 'Good' as an adjective, on his view, is most naturally applied to a virtuous disposition or its possessor, whereas 'good' as a substantive signifies necessarily a good to someone, and bears no implication of intrinsic value.[2] It means in fact someone's happiness, and that again on Pritchard's view means someone's pleasure.

Taking his defiant stand on the bedrock of obligation, Prichard scours its surface to remove any slippery matter which might imperil his foothold. He asserts that to the obligatory character of an action which someone ought morally to do, its motive (though it must have a motive), its consequences (though it must have consequences), and the question whether it fits into any system of conduct in which other moral agents are concerned,[3]

---

[1] I well remember him saying, 'I once spent six months reading nothing but Spinoza. I came to the conclusion the man was muddled.'

[2] See *Moral Obligation*, 1949, pp. 114 ff. I draw in this chapter mainly on the essay in that volume which bears the same title.

[3] Or, I think, any system connecting the agent's own actions.

P

are all totally irrelevant. This leads him to deny implicitly that
knowledge has any part in virtue, by committing 'us' to a view
which I doubt if many of 'us' do in fact hold, namely, that a
conscientious action is *eo ipso* a morally good action. 'We think,'
says Prichard, 'that the question whether some act was morally
good is quite independent of whether a man is right in thinking
he ought to do it. Again, provided we think, for instance, that
an inquisitor was acting conscientiously, we think his action
morally good however misguided we think his idea of his duty.'[1]

Thus Prichard agrees with the utilitarians that the good which
men pursue is their happiness, and that happiness is a synonym
for pleasure. Like them he looks through economic spectacles
and sees a world of singular self-enclosed individuals whose
moral actions and whose 'goods' constitute no system, a world in
which everything is just itself and not another thing.[2] The utilitarians tried to elevate economic action into moral action without
changing its nature, without any clear understanding of the relation between the two. They stretched their hands, especially
John Stuart Mill, in vain longing for the further shore. Prichard,
on the other hand, was very certain that his feet were firmly
planted on it. He had his own clear-cut conception of morality
as something unique and much too precious to depend on anything else, and as therefore standing in a perfectly external
relation to economic action.

If we now watch Prichard developing this 'deontological'
theory, as J. H. Muirhead christened it, through criticism of what
he calls the teleological view, I think we shall conclude that his
position is quite untenable as it stands, and that the elements
which he excludes are in fact integral to morality. But we shall
also have to allow that Prichard's errors in many cases point to the
fact that the self-transcendence which is human morality cannot
be envisaged as complete, that there is in moral conduct a residue
from a lower level of human nature always surviving at once to
subserve and to hinder.[3] It is a residue of unresolved contradic-

---

[1] Op. cit., p. 155. How this view would have shocked the inquisitor!

[2] Prichard is yet more atomistic than the utilitarians, who did at least believe in a
summum bonum in which each individual's good contributed to an aggregate, if not a
system, which it was every man's duty to increase, even if their conception of every
man's good as his pleasure made equal nonsense in this context of aggregation and
duty.

[3] In conduct conspicuously, but in all other kinds of value-experience as well,
this residue has the form of a lower self or personality. That is why it is so easily and

tion, very repugnant to a man of Prichard's temperament, but there could be no morality without it.

Among those who hold a teleological theory of moral obligation[1] Prichard numbers Plato, Aristotle, Bentham, T. H. Green, Bernard Bosanquet, and H. W. B. Joseph, and clearly the list could be lengthened. The teleologist, says Prichard, maintains that those actions are obligatory which conduce to a single final end. This end men call their own good, and whatever precise shape it takes, it must mean their own happiness. Prichard assumes, as we have already seen, that happiness is a synonym for pleasure, and he also takes for granted that a man's own good cannot also be the good of anybody else; for he believes that the notion of a common good involves the flat contradiction of identifying one person with another, and to him an *alter ego* is a nonsensical phrase. From these premisses he not unnaturally concludes that the teleological view reduces to egoistic hedonism, substitutes the non-moral 'ought' for the moral 'ought',and affords no means of distinguishing a good man from a bad.

The utilitarians are doubtless open to these criticisms, but not the remainder of Prichard's named opponents, none of whom identified happiness with pleasure nor regarded one man's happiness as necessarily excluding from its content the happiness of another. We must therefore consider how the teleologists have in fact met these criticisms. No doubt they differed among themselves in some respects, but since we are concerned primarily to reach a view of our own and not with historical exposition, we have a right to select within what, if we except the utilitarians, is a general community of outlook. In Aristotle's view, man is only definable in terms of a specific function which differentiates him from, for example, other species of animal or from a plant. It consists, so far as man is practical, in the doing of certain actions which actualize certain innate impulsive capacities, and these capacities are, by repeated action of the same type, developed into a more or less fixed disposition which is his character. The end ($\tau\acute{\epsilon}\lambda o\varsigma$) to which these actions tend, if they are good actions, is the consummation of this functional nature, its perfect functioning.

---

commonly mistaken for a man's 'real' or 'fundamental' personality. His developed self then appears as an adventitious epiphenomenon, the 'mask of civilization', perhaps.

[1] Prichard 'of course' gives his own slant to the discussion by assuming that any moral theory is primarily a theory of moral obligation.

Practical man, that is, cannot be defined without reference to an end which always to some extent lies beyond him, but is at the same time within him, ideally conceived, as his supreme end in the sense of his ultimate purpose which he has still to realize. He is thus by definition self-transcending. It is his essential nature *qua* practical to aim at the perfection of his own present and actual nature. To strive in his functioning towards perfect functioning is, in Spinozistic language, his *nisus in esse suo*. This end is said by Aristotle to be εὐδαιμονία, which may with tolerable accuracy be translated 'happiness', and to be the human agent's supreme good.[1]

So far I have said little to defend Aristotle from Prichard's contention that the teleological view reduces to egoistic hedonism, substitutes the economic for the moral 'ought', and offers no means of distinguishing a good man from a bad. Be it, however, first noted that by making this concept of defining function central and fundamental Aristotle links intelligibly the various applications of the word 'good' in ethics and does not leave it a quite inexplicable equivoque. The agent's supreme end is his good. His motive, which is this end ideally conceived as his purpose, is good if and only if the end is truly conceived. His actions are good if (*a*) his motive is good and (*b*) they conduce to realizing this end. Nor are (*a*) and (*b*) really two separate conditions of good action, since unless the motive is good what is achieved is not the realizing of the end except by accident,[2] and if the action in itself and essentially contributes to realizing the end, the motive

[1] A small minority of men, according to Aristotle, find their supreme happiness in a yet higher εὐδαιμονία of purely contemplative activity, but in so brief a sketch this may be ignored.

[2] I think Aristotle's position may be fairly expanded as follows. Every (moral) action sets up a train of consequences which, since every action is also economic, are in some degree contingent. Some foresight as to what is likely to happen, and some efficiency in controlling the event, are a part of morality—the moral agent has a duty to cultivate his skills—but the part played by luck cannot be altogether eliminated in assessing moral worth. By good fortune some consequence of an action with a bad motive may promote the moral good, and by bad fortune some consequence of an action with a good motive may damage it. The moral quality of the action is unaffected in the first case, and in the second, too, provided that the agent's efficiency cannot be questioned. Thus fortune can be called good or bad only in a remotely derivative sense of the terms, but not in a purely equivocal sense; for Aristotle is quite clear that some measure of the 'goods' of fortune is needed for the making of the morally good agent, and is a neccessary though minor condition of εὐδαιμονία. Moral goodness remains intrinsic, because it is the goodness of perfected human nature; as a criterion it is immanent as well as transcendent. But it is not fully intrinsic, because morality is *ex hypothesi* a striving, and the end, the final perfection, is never fully achieved.

must have been good. In other words, the two conditions are inseparable because the good motive is the end truly conceived and operating as final cause of the action. Again, the agent's character is morally good only in so far as it is formed by habitual good action, and finally those actions which the agent ought to perform are obligatory upon him in so far as they are such as to contribute to the moral end.

We must try to expand this account of the moral agent to meet Prichard's charges. Is Aristotle a hedonist? He identifies happiness not with pleasure but with certain activities which define human nature. These activities, like any activity, are pleasurable so far as they are unimpeded, but the pleasure takes its character from the activity to which it is appropriate.[1] On this view, the pursuit of happiness is never the pursuit of pleasure except indirectly, and it is not the pursuit of selfish pleasures unless happiness be identified with economic satisfaction. The happiness of the practical agent is in fact, according to Aristotle, the control and development by a rational self of that appetitive self which seeks economic satisfaction. This rational self is inseparable from the appetitive self, which it presupposes. Its distinction within the whole self from the appetitive self is obvious and painful in moral conflict, but this very pain is evidence of their unity within the whole practical self. If this whole self is functioning truly, the rational self is (a) playing the role of economic observer and efficiently directing the skills which belong to the active or responsive side of man's appetitive capacities, (b) controlling and sometimes suppressing his appetitive impulses, and (c) conceiving a rational end and developing the lower, economic self into an instrument which shall subserve this rational end and, so far as is humanly possible, realize its own nature actively in this service. In short, Aristotle's 'happiness' is a rational activity in which economic activity is presupposed and modified, though notoriously not without a residue which may become a conflicting element.   While it is unimpeded it is pleasurable with its own peculiar pleasure, and a symptom by which you may know the really good man is the pleasure which he takes in his actions, his enjoyment of 'the luxury of doing good'. His goodness will spare him pain in repressing his economic lusts—their urgency, when it would be wrong to indulge them, will tend to vanish as good

[1] See pp. 63–4.

character forms—but he will not shirk the inevitable pain of real
self-sacrifice when some activity, otherwise worthy, has to be
checked or even crushed in the interest of a higher purpose.
He may even have to accept torture and death on these grounds.
Happiness, then, *is* a man's own good, but it is not pleasure, and
since it is not economic satisfaction, the man who practises it cannot be a singular self-enclosed individual save in so far as the
economic element remains incompletely absorbed and developed
in him.

Prichard's contrary opinion perhaps springs partly from the
idea that a man must be held fully responsible for his own conduct,
and that it would be ignoble to suppose that morality can owe
anything to external influence, either to purely contingent
circumstances or to the influence of other moral agents. This
would certainly be a defence of morality as an intrinsic value,
but it would be a quite wrong-headed defence. It may be true
that if ever a man did a good action he did what was obligatory
upon him, whether or not he was conscious of the obligation;
but absolute moral responsibility, like absolute freedom of
will, of which in a moral agent it would be a consequence, is not
a human attribute. A man's moral problems do not begin—he
does not exist as a moral being—until he is born with a nature
which he can only modify within certain limits, and he cannot
escape experiencing certain external advantages or disadvantages
which we are bound to take as contingent but as not wholly
irrelevant to morality. For the moral presupposes the economic,
and the economic involves the contingent. Moreover, to admit
the influence of other moral agents as a vital factor casts far less
slur upon a man's morality if the moral self is not taken to be a
self-enclosed atom; and to deny it leaves little room for any moral
action at all. The moral life is not a prize competition in which
candidates are bound by a rule to put in nothing but their own
unaided work.

A second assumption on which the error may rest is one to
which Aristotle equally little lends countenance. Practical
reason may be conceived intellectualistically on the pattern of
its own lowest phase, economic observation. A man will then
be supposed to know a good end from a bad end, or to discrimin-
ate between what he ought to do and what he ought not to do,
in the same 'detached' way in which he knows chalk from cheese

when he is ascertaining how the land lies before he acts. And if his judgment is obscured the reason assigned will be that some naughty desire has knocked his reason off balance, and it will be held that desire may subdue his reason until it becomes the slave of his passions—which is possible in a sense, but not in this sense. Aristotle did not suppose virtue to be knowledge of that kind. Practical reason as he conceives it is knowledge embodied in action, and in it desire is transcended to become rational wish, which is desire of a good quite other than simple economic satisfaction. Conversely, on his view, a man cannot even desire economic satisfaction, though he may feel an impulse, without in some degree setting its object ideally before him as a quasi-rational aim.

We have said enough to acquit the teleological view of substituting the economic for the moral 'ought'. Can it distinguish between a good man and a bad? If the practical self is functioning untruly, failing of its genuine nature, the defect, as Aristotle sees it, will lie somewhere on a scale between weakness and perversion, but it will never be wholly the one or the other so long as a man remains a moral agent. Aristotle's conception equally of the good and the bad self depends on the assumption that both in seeking economic satisfaction and in seeking his supreme good man reasons and desires in one activity. In so far as he is perverted, man misconceives (but also, as it were, 'mis-desires') his good, and the whole hierarchy of his functioning then serves the ends of his economic nature as if they were the ends of his whole nature. The good man and the bad both actively realize their own nature and pursue their own good, but the bad man's 'good' is a perversion which not merely fails to satisfy more than his own economic nature but sets this up to dominate his whole nature. It is in that sense that reason can become the slave of the passions, and the doctrine is that which Plato taught when he described the internal constitution of the bad man as a tyranny of which he himself is the victim.

We have seen that satisfaction in happiness as Aristotle conceived it cannot be the satisfaction of a singular self-enclosed individual, but we have still to give εὐδαιμονία a content. Most moral philosophers spend a good deal of time discussing particular instances of action, and they very commonly forget that every real act has a context. Character issues in particular acts, because action is in the first instance economic. These acts catch our attention, and on them we pass judgment. But the moral end is not a heap of separate acts but a way of life embodied in action, and moral judgment passed upon an act without reference to the character from which it issues and the end to which it contributes has little value. The only life in which a moral agent can function well or ill is, in Aristotle's view, a social life. Only as a member of a community can man be a moral agent.[1] The cardinal virtues of temperance, courage, justice, and wisdom, which a man acquires if his natural capacities are truly developed and not perverted, and also φιλία, which covers all forms of love and friendship and in its highest form transcends virtue—all these, which together systematically constitute the good moral personality, have no scope for their exercise, and therefore no existence, no meaning as words even, outside the community. This Aristotle expresses by saying that in the real nature of things the community is prior to the individual, meaning not that the community is all and the individuals nothing, but that in the community which they constitute the mere singular individuality of its members is at least partly transcended. Aristotle thus makes quite clear both why and how an act to be good must fit into a system of such acts. Prichard's retort when Joseph puts forward a similar view is either naïve or obstinately blind: 'To attribute a character to the parts of a system only as parts of that system is really to attribute the character to the system and to deny it to the parts. Thus, to assert that the parts of a picture are beautiful only as parts of the picture is really to attribute beauty to the whole picture and to deny it to its parts.'[2]

On the teleological view, if I have not misinterpreted it, morality is an activity of self-transcendence and self-realization, which man can never quite perfect because, if an unabsorbed residue of his economic self did not persist, he would not be a moral being at all. Man is not self-sufficient, and his morality involves a contradiction which the moral philosopher makes no progress by evading. The category of means and end, under which Aristotle, rightly as I believe, conceived moral conduct, inevitably presents human morality as a never complete transition from the economic to the moral.

[1] That Aristotle's community is the Greek city-state does not affect the argument.
[2] Cp. op. cit., p. 149.

None of his successors has made this so clear as Aristotle, and we shall do well to follow him further. What I have called in general 'economic action' he considers in its special and developed form of τέχνη, which means art in the sense of craft, the exercise of trained skill to modify an object which is in varying degree external to the agent.[1] The object may be wood or stone for working with a tool; it may be the living human body, as it is in the art of the dancer, the gymnast, or the physician; it may be an army of trained men led by a general; or finally it may be a whole community of men governed by the art of the ruler. Not only, moreover, is the object modified always external to the agent, but the modification—the finished material artifact, the trained dancer or athlete, the healed body, the disciplined army, and even the civilized community—is never a complete end in itself. The artifact is for use,[2] the dancer dances to entertain, fitness and health exist to serve all the serious purposes of life, the disciplined army and its general have wars to fight, and the ruler makes war for the sake of peace. In every case the product is not only external to the producer but is designed for an end which again lies beyond it and is so far external to it. Both these externalities vary in degree. Neither is ever absolute, but neither is ever quite overcome. The technical undertakings of a civilized community do, as my examples have suggested, form in principle, and roughly in practice, a hierarchical system of ends, the lesser serving the more important and wider in scope under the architectonic art of the ruler, who exercises a general control over them all. But the system is not a closed system. The final end of it is the 'economic' life of the community as a whole, but as within this final end every purpose has a further purpose, so even the final end itself is only relatively final.

Between moral conduct and the exercise of a craft Aristotle draws clear and familiar distinctions. Although craft develops in response to desire, its object is external, whereas the moral agent reacts to and upon his own impulsive semi-rational self: his own character is the product which he shapes.[3] Accordingly, the craftsman is judged good if and only if his work is good, bad

---

[1] Cp. pp. 22–3.

[2] That Aristotle confused fine art with craft is not here relevant.

[3] Even the physician healing himself acts only on his own animal nature, and so on something which from the moral point of view is external. Aristotle would have found psychiatry an interesting intermediate between medicine and moral training.

if and only if his work is bad. Although he is not to be judged at all until his works proceed from a settled habit of skill developed by exercise, the criterion to be applied is simply efficiency. He is not good or bad in himself but good or bad at making or doing something. The moral agent, on the other hand, is judged by an immanent criterion. While the craftsman cannot be morally blamed for making or doing badly, the moral agent's worth, if he is good, lies in his good activity, and if he fails in action he can plead in extenuation that although he was inefficient his intention was good.[1]

This distinction between craft and moral conduct is a special instance of the general Aristotelian distinction between process, which covers any sort of change, and activity in Aristotle's special sense of the word. The former, whether natural or artificial, always has an end beyond itself, whereas 'activity' is complete and perfect at any and every moment of itself. If this distinction is made absolute in ethics, the result is the complete severance in respect of values between the moral and the economic, and even the heroical absurdity of Prichard's *fiat obligatio ruat caelum* becomes hard to escape. But the full context of Aristotle's doctrine shows quite clearly that the distinction is not, in his view, absolute in ethics. When he draws it he is, in the language I have used, making provisional abstraction of the economic agent and the moral agent in order to draw a relative contrast between them, a perfectly legitimate procedure. His final view is not in doubt. We have already seen that in an ordered community the crafts form a single hierarchy within which every end is relative to a wider end and so itself still a means, and we have seen that the system is not a closed system, because even the ruler's art is not fully an end in itself. Aristotle applies exactly this same analysis to the deliberately willed action of the indivi-

[1] Only in extenuation, because in the moral action the economic action is contained. Aristotle would certainly have denied that conscientiousness is enough by itself to make an action morally good. He does not deal explicitly with such a case, perhaps because ancient Greece produced few fanatics, though the notion that the Greeks had no true idea of conscience is a piece of puritan bigotry. Socrates very obviously had a conscience, and a very clear idea of what a conscience is. Aristotle would have regarded Prichard's inquisitor as viciously ignorant of the good. He would have asked, as he asks of the profligate, How did he get into that lamentable condition? The difference between the two would be that the profligate sins through passion, which in the end blinds him, whereas the inquisitor does not lose reason but perverts it, which was, incidentally, the precise ground on which inquisitors burned heretics.

dual, without distinction in this respect between moral and economic action. In *all* deliberately willed action the agent first conceives and desires an end which is, as a rule, not immediately
feasible. In that situation he deliberates to discover what, if it
were done, would lead at once to the realizing of his ultimate
end. If that is still not in his power, he deliberates again until he
finds a means which he can here and now take. Aristotle describes this deliberative process as analysis of the end. The whole
series of means, that is to say, are relative ends and constituents
of the ultimate end from which the deliberative process started,
and this holds equally for economic and moral action. The
difference between moral action and purely economic action is as
deep as any in human experience, but we make nonsense of it if
we try to make it absolute. If we still doubt whether Aristotle
did so or not, we have only to consider what he says of the ruler
or statesman, the πολιτικός. The truly wise ruler is for Aristotle
the happy man *par excellence* within the practical life. If the ruler
is the right man in the right place, he has the fullest capacity and
the fullest scope to exercise all the virtues of character and that
practical wisdom which at once irradiates and crowns them.[1]
Practical happiness is the supreme and embracing end of the
practical life, that for the sake of which all lesser ends are desired.
It is blessed and to be praised even above virtue. The wise ruler
is the happiest man, and if any man's practical action can be a pure
activity and possess absolute moral worth it must surely be the
active life of the good and wise ruler. But the ruler, although his
profession is explicitly moral, as that of the ordinary craftsman
is not, is *ex officio* the master craftsman. Even in *his* life the moral
factor can neither loose itself from the economic like a disembodied soul, nor absorb it without residue.

Aristotle states his doctrine of moral conduct very simply in
terms of his own causal theory. When the moral agent realizes
the series of means into which he has analysed his ideal end, his
act of will may be called either 'appetitive reason' or 'rational

---

[1] One could, I think, exhibit practical wisdom (φρόνησις) and the various virtues
of character which Aristotle discusses in the *Nicomachean Ethics* as constituting just
such a hierarchical system as the crafts or the stages of means-taking which constitute the practical agent's realizing of his end, a system in which each stage transcends its predecessor but not absolutely. It is of historical interest that in the nineteenth century φρόνησις was usually translated by 'prudence'. The mistake was no
doubt due to the influence of utilitarian ethics. The intellectualistic interpretation
of Aristotle's practical reason is still common.

appetition', and 'such a source of action', says Aristotle, 'is a man.' But he also says that the originative causes of things done are the ends at which they are aimed. In other words, man is the efficient cause of his own action—he is by nature an active agent —while the final cause of his action is the end which he conceives ideally, and with which he identifies himself as with his own developed nature. Thus, if we abstract from contingency, the difference between the efficient and the final cause of moral action is simply the difference between two stages in the agent's self-transcendence. They are the *termini* of transition through a phase of his self-realization. Yet we cannot in fact altogether abstract from contingency. In economic action, which modifies an external object, the efficient cause of change resides in the agent, and for the modified object the change is largely contingent, because it does not in the main follow from the object's nature as a necessary development of it. In moral conduct the object modified is relatively internal; it is a man's own self. Consequently the efficient cause is here much more nearly identical with the final cause. But they still cannot completely coincide. If moral conduct could really be an activity perfect at any and every moment of itself, efficient and final causes would fully coalesce, but that would be the end of morality.

Within its limits, this theory of moral conduct as incomplete self-transcendence, elaborated by Aristotle from the Platonic distinction between craft and conduct, has never been greatly bettered. If we wish to reflect philosophically on human conduct as it springs from its natural roots, neither making of morality an object of economic observation which has no goodness in itself, nor treating it as so absolute a good that it cannot be seen until it is scraped clear of economic dross, then something like Aristotle's developing series is indispensable as a method. The problems which cry loudest for its application today are perhaps those revealed by the genius of Freud, who was the first investigator to give any sort of precision to the level of psychical activity which lies between the physiological and the moral. The concepts of psychical integration and adjustment to life lie halfway between health and morality, and it is only when they are so envisaged that they acquire a philosophical interest. It may be sometimes useful in psychiatrical practice to forget this, but in philosophy a one-level view is always abortive, and to isolate a concept by analysis is only the first step towards its philosophical clarification. There are plenty of old problems, too, which such a method illuminates. Between *utile* and *honestum* the relation is something much more subtle than sheer contrast. Why, for example, do we so often tell an immoral young man that he is being foolish and imprudent? Partly, no doubt, we are being euphemistic because we fear to alienate him by preaching, but partly we tell him that honesty is the best policy because we hope that the threat of economic disaster will act as a deterrent. The argument is not moral, but it is neither irrelevant nor cynical, because the economic is contained in the moral and human motives are very intricately mixed. Again, the retributive factor in punishment is a part of its reformatory purpose, since a man cannot recover his morality until he has willingly suffered some equivalent of the wrong which he has done.[1] There is no such thing as painless repentance. Yet again, the relations of the legal to the moral and of private to public morality raise a thousand questions which cannot be answered by treating the terms as *distincta* which have simply to be disentangled and contrasted. In a world in which everything was one thing and not another thing these problems would not arise; but they do.

I have extolled Aristotle's theory as excellent within its limits. It might well be objected to his doctrine, at any rate as I have so far expanded it, that the city-state is a thing of the remote past, and that in any case no sort of political community could provide full scope for the whole of a man's moral life: the good citizen must always fall short of the good man. That, I am sure, is true, and I would go much further. Even if it be granted that, although the virtues are all social, the community in which they are exercised is not confined to the state, and that they may find their

[1] The desert of the criminal and not the compensation of the victim is the important aspect of retribution. Neglect, even denial, of the retributive factor in punishment is a typical sign of our times. We are eager to construe moral delinquency as mental disease, and the modern murderer confidently pleads that he had a blackout when he stabbed or strangled after rape. We virtually decline to credit the possibility of suicide unaccompanied by at least temporary mental derangement. For this reluctance to impute moral responsibility the worser psychiatrists are heavily to blame. The theoretical error in it is the false interpretation of a higher level in terms of a lower. But its cause in the first instance is the emotional reaction of weakness to the profound experience of evil through which we have lived. In England, it results chiefly in governmental concessions to sentimental petitions against capital punishment, but in Russia it has led to the annulling of human personality and produced the 'confessions' of the brain-washed. Cp. Mr. J. D. Mabbott's excellent article in *Contemporary Philosophy*, Third Series.

scope in several independent or semi-independent non-political communities, yet if the moral end is confined to self-realization in any sort of finite community or communities the problem of defining morality is not more than half-way to solution. For finite community may become the merest camouflage for selfishness if it claims absolute value and has no end beyond itself. A marriage can be *un égoisme à deux* and a family the worst of cliques. The Nazi state drew loyalty and self-sacrifice from its citizens, but because it had no end beyond itself, the very virtues of its members made it the foulest of perversions. If you conceive a single social community extended to cover the human race you still cannot show that, even ideally, its practical activity would possess a more genuinely intrinsic value than the activity of a world-wide ant heap. A man would not become moral by fulfilling the duties of his station, if he did not by nature partake in an infinite activity which cannot be theoretically reached by summing, or even by synthesizing, his finite communal activities.

A moment's reflection makes this clear. Morality is practical, but the will operates in all activities whether their essence is practical or not. It is a commonplace that aesthetic, philosophical, and scientific activities are ruined if they are set to work under a moral directive, but this does not remove the moral obligation on a painter to quicken his vision and improve his art, on a philosopher to think straight, on a scientist not to falsify facts. Each of them has a moral duty to resist interference from outside his profession, but each soon enough finds his conscience working within it. It is in the awareness of the good will as in this sense ubiquitous that the moral agent first discovers his practical activity to be not simply finite, and that, I think, is the beginning of the religious consciousness.

That the intrinsic good is eternally real and complete but nevertheless also in temporal process of fulfilment by human beings is the assumption made by the Christian religious consciousness, and it is an apparent contradiction. So far, however, religion is not unique among the kinds of value experience. The artist makes an analogous assumption in respect of beauty—if beauty is the right name for what the artist both sees and creates— and the philosopher in respect of truth. In its general nature this contradiction permeates all our experience of intrinsic value, because it is a constituent of our nature and we can never tear it out of ourselves to confront it squarely and conquer it once for all. By the very solving of it as we find it in us we re-create it and ourselves afresh, equally in action, thought, and aesthetic imagination. Everywhere the ideal is taken as real because it is in part realized, and perfectionism can become a vice which hampers achievement. But the philosopher, the artist, and even the moral agent who is not explicitly religious are not compelled to envisage in a definite and concrete shape the ultimate nature of the reality which works in them. Religion, on the other hand, if it is neither pantheism nor the worship of an Aristotelian God unconcerned with human affairs,[1] presents a contradiction far harder to accept. Religion is essentially practical, *per se* and not *per accidens* a matter of the will. Therefore the good will must, I think, be envisaged by the religious consciousness as a real person, a person in whose nature, if he is to be worshipped, omnipotence and omniscience are consummated in love and wisdom. It then seems inevitable that the reality of this person should be regarded as verifiably manifest in action in which he is the agent, and here the difficulty begins. The action of the deity is conceived, at any rate by Christians, as entailing miracle, and that, too, seems inevitable on the premises. But all action at its lowest level is economic action which issues in events open to economic observation, and the world of the economic observer behaves according to rules. These rules are doubtless extremely provisional as we formulate them; they can with some plausibility be regarded as merely 'prescriptive', as indicating the way we should take our data if they are to help us to predict. But these rules, whatever they are, do not admit of miracle. For an alleged miraculous event is not an exception to a current scientific law or rule which in principle necessitates modification of the rule: it assumes both the validity of the rule and the breaking of it, and a miracle scientifically explained would not be a miracle at all. A miracle does not embody the fruitful contradiction which is the spring of all experience of value and the reason why a human action can be both economic and moral and yet not miraculous; it is a flat contradiction of science at its own level. Science offers an abstract

---

[1] Neither of these seems to satisfy the western religous consciousness. Aristotle, in that all the imperfect activities of the changing world pattern themselves upon the eternal activity of his God, does provide some end beyond society for human conduct, but on the whole he seems to conceive his God as totally transcendent and man's nearest approach to him as through contemplation rather than practice.

and highly provisional account of the world, which is transcended in value and ultimately meaningless without value, but value conversely presupposes the world of scientific fact. Philosophically, miracle is a gross misconception of transcendence, and any consent by science to weave miracle into its own texture or accept heterogeneous patches of miracle would entirely wreck its purpose.[1]

The short way out of this dilemma is to dismiss miracles as superstition and religious consciousness of the Christian kind as a delusion, but the objections to taking this course are weighty. To say nothing of the experience of ordinary men, the lives and achievements of the better saints, canonized or not, show a value which does seem to transcend non-religious morality, and the faith which inspired them would pretty clearly have failed if it had not included belief in certain past and future events which must be called miraculous. Art with a religious content presents another objection. No work of art as such, even the *Credo* of Bach's B minor Mass or of Beethoven's *Missa Solennis*, either states or argues anything, but if the emotion expressed in countless masterpieces of music and painting was engendered by a quite illusory faith, it becomes hard to tell in what their greatness consists. Moreover, the rejection of the religious consciousness as a delusion would still leave us without a supra-social end for human conduct, and not only have we too often seen the social end which transcends individual selfishness but is not itself in turn transcended lead to practical enormity, but such an end is also a theoretically indefensible ideal.

Perhaps the likeliest of philosophical solutions is to take a hint from the myths of Plato and rather more than a hint from Hegel. We might insist that the religious consciousness is essentially practical and interpret all theodicy as symbolic, as truth which must be grasped in this special imaginative form if man is to climb certain summits of the practical life. But although we might thus explain the power of religion in men who took the symbols literally as historical fact, could we suppose that symbols consciously accepted as symbols have the driving force which impels saints and martyrs?

[1] It is futile for theologians to argue that one scientific hypothesis rather than another makes plausible a religious belief in a miracle; that the modern conception of matter, for example, lends more support than the Newtonian to faith in the resurrection of the body.

I have contributed little but commonplace to this well-worn topic, and I will leave it with this scarcely novel remark. If religion begins in the awareness that morality covers all life, at least it follows that cultus is not the only exercise of religion, and conversely that no cultus centring round a special creed can claim authority to loose and bind in any other sphere of special activity.

CHAPTER XII

AESTHETIC EXPERIENCE

THERE is in these days among persons strongly interested in art, if not among modern British philosophers, a fairly wide acceptance of the view that art, like any other intrinsically valuable activity, is both all-pervasive and autonomous; that the content of art, that is to say, in principle excludes no material as alien, and that the artist at work owes no allegiance to any but aesthetic standards. Neither would many people deny that aesthetic experience, whatever distinction be drawn within it between creation and contemplation, is a function of the imagination, not a practical doing or making but a vision essentially unconcerned with any but its own distinction between truth and falsity, and therefore blind to the difference between fiction and historical fact. All this has been ably argued, and I need not dwell long upon it. Our chief concern in this chapter must be to show that aesthetic experience, like other forms of value-experience, is self-transcendence, and to ask what form the infinite activity, which we have assumed to be present in all human experience of value, could be said to take in aesthetic experience. To begin with, however, I must expand and try to clarify the notion of artistic imagination, and I think I must not end without having considered a charge which is sometimes brought against idealist philosophers. It is said, not quite implausibly, that they often fail to distinguish intelligibly between the coherence in which they take philosophical truth to consist and the coherence which distinctively characterizes a work of art. If we fail altogether to distinguish between logical and aesthetic coherence we shall find ourselves in difficulty when we come to discuss philosophy as an experience of value.

The early days of British empiricism produced a doctrine of the artistic imagination which in its shortcomings provides an illuminating foil to the kind of theory which we shall be trying to develop. 'Experience', wrote Thomas Hobbes,[1] 'begets Memory; Memory begets Judgement and Fancy; Judgement begets the strength and structure; and Fancy begets the ornaments of a Poem. The Ancients therefore fabled not absurdly, in making Memory the Mother of the Muses. For Memory is the World (though not really, yet so as in a looking glass) in which the Judgement, the severer Sister busieth herself in a grave and rigid examination of all the parts of Nature, and in registring by leters, their order, causes, uses, differences, and resemblances; Whereby the Fancy, when any work of Art is to be performed, findes her Materials at hand and prepared for use, and needs no more than a swift motion over them, that what she wants, and is there to be had, may not lie too long unespied. So that when she seemeth to flye from one Indies to the other, and from Heaven to Earth, and to penetrate into the hardest matter, and obscurest places, into the future, and into her self, and all this in a point of time, the voyage is not very great, her self being all she seeks; and her wonderful celerity, consisteth not so much in motion, as in copious Imagery discreetly ordered, and perfectly registered in the memory.'

On this empiricist view, the artist's memory is stored with countless images derived from his own or other men's intelligent observation of Nature, especially human nature, and his imagination selects and rearranges what it requires out of these hoarded relics of decaying sense. Thus, 'when any work of art is to be performed,' the artist's materials are copies, mirror images of a ready-made independent Nature, and his work is not creative in any sense beyond that of 'discreet ordering'. Moreover, this second-hand imaginative product is nothing but a garnish. It merely ornaments an already firmly founded structure. Art, therefore, creates nothing, and it has neither autonomy nor intrinsic value. Its function is to provide a cosmetic, as Hobbes later says, 'to adorn Vertue and procure her lovers', and this debasing of art from end to means does not differ in principle from the Lucretian use of poetry to sweeten the bitter draught of scientific instruction.

What is the fault in this doctrine? We must cast back. In discussing the logical genesis from undifferentiated feeling of a finite subject distinguishing himself from the objects of his primi-

[1] In his Answer to the Preface of Davenant's *Gondibert*.

tive appetites[1] we were primarily concerned with the emergence of a world of sensuous fact which a man must get to know if he is to satisfy those and subsequently developing appetites. For brevity's sake, however, we ignored a phase in that process, which follows the distinction of self from not-self but precedes the establishment of detached objective fact. Economic observation, because it involves a kind of thinking, entails a decision between the merely apparent and the (practically) real, and this decision presupposes a phase of sensuous experience in which, just because the decision has not yet been made, the content is present without distinction of apparent and real. In that respect the content is indeterminate, but only in that respect. It comprises the whole diversity of sensuous distinction as such, and on that already diversified world the decision between apparent and practically real operates, transforming it into the object-world of economic observation. But the factual decision need not operate. The sensuous diversity can develop autonomously in, or rather as, free imagination, and there begins aesthetic experience.

It is vital to understand this bifurcating development of sense. The economic observer assumes that all his object-world is real, and that when his factual decision has operated, what he then judges only apparent is what he had before either doubted or misconstrued. Appearance, that is to say, is to him simply subjective. If anyone else continues to misconstrue it, he condemns this unreal construct as a fiction. Within his own practical sphere this contrast which he makes is entirely legitimate, but it is a contrast only valid after factual decision has occurred. What the deliverance of sense is apart from factual decision the economic observer cannot tell, because only in the act of decision are he and his objective world logically born, and when philosophers borrow his economic spectacles they cannot tell either. Are they to put the cart before the horse and assume an independent real world which causes correspondent impressions of sense? Or are they to embrace a phenomenalism which cuts the ground from under any distinction between true and false? In short, the economic contrast of real and apparent has no place outside practice, and the content of sense is more than a mere indeterminate somewhat awaiting factual decision. There is a world elsewhere.

[1] See pp. 175–6.

Factual decision mutilates as well as determines its material. In economic observation the sensuous content consists of what R. G. Collingwood aptly called 'sterilized sensa'.[1] It is mere datum for economic cognition, entirely stripped of the emotion which is integral to all sensuous content unemasculated by economic abstraction. In the economic observer, imagination supplements and develops the sterilized datum until it presents him with the complete factual object. He sees a flat surface and imagines the invisible solid of which it is a surface. He sees or hears intermittently a moving object, and his imagination fills the gaps, constructing its continuous path. Imagination binds the data of his several senses, and nearly all the world of fact which he builds is imagined.

The free imagination, too, constructs a world, but it is not the detached world of economic fact. Subject and object are not, in the experience of it, severed as in a practical attitude they must be. On the subjective side, the free imagination functions to bring to open consciousness and express the feelings, the rudimentary emotions, which belong to all unsterilized sensa, to mature them until a man knows what it is that moved at first obscurely in him.[2] But on the other side it develops a sensuous world which is no less real and objective than the economic world. It is not a world of fact, and it is therefore not abstracted and detached from the emotion which is inherent in it, but it is not for that reason a subjective, in the sense of a capricious, construction. There is nothing arbitrary in the freedom of the aesthetic imagination, and its subjective function of developing emotion in conscious expression is not an idle private gratification but a kind of knowing. For emotion and this kind of knowing are not two but one, because the truth so known is not fact but value.[3]

Even to a reader who takes quite seriously the autonomy of aesthetic experience this separation of fact and value may seem too sharp. He may think that if the imagination bifurcates in two alternative activities, the one economic and the other aesthetic, then the reality grasped in aesthetic experience is bound to become a world so utterly different from the world of economic fact that its

[1] *Principles of Art*, 1938, p. 162, a work to which I owe much in this chapter.
[2] This is, of course, something quite different from giving rein to one's emotions in behaviour, a process which may afford relief but does not bring understanding.
[3] Collingwood's metaphor of an emotional charge on sensa is not quite adequate to the intimacy of the connection.

claim to be real will dissolve in the fog of a quite irrational mysticism. He will tell me that in the end this path must lead back again to the old idea of aesthetic experience as merely subjective, merely make-believe, perhaps to the Hobbesian notion of art decorating a structure which copies fact with capriciously combined memory-copies of other facts.

If I have deserved this charge, it must be because I have not sufficiently emphasized a point on which I have already dwelt. I have said that a man enters whole into every act and passion which can be fairly called his.[1] His identity permeates his several activities and becomes explicit in their differences. The economic agent was an abstraction, and the economic observer a double abstraction. We must not speak, as I may perhaps have seemed to speak, as if the free and the factual imagination were two totally severed faculties constructing two quite mutually alien worlds. There is, indeed, very clear evidence that they are not. Its sensuous medium is a differentia of aesthetic experience, but it is obvious enough that aesthetic experience can none the less contain non-sensuous elements. I have already called the aesthetic imagination a kind of knowing, and art would be of small value if it involved only the senses. A poem moves in the sound of words and a painting in colours and shapes, but the emotions which they express are not confined to those rudimentary emotions which are an aspect or moment of all unsterilized sensa. Intellectual activity has its own emotions which demand aesthetic expression. Most great poetry in fact expresses emotions generated in the intellectual apprehension of human situations which are already in their own right emotional, whether that emotion is practical or intellectual. In good Nature poetry, and in landscape painting, the human condition does not obtrude itself, but it enters at least by implication, and although abstract painting and sculpture may possess a special merit of freedom from the sterility of economic observation they lack the scope and ripeness of great art.[2] The eye of the artist is 'innocent', but it is synoptic. It therefore sees the economic observer's world, not in abstraction as he sees it, but as transcended in a world of aesthetic value. A poem is not fact or fiction, but there may be both fact and fiction imagined inside it. Thus imagination in the artist and in the economic observer—and for that matter in the economic and the moral

[1] See p. 196.   [2] See Chapter I, p. 13.

agent, since imagination plays its constructive part in all human activities—is not simply different, and the reality which in its several functions imagination differentiates is for that same reason the same reality. Aesthetic experience, like any other intrinsic value, is autonomous but also all-pervasive. Experience in all other forms can enter into its content, and it does so by virtue of the emotions which those other forms of experience generate.[1]

I am committed to asking in what special form an infinite activity is manifest in aesthetic experience, but I fear I may have raised a hope I cannot satisfy. The characterizing of any form of value-experience is bound to be largely deictic. It is a commonplace that you cannot make morality intelligible to a man who has no moral consciousness, and if a man has it you cannot help him to a better understanding of it without pointing to such moral experience as he acknowledges himself to possess and persuading him to develop it in reflective thinking. That is because all experience of value is self-consciousness. Aesthetic experience, however, is not only self-consciousness but also essentially sensuous in its medium and essentially itself expressive. Art is language, and there is no other language into which it can be translated. The deictic element is therefore bound to play a larger part in the discussion of aesthetic experience than in that of any other value. We all know how easily the frustrated critic of one art (especially the musical critic) slides from direct analysis to draw analogies from other sorts of art, even from other forms of experience, and the aesthetician cannot do much except try to relate aesthetic value to other values. If I am pressed for a positive definition of the infinite activity which, I have alleged, constitutes itself in human aesthetic experience, I can do little more than call it an infinite activity of sensuous self-manifestation, and ask the reader to consider whether his own experience does not contain some such intimation.

Can we find a special sense in which aesthetic experience is

---

[1] Science is an exception, because science as such generates no emotion: the sensa involved are safely sterilized. A scientist worrying about his science, wrestling with a moral, religious, or philosophic problem in which his scientific convictions or hypotheses come into conflict with something else, could no doubt be the subject of a poignant poem, but not a scientist simply absorbed in scientific thinking. Lucretius was perfectly right when he said that he was using poetry as a means to sweeten the bitter draught of learning, but that is a practical process and not artistic creation. His science enters the content of his poetry only in his passionate vindication of physics as the vanquisher of superstition and the fear of death.

self-transcending? At least we can distinguish it in this respect from moral activity. Between the poles of privacy and universality the succession of phases in aesthetic self-transcendence is not *in se* a strenuous passage through conflict, as it is in the transcendence of the economic by the moral life. For the will is involved in it only incidentally. The language of conation does not properly apply to a theoretic activity. An artist or a philosopher may talk of himself as striving and failing or succeeding, but his strife can only be the effort to achieve practical conditions which make philosophic thinking or creative imagining possible. That can be hard enough. It may need the sternest effort of will on the part of an artist to foster and discipline his natural energies in the development of his technique, and to withdraw his attention continuously from non-aesthetic distractions; but aesthetic imagining, whatever be its relation to technique,[1] is not in itself a movement of the will.[2] We have already called it a kind of knowing, and we must try to compare it with other kinds of knowing.

In one respect the free imagination must be analogous to any other kind of knowing. It must possess in some form that dual character which belongs to any true judgment. If you or I judge that $2 + 2 = 4$, that truth is part of the content of an individual mind, but it also holds true objectively beyond the private judgment of you or me or of any other finite individual mind. One may fairly say, with a caveat that the whole economic world is an abstraction, that the mathematical or scientific proposition holds true independently of any finite judging subject, and that its truth, like that of all propositions in economic thinking, is the truth of correct correspondence to fact. As finite thinking develops in spheres where value enters, it becomes no longer plausible to regard the relations between these two aspects of truth as consisting in independence and correspondence. In philosophical thinking, and perhaps in serious historical thinking, finite judgment, so far as it is true, clearly does not copy and correspond to anything: it manifests and actually sustains the objective world which gives it content. Outside the world of economic observation, truth in its universal, non-private aspect is an infinite activity which constitutes itself in constituting finite

---

[1] See p. 237.
[2] If an infinite activity moves in it, the metaphor of 'inspiration' hits here more of the truth than any hint of domination or guidance.

minds, not a character of independent fact nor a relation of correspondence between independent fact and finite human minds, and its universality is concrete, not merely general. In such thinking the self-transcendence of the individual finite subject is easy to mark. The finite thinker progresses always and only by cancelling a prior opposition between his relatively private idea of the world he is coming to know—his inadequately grounded opinion, that is, or his imperfectly verified hypothesis—and that objective world itself. At the same time, the cancellation is never complete; opinion is never transcended quite without residue into knowledge.

The aesthetic process is certainly analogous, but let us first consider the difference. The privacy in which it begins is not opinion, not a hypothesis entertained without commitment; it is an unclear emotion. Analysis of that emotion would certainly reveal an objective situation—of course not an economically factual situation: it might equally well without distinction of fact from fancy be the pattern on a dirty whitewashed wall, the rape of Leda, or the love of three oranges—but the initial urge which sets the artist imagining is the urge to clarify by expressing it the feeling in himself which his apprehension of the situation has generated; it is not a direct urge to understand that situation. On the other hand, as the painter, the poet, and the musician compose they do not merely find out more and more clearly what their emotion really is: they also, within the same process and quite inseparably, develop what turns out to have been initially an undeveloped and merely suggestive situation. The painter is obscurely moved by some glimpse of harmony or balanced conflict of shape and colour in a landscape, or in some image which has arisen in his mind through conscious or unconscious memory, and if he is a genuine artist his picture when painted will show him his own emotion as no longer a half-hidden and capriciously private and subjective feeling, but as developed and embodied in an unpredicted world. The musician and the poet in their own media experience a like transition from private feeling to a universal and communicable world in which emotion is present, not as a comment added but as an integral element. That world is not sterilized fact; yet more surely is it not fiction. It is made of emotion and imagination, but it is objective and more real than fact because it has intrinsic value. Any genuine

work of art gives an impression of timeless value. If one goes
to school with the greatest works of art to test that impression,
one finds it become explicit in a more and more solid and deeply
founded world; and the value which becomes explicit is not
simply that which we call 'beauty' when we want to distinguish
aesthetic value from other values by its form, for the intrinsic
values are autonomous not in spite of their interpenetration but
because each pervades the others. The imagination of Shakespeare in his great tragedies so dominates the clash of good and
evil, so colossally bestrides the gulf between optimism and pessimism, that the eternity of moral values is forced upon you as you
read. You may accept it with thankfulness or terror, but you
cannot escape it except by ceasing to take in what Shakespeare
communicates. You have listened to no philosophic discourse,
but when you have finished *Othello* and *Lear* a subjective theory
of value has become ridiculous: if it were true there could have
been no Shakespeare. Every great artist, whatever the codes and
canons which critics may prove to have governed his work, makes
it plain that value is timeless and objective.

Artistic creation, then, like other kinds of theoretic activity,
moves from privacy to an objective world—these are its termini—
but its distinctive character is this: the objective world it attains is
manifest in an original unity of imagination and emotion which
remains the final form of the work of art, of the full expression,
that is, in which the activity culminates. Science aims at superseding its sterilized imagery by abstract thought, and philosophy,
too, in its own manner transcends imagination. In art, on the
contrary, this relation is reversed. Intellectual thinking is neither
the medium nor the goal of art, but thinking which generates
emotion[1] can, and in the greatest art a vast range of it does, enter
the content of art, becoming subordinated to the imaginative
form.[2] Art by virtue of this power shows itself to be a rational
theoretic activity, and for that reason I have ventured, perhaps
rashly, to call the aesthetic imagination a kind of knowing;[3] but
any intellectualistic theory of art is foredoomed to disaster.[4] On

[1] Not, therefore, scientific thinking.
[2] This is, of course, quite different from the *subordinate* aesthetic aspect which
philosophy, science or mathematics possess just because they are expressed in language.
[3] One might stretch language in the opposite direction by calling art 'objective
emotion'.
[4] Disaster even worse than that which befalls the thinker who tries to intellectua-
lize morality.

the other hand, within the always imaginative process of artistic creation from privacy to objectivity we shall again find, I fancy, the residual persistence of a lower level surviving indispensably to subserve a higher, although the higher level aims in principle to constitute itself out of the lower by absorbing and superseding it.[1] In that, perhaps, may lie the solution to a puzzle which Benedetto Croce made poignant, the vexed problem of the bodily work of art.

Croce held that the real work of art is a complete and finished intuition-expression within the artist's imagination, and that the bodily work of art is a secondary economic product, a mere means to communication and construction. This view has a show of truth if it is set in contrast with a crudely realistic technical theory which conceives art as imitation and finds the essential work of art in the pigmented canvas or the modelled bronze. On the other hand, it comes near to the opposite error of subjective idealism, and one may suspect that the processes of painting and modelling play a more important role in aesthetic creation than Croce allows.

Let us attempt the difficult and hazardous task of analysing such a process. Clearly a painter must cultivate a certain practical skill in manipulating pigments with brushes, and in order to exercise it effectively he must have a knowledge of certain economic facts about brushes, pigments, and types of canvas. But this knowledge and the exercise of this skill, which together constitute craftsmanship, are not in essence aesthetic creation, for the sufficient reason that craftsmanship is practical, whereas the artist's activity is theoretic. For the same reason it cannot be true to say that in the artist the economic agent *qua* craftsman is transcended with residual persistence *precisely* as the economic agent is transcended in the moral agent; for the latter transition is wholly within the sphere of practice. So it might seem that Croce is right after all, and that artists exercise craftsmanship only from the practical motive of communicating and educating, reinforced no doubt by the yet more directly practical motive of earning a living. It is much to be doubted, however, whether practising graphic and plastic artists would support this view. Most painters would probably maintain that they paint primarily in order to see, and to see more clearly, to develop a relatively inchoate imaginative

[1] See p. 29, and pp. 202–3.

experience, not simply to record for practical purposes an already
consummated vision. Surely they would be right. Surely a
painter's imagination is developing and reconstituting his (unsterilized) sensa while he paints, and his emotion is attaining to
clarified expression gradually. Morover, sensation persists residually in his imagining, and his imagining is, furthermore, being
constantly enriched by new material. Fresh sensa keep occurring
to him all the time as he looks with shifting attention at a landscape, and also as he looks at the unfinished picture on his easel.
Even if he is painting from conscious or unconscious memory in
the studio, he is constantly receiving fresh suggestions from what
he has so far made visible on canvas or paper. There is another
source, too, of fresh sensa which could not have been anticipated
while the canvas was still blank. His bodily feelings as he wields
his brush enter continuously and not irrelevantly into his work.[1]
In a drawing this is often as obvious as it is in the analogous case
of a dance which develops and expresses the physical sensations
of the dancer. No doubt one artist creates more fluently and
quickly than another, but it approaches absurdity to suppose that
any artist can know fully and precisely from the start what, saving
a lapse in technique, is going to appear at the end.[2]

The conclusion to be drawn, so far at any rate as the graphic
and plastic arts are concerned, is perhaps this. The painter is a
craftsman, and his technique does produce a physical thing. This
can be examined scientifically in the bowels of the National
Gallery; it can be bought and sold; it is a means of communication and education. But that physical thing is a practical product
and, with a qualification to be added later, falls outside aesthetic
experience. Technique, I suggest, serves also a second purpose.
I spoke of the artist's struggle to achieve practical conditions
which make creative imagining possible,[3] and it might be said
that his exercise of craftsmanship plays a special part in this
struggle by liberating the flow of his imaginative expression. But
at this point it becomes impossible to keep the barrier between
practical and aesthetic quite intact, unless one is prepared to say
that defective technique has no bearing at all on the character of
imaginative creation, and does nothing worse than hamper the

---

[1] A bad artist can also force factitious excitement into his work.
[2] Unless, of course, he is virtually repeating himself or another artist, and in that
case he is not engaged in aesthetic creation.   [3] See p. 132.

construction of the bodily picture as a practical means of communication and a saleable article. May it be that technique within the whole process of painting is a lower level transcended in aesthetic creation, but transcended incompletely? The relation between technique and artistic creation would then after all bear some analogy to that between economic and moral action: virtuosity may corrupt an artist somewhat as the economic satisfactions may corrupt a man morally. But the two relations will still not be the same. No man by a positive effort of will can lift his technique to aesthetic creation as a man can by effort moralize his economic nature. He can only improve and adapt it in the hope that the inspiring Muse (not, please, the subconscious) may transform it. In support of this position let me here qualify, as I promised, my statement that the bodily work of art falls outside aesthetic experience. If this were wholly true, the painted plane and the fashioned solid could hardly be a means of aesthetic communication. We can of course put off our economic spectacles to look aesthetically at any set of coloured patches on a wall, but we shall not see something which at once communicates an artist's imaginative creation. The pattern on the wall may inspire us to paint like Utrillo, but it will be nothing like da Vinci's *Last Supper*.

Pictures and statues, if I am right, have the ambiguity of any phase in self-transcendence. They persist residually from a lower level both in the artist's and the spectator's experience. But in both they are partly transcended in aesthetic imagination, and to this their power of enabling communication testifies. In music and poetry it is harder to say just what the communicating work of art, the analogue of the bodily picture or statue, really is, and in trying to do so we may easily lose sight of principle in empirical detail. We might take the work of art as the actual performance of the symphony, the opera, or the tragedy, or as the actual recitation of the lyric. Here is something still obviously within aesthetic experience, creative or communicated. Here in fact, if we think of Mozart writing the Queen of the Night's arias for his sister-in-law or delightedly exploring the resources of the newly invented clarinet, or again of Shakespeare creating heroic roles for Burbage to play at the Rose or the Globe, the technique of making seems to be as integral to the imaginative creation as the manipulation of his medium is to the painter and the sculptor.

There is even, perhaps, an ideal speaker for every lyric.[1] I cannot believe that there are 'ditties of no tone' complete 'in the head' of the reader or even of the poet himself. Heard melodies are less sweet than unheard only if they are badly sung. The aesthetic imagination must find its consummation as well as its beginning in actual sense.

If we reduce the 'work of art' in music and poetry to the score and the manuscript, we reach something which, unlike the picture and the statue, can be mechanically copied any number of times without the slightest loss of communicative power,[2] and it is a mark of any technical product that, having no genuine individuality, it can be reproduced without essential loss. But even at this lowest level I think we have something which does not fall entirely outside aesthetic experience. Communication of any sort between human minds has two conditions. It presupposes in men a concrete identity working itself out in their difference— atomic particulars could not communicate—and it does not occur without a medium which is material and economic in so far as it is a means; but the medium which serves aesthetic communication is not wholly independent of what it communicates. If I look into Chapman's Homer I do not see merely what the printer saw when he ran off the first proof and read it.[3]

We are left at length with the task of distinguishing between aesthetic and logical coherence, and it may help us if we first pick up the thread which we dropped in order to discuss the bodily work of art. We had found, briefly, that aesthetic creation, like other forms of theoretic activity, moves from the private and subjective to the objective and universal, but that it none the less remains in its final form imaginative and emotional, thus reversing the relation between imagination and intellectual thinking which obtains, though with a difference, both in science and philosophy.[4]

---

[1] Who is not always the poet himself.

[2] Though perhaps a collector of first editions might not agree.

[3] The ambiguity of the material medium in aesthetic experience is intriguingly illustrated by Ruskin's anecdote of the unknown Alp: 'I saw in the clouds behind the houses an Alp which I did not know, a grander Alp than any I knew, nobler than the Schreckhorn or the Mönch; terminated, as it seemed, on the one side by a precipice of almost unimaginable height; on the other, slipping away for leagues in one field of lustrous ice, clear and fair and blue, flashing here and there into silver in the morning sun. For a moment I received a sensation of as much sublimity as any natural object could possibly excite; the next moment I saw that my unknown Alp was the glass roof of one of the workshops of the town rising above its nearer houses and rendered aerial and indistinct by some pure blue wood smoke which rose from intervening chimneys.' *Modern Painters*, IV, x, §8.   [4] See pp. 232–4.

From those differences at the root between aesthetic creation and other theoretic kinds spring these differences in the fruit. In scientific thinking opinion passes into scientific knowledge, which is purely general, abstractly universal. The private and subjective element vanishes, or seems to vanish, without residue, and the process from beginning to end bears no mark at all of individual personality. The only trace of privacy and subjectivity in scientific knowledge lies in the speed with which it becomes outdated. In philosophical knowledge—if that term may be applied to whatever we happen to regard as the best achievements of human philosophizing—the aspect of individual personality is never absent. In a great philosophical thinker the element of *mere* subjectivity, of inadequately grounded and perhaps capricious opinion, dwindles as he progresses towards a final view, but his individual personality persists always in his work, and it develops in depth and intensity so long as the vigour of his thought is unabated. A body of knowledge or a way of thinking in science or mathematics betrays no origin in personality, but a Plato or a Spinoza, although his goal be a synoptic vision of all time and all being, does not become less Platonic or less Spinozistic as he approaches it. Philosophies are never impersonal, and that is no fault in philosophy. It is so because the universal which the philosopher seeks is not the abstract universal flatly identical in its bare particulars, but the concrete universal of value which is individual and subject.[1] For that reason philosophies do not perish with the same speed as scientific theories and methods. There is an endurance in human values which there is not in human facts.

The work of an artist more plainly proclaims its author's personality than does the speculative construction of a philosopher; yet, for all the wastage and evaporation of second-rate art, the greatest art on the whole abides more surely than the greatest philosophy, at any rate in the original shape in which it was created. If persons were singular individuals and personality connoted the subjective, the capricious, and the idiosyncratic, this would present an odd paradox. We should have then expected Greek science, for example, to be still taken for incorrigible truth, Greek poetry to have perished long ago, and the survival value of Greek philosophy to have been intermediate. If, however,

[1] Cp. pp. 198-9.

human personality will bear the meaning which I have given it,[1] the case is different. Then the transience of scientific theory becomes intelligible, and we can see that both philosophy and art endure by virtue of the personality which each in a different manner exhibits, and not in spite of it. But the difference of manner still sets a problem.

A philosophy must claim from the first to be in principle all-comprehensive.[2] A philosopher writing 'Finis' may confess that he has left many gaps and failed to touch on many relevant topics, but even where he has remained silent he has already committed himself by implication. A work of art, on the other hand, originates in the emotional imagining of a situation. One emotion cannot contradict and nullify another emotion, and a work of art does not wait to develop until the situation becomes all-embracing. The situation—we might call it the unsterilized fact—may be a complex of shape and colour, or it may be that which provides an epic or a play with its content. How great its extent must be in order to generate an emotion expressible in art is a question to which there is no *a priori* answer. Certainly it must be a complex of elements, and one work of art may reasonably be compared with another as greater in 'depth' or 'reach', or 'suggestiveness'; but how big a thing a work of art is depends upon the scope of the emotion which on this or that occasion possessed the artist, and however great this may turn out to have been when it has gained its final expression, the resultant work of art enters into no kind of logical competition with any other artist's work.[3] That must be so, since in art imagination is the dominant form, and any intellectual thinking which enters into the content of art is subordinated to that form. You cannot imagine, factually or aesthetically, an all-comprehensive totality. You may believe that reality is such a whole, and you may argue that it must be, but if you do, your belief and your argument are a matter primarily of conceptual thinking and not of imagination, even though it be not possible to think without imagining. A great work of art is for that reason *uniquely* personal. It expresses its creator and no

[1] See pp. 195–8.
[2] Even one which claims to be no more than a method must claim some sort of ubiquitous applicability.
[3] When the Alexandrian poet complained, ἅλις πάντεσσιν Ὅμηρος, it only meant that contemporary poetry was not good enough aesthetically to compete with Homer, not that there was nothing new to say.

other man because, however much intellectual thinking is sub-ordinated within its content, it sprang from one emotion and its final form is imaginative, even actually sensuous, not intellectual. As an imaginative creation, a work of art is a sort of monad, but it is not a windowless monad; the universal is in it implicitly. It neither excludes, limits, nor complements any other work of art, but it is not subjective or capricious. A philosophical system, on the other hand, is less intensely personal, because its universality will always in some measure fail in concreteness. Thought, transcending imagination incompletely, falls so far short of the concrete universal which its own nature demands, and it cannot accept the sensuous concreteness of imagination as a substitute.

We can now restate this difference between art and philosophy as manifestations of personality in terms of the difference between aesthetic and logical coherence. It is in effect the same difference.

The simplest poem, painting or musical composition is a con-crete unity in and through difference. Any element of it deter-mines and is determined by every other element. In so far as it is genuinely a work of art, every element in it is in a golden mean between excess and defect, and we are merely repeating the same thing if we say that the whole at once gains its own nature from its elements and contributes their nature to its elements. A work of art has that general character of coherence because it is rational, but its special aesthetic coherence is an intimacy of sensuous-imaginative interpenetration which defies further intellectual analysis. If one has experienced it and compared it reflectively with other forms of rational experience, one knows what it is, and one knows it as rational. This knowledge, which is philoso-phical knowledge, can be deepened and expanded, but only if aesthetic experience is deepened and expanded within it. There is no harm in using aesthetic coherence to illustrate the nature of logical coherence, if it is realized that at a certain point the analogy breaks down. In aesthetic coherence the unity in difference re-mains sensuous-imaginative in form even when the emotion which a work of art expresses was largely engendered by intellectual apprehension. Moreover and in consequence, a work of art has not to satisfy any criterion of comprehensiveness in order to be 'true'. Logical coherence, on the other hand, as the essence and the criterion of intellectual truth, cannot be divorced from

R

comprehensiveness. We accept as true a philosophical system, or any system having reference to value, in so far as it is not only internally coherent but also comprehends the erroneous interpretation which as such it contradicts, reshaping that error as a part of its own truth.[1] The internal coherence of such a system is not the mere consistency which formal logic offers—system must not be mistaken for its ghost—and it is not purely relational truth grasped in a merely discursive thinking. It is synthetic as well as analytic, and to grasp it is to grasp the universal as individual, as must be so if insight into it is insight into value and therefore self-consciousness. In other words, there is an intuitive element in the grasp of such a system.[2] That element of intuition recalls analogically the direct immediacy of sense, and we can safely say that aesthetic coherence is transcended in logical coherence. Without it we could not make clear to ourselves the notion of philosophical thinking. But the transcendence is incomplete. Aesthetic experience retains the autonomy to which it owes its perfection, and for that reason philosophy can never fully penetrate its essence. Earlier in this discussion I tried to define the infinite activity which constitutes itself in human aesthetic experience as an activity of sensuous self-manifestation.[3] The objective character of aesthetic creation makes clear the presence of it. Works of art express emotion and do not, like statements, agree or disagree with one another, but the emotion imaginatively expressed is not capricious but necessary and real beyond any contingent subjectivity. Yet I do not know how to improve my definition.

[1] System in this sense would include any historical interpretation which goes beyond fact to value, and even system so far as science makes use of it.
[2] For that reason we cannot say with Collingwood that art pursues a truth of individual fact, intellect a truth of relation; see *Principles of Art*, p. 228.
[3] p. 231.

CHAPTER XIII

PHILOSOPHY

I HAVE contended in this book that of two things one must be
true. Either philosophy is concerned primarily with intrinsic
value, and with the world of science and practical (or, more
precisely, economic) common sense only as embodying the privation, the significant absence, of intrinsic value; or else philosophy
has no function that is not better performed by this or that special
discipline which is innocent of philosophic pretensions.[1]

The present need to urge this disjunction has seemed to me
desperate, even if there can be found no better way of philosophic
thinking for Englishmen; even if the conclusion to be drawn is
that our philosophers should recognize their redundance and seek
other employment before their profession becomes quite discred-
ited. On the other side, I readily admit that there is plenty to
be said against the rough-and-ready exposition of idealism and
transcendence with which I have filled the last four chapters. It
will appear both unoriginal and in itself doubtfully consistent.
The unity of value with reality and truth is a doctrine which owes
its origin in Europe to Plato, and the main tradition of western
philosophy is founded upon it. But I have picked and chosen
eclectically among its inheritors, the nineteenth- and twentieth-
century idealists. The notion of truth as coherence, and of all
experience of intrinsic value as self-transcendence, I took in the
first instance from Bradley and Bosanquet, but both those
thinkers, particularly Bradley, seem to me to retain too much of
the empiricism which they set out to counter, and unduly to
assimilate philosophical to scientific thinking. In trying to relate
economic to moral experience and the aesthetic imagination to

[1] This is not to deny that if there was to be a British philosophy it was bound to
begin in empiricism, nor that the classical period of British empiricism provides an
indispensable means to a critique of the economic attitude. I mean merely that the
twentieth-century return of British philosophy to a second childhood makes it both
otiose and tedious.

philosophical thought, I have been largely influenced by Benedetto Croce. There is much, however, in his views which I find
it difficult to accept. Without doubt the natural scientist thinks
abstractly for an economic end, but I think it is possible for the
philosopher to look, as it were, in the opposite direction and view
Nature as a *graded* privation of value. It is, I believe, just this
procedure in opposite directions which makes the characteristic
contrast between philosophy and science. In rejecting Nature as
no more than the pseudo-conceptual construct of science Croce
seems to cast empirical fact into an outer darkness impenetrable
to any gleam of reason, and so to press distinction into irrational
separation. By the same token I begin to find less and less satisfaction in his suspiciously subjective doctrine of the work of art
as complete without material embodiment.[1] I have been tempted
to disturb the brilliant simplicity of his circle of spiritual 'distincts'
with a bifurcation. I have suggested that between the artist's
technique and his imaginative creation there is a tie analogous
to the relation between moral action and its economic antecedent.[2]
If I am right, it is not altogether futile to attempt to grade philosophically periods or types of artistic creation, or again the arts
themselves, even if we must frankly admit that philosophical
construction on these lines can never rise wholly above empirical
classification with all its ambiguities of contingent cross-division.

Behind the later idealists looms the giant figure of Hegel as
something much more than their background or their starting-
point. There are more ways than one of stating Hegel's position
in relation to theirs. One might perhaps compare the idealists
in terms of the degrees to which they severally believed it possible
to make explicit the immanence in human experience of a totality
of spirit which at the same time transcends it, but it may here be
more helpful to make an approach from outside explicit idealism.

Any philosophy which recognizes intrinsic value as rational
is logically bound, I think, to entertain the notion in some sense
of a monistic Absolute. In pre-Hegelian thought we can conveniently take as opposite poles within which the expression of
this notion varies: (1) the Platonic Forms as the utterly transcendent entities which Kant supposed them to be, and (2) the
Ideas and Ideal of pure reason in Kant's own philosophy, sum-
marizing the latter roughly as the notion of that which is

[1] See p. 235.   [2] It is only a suggestion.

absolutely self-conditioned or, as Kant cautiously preferred to understate it, unconditioned. Plato regarded the Forms as fully real and fully knowable, whereas Kant held the unconditioned to be unknowable, and to be a purely regulative and non-constitutive, though indispensable, notion in human experience. Kant may no doubt be judged wrong in his interpretation of the Platonic Forms as utterly transcendent, but these two positions well express the dilemma: Any attempt to characterize directly the Absolute inevitably denatures it. Any predicate applied to it limits a subject which is *ex hypothesi* infinite. For the Absolute is revealed only within human experience, but human experience provides only finite predicates. If, for example, the Absolute is said to be 'one', there is seemingly no answer to the retort, 'one what?' On the other hand, if the Absolute is taken as no more than a regulative notion within human experience, that notion will not bear criticism. For a mere idea or ideal which constitutes no object and claims to refer to (be the mere thought of) an Absolute (or in Kant's terminology a thing in itself) which *ex hypothesi* cannot be known, could possess no authority to regulate. If it is in no sense constitutive, it is null and void.

Hegel's solution was to contend that to recognize a limit is already to have surpassed it; that the infinite must be known in knowing the finite and the real in knowing the apparent, because the finite and the apparent could not otherwise be known to be such. The real and infinite is genuinely immanent and constitutive in the apparent and finite, and it is the task of philosophy to make progressively explicit the immanence of the transcendent (or, alternatively, the self-transcendence of the finite), until, logically, the antithesis of finite and infinite, or apparent and real, is cancelled. Thus for Hegel philosophy must reveal a universe of activity in logically developing phases of progressive self-transcendence. How far Hegel believed that his own dialectical system had reached towards achieving the synthesis of finite and infinite through the cancellation of their antithesis is a question which I have struggled to answer in *A Study of Hegel's Logic*. Here it is beyond our scope, but Hegel had certainly far greater confidence in the possibility of positive philosophical construction than had the British idealists who followed him. The main achievement of F. H. Bradley, beyond his destructive criticism of the contemporary British empiricists, was perhaps the establishment of the notion of truth as coherence. Bradley's 'coherence' became a half-way house—indispensable to the student as a hut to spend the night in is to a climber scaling a major Alp—between the notions of truth as correspondence and truth as genuineness achieved in self-transcendence.

That I have borrowed largely from Hegel in these latter chapters will be obvious enough. I have no doubt that his system is truer in his own sense of *Wahrheit* than anything which his successors, sympathetic or hostile, have achieved; but philosophy, as Hegel knew well, even if he sometimes forgot it, is the product as well as the criticism of its own age, and any claim it might make to finality is *a priori* absurd. If one contemplates Hegel's philosophy as a finished system it at once reveals not finality but finitude. I shall not, as I come to the close of this book, even follow Hegel in attempting to present philosophical thinking as itself the supreme and all-embracing form of intrinsic value, the highest phase of that self-conscious activity in which intrinsic value consists. Such a position may seem to be not only Hegelian but entailed by what I have so far said, and perhaps, despite the feebleness of so much human philosophizing, it is not wholly untenable. But what abides in my own mind after some study of Hegel and his idealist successors is not so much the detailed articulation of a unitary system as two convictions to which I find myself always coming back. The first is that no subject of enquiry reveals itself to philosophical insight except in terms of some kind of developing series or *Stufenleiter*. On this assumption Aristotle construed and synthesized his universe by applying an analysis which itself ascends in three stages of developing complexity: matter and form with their respective correlates potency and actuality, fourfold causation, temporal process and timeless activity. It is a fair, though very obviously incomplete, interpretation of Hegel's system to call it a reconstruction of the Aristotelian universe in terms of self-consciousness, and to see Hegel's dialectic as an incomparably subtle and powerful attempt to consummate Aristotle's triple analysis.

Hegel, like Aristotle, offered a system which, at any rate *prima facie*, does make some claim to finality. It has met with much abuse from critics who have not understood that the criterion of truth by which it demands to be judged is not correspondence, nor even internal coherence, but genuineness. Nevertheless the second conviction which the study of idealism has left with me is a mistrust of philosophical system unless it is explicitly offered in the form, as Collingwood put it, of an interim report. I am conscious always of that ambiguous duality in human experience which at once makes it what it is and denies it the full reality of its own nature, that contradictory persistence of contingency in human thought which makes it a limping activity and dooms it at once to incomplete success and to that critical knowledge of its own failure which is inexplicable on any positivistic hypothesis. Reflecting on Hegel's system, I recognize that one cannot after all, in considering possible criteria of truth, simply reject correctness depending on correspondence in favour of coherence,[1] nor altogether substitute Hegelian *Wahrheit* for mere coherence. Rather there are three phases in the notion of human truth such that the first persists not fully absorbed in the second, at once hindering and helping, and the second similarly in the third. Hence I find myself less inclined to try to set system against system than to select this or that conception of developmental order from this or that philosopher and see whether it seems to yield insight when applied as a method in a given field of experience.

It may be that this is sheer weakness. The world stands in bitter need of a new and genuinely positive development of speculative thinking, but that will only come—and I can at present see no sure sign of its advent—with a new and genuine advance of the human spirit, which will not in its first shape be philosophical. A new philosophy, as I have said, is the product as well as the criticism of its age. The recrudescence of empiricism is a symptom of general philosophical impotence which afflicts us all. Am I then, like many better thinkers, after all tinged with the errors I try to combat? Am I lapsing with the moderns towards anarchy and the despairing acceptance of philosophy as a mere method of analysis indifferently applicable to any content? On the whole I think I am not. Doubtless I have recoiled without conspicuously leaping. I freely confess that weakness, which I would cure if I could, but I should repudiate the charge of mere negative reaction. Towards the end of an earlier work I adumbrated the notion of human experience as incomplete self-transcendence, presenting it as an attitude reached through

[1] If we could, science would be not the privation of value but its mere absence.

criticism of Hegel.[1] I called it a policy rather than a position, a method of diagnosis rather than a solution.[2] It is not, however, a mere method. At least it implies the general view of their own nature and of the universe they live in which normal balanced men have held since the beginning of civilization. But I press it here and now because in its negative aspect, too, it seems to me to have in it something which abides and must outlive the modern rage. I believe it to be not only the one theoretically possible starting-point from which philosophical speculation can advance without certainty of shipwreck, but also the dilemma which always will, as it actually always has, set men philosophizing. Hence I do not mind if I am called either outmoded or eclectic. There is, on the one hand, no substitute for new thinking, and the great systems of the past cannot serve us as they stand. They can only provide us with weapons for a fresh battle with the human dilemma; weapons, too, which though indispensable will themselves inevitably need retempering as old problems change their shapes in new contexts. On the other hand, methods are constitutive moments of the systems from which we abstract them for adaptation, and the systems of the past cannot serve us at all unless we study them as they stand. The concepts of the great thinkers will not work for us in new contexts unless we have already understood them in the contexts in which they were first conceived. To gain what the masters of philosophy have to give, a man must first submerge himself in their major works. Happy to be in contact with greatness, he must read with sympathy and with historical imagination before he passes to the criticism which is the purpose of his reading. He will merely lose his way if he attempts a short cut through textbook digests and conventional histories of philosophy. These by themselves will only fob him off with abstractions and fragments. He will make less progress still if he does no more than tear (or get torn for him by his teacher) famous dicta, or what may appear superficially to be self-contained arguments, from the contexts to which they belong, and try to subject them to 'powerful logical techniques'.

At the beginning of the century this would have seemed a commonplace too trite to deserve fresh mention in print. Every philosophical teacher gave this warning once to his pupils and no more. But the fashion has changed. Plato charged the

[1] See *A Study of Hegel's Logic*, Chapters XIX–XXII.   [2] Ibid., p. 367.

Sophists with corrupting the young to evil practices. No one could justly so accuse our respectable troglodyte teachers of philosophy, but in the last few decades British philosophy has become a major educational disaster, if only because it has been fundamentally anti-historical. No study has a very high educational value unless it compels critical but sympathetic contact with the great masters of a great subject, teaching clever young men not only to think but to be a little wise. The prestige of *Literae Humaniores* once rested on the very widespread belief that this was what 'Greats' above all other final schools at Oxford achieved, and their Ancient History colleagues allowed the greater share of the credit to the teachers of philosophy, in whom they quite often recognized and respected the sage as well as the expert. More than once in recent years the Greats examiners have, with the queerest naïveté, complained in their reports that candidates have tended to treat the works of Plato and Aristotle as of merely antiquarian interest. What but the purest intellectual parochialism could be expected from the pupils of any but a tiny dissident minority of Oxford's present-day teachers of philosophy? It was Professor Ryle who coined the phrase 'philosophical paleontology'. The examiners had perhaps hoped that candidates would, like sparrows pecking at horse-dung for the occasional oat, scavenge the writings of 'the teachers of mankind' for rudimentary linguistic and logistical puzzles, and perhaps the young men had found it tedious.[1] That would be small matter for regret. Speaking of ordinary history, G. M. Trevelyan wrote: 'What we know is indeed an infinitely small part of what has been; but it is all that is left to us now; and by it we can still in imagination escape from the decree passed against each one of us at his birth, that he should not issue forth from his narrow span of years, with its little circle, that looks so large, of modern thoughts and sights and sounds.'[2] Apply these words, *mutatis mutandis*, to philosophy and they are doubly true, because our legacy of

[1] Formerly, when a Greats candidate whose class could not be determined on his written work was given a long 'viva' in philosophy, the custom was for the Ancient History examiners to be present at the interview. Their interest in philosophy had persisted, and their judgment of the candidate's performance was often of value. I am credibly informed that now they seldom attend. Clearly philosophy to them is either a narrow specialism which they dropped without reluctance when their own schools were over, or something, if they belong to an older generation, so alien to what they learned themselves as to be unintelligible.
[2] *England under the Stuarts*, pp. 516–7.

philosophical writings from the past is rich. To science they do not apply. Old theories in physics or mathematics are, quite naturally and properly, yet more outmoded than their practical products. They rest on their shelves less regarded than old astrolabes, or than the motor-cars of the 'nineties, which at least excite a mild interest in social history when pulled out for a rally and a drive to Brighton. In this there is no loss to science. In science problems can be solved and done with, but in philosophy they cannot, and to bring philosophy in line with science in this respect it has to be assumed that most of its problems never really existed. No age but ours could have taken Mr. Russell's account of the great thinkers in his major pot-boiler, *The History of Western Philosophy*, for serious historical scholarship, nor greeted with respect and not ridicule a work based on such extensive ignorance and misconception as Dr. Popper's *The Open Society and its Enemies*. It may have been arrogant in Aristotle to call his predecessors lisping Aristotelians, and in Hegel to claim the main philosophies of the past as moments absorbed and transcended in his own system; but the self-knowledge of great men sometimes outruns their modesty, and Aristotle and Hegel had not only read and reflected deeply on their predecessors' work but were respectively the first and the last great historians of philosophy. Their pride pales to humility beside the conceit of those who argue that the sages of the past talked mainly nonsense (because theirs was not the way to talk), and even offer their outmoded epigoni a course of psychotheraphy, a philosophical brain-washing, to relieve them of anxiety complexes induced by wrestling with pseudo-problems.

Of late our philosophical writers have a little mended their manners. The early logical positivists came talking the talk of Plato's little tinker who has had his chains knocked off and married his master's daughter. Their successors are a trifle bewildered, less confident, and accordingly more civil. There even appears on the last page of Mr. Urmson's *Philosophical Analysis* a phrase which has nowadays an almost archaic ring: 'the great, dateless works of philosophy.' *Lateat scintillula forsan.* Yet at present if I had an intelligent son coming up to Oxford, I should not regret it if he turned his face away from all the three Honour Schools that include philosophy, even from Greats.

SUBJECT INDEX

Psychiatry, Psycho-analysis, 16, 80, 217, 220, 221, 250
Psychology, 73–80, 91ff.
Punishment, 221

Realism, 33, 151, 156, 166, 167
Reality, 24, 28, 33, 136, 144, 162, 164, 228
Relations, 99, 189–90
Religion, 222–5

Science, Abstractive tendency of, 28, 45–6, 183–4
Science, Economic Character of, 54ff., *passim*
Science, 'Social', 57
Sculpture, 6–7, 14
Self and Not- Self, 30, 74–5, 194–5
Self-consciousness, 153, 174, 194, 231
Sensa, Sterilized, 229, 231
Sensations, 88ff., 95
—) (perceptions, 96–8, 151–2
See also Sensa, Sense-data
Sense-data, 51, 100, 137–40, 151–2
Sensibilia, 88ff.
Similarity, 110, 126, 159, 196, 201
Solipsism, 25, 86, 95, 99, 136, 166
'Specious present', The, 102, 104
Stufeuleiter, 130, 168, 207, 246
Subconscious, The, 16, 17, 117, 237
Subject and Object, 167, 176, 195, 201, 229
Syntax, 10, 128, 129, 130, 141
System, 25–8, 120–1, 133, 173, 183–8, 242, 247, 248
— and Value, 199
See also Coherence

Tautology, 141, 186–7
Technique, 235–8
See also Craft
Transcendence, 165, 178, *passim*
Truth, 113–16, 130–1, 183–90, 247
— as Coherence, 114, 162, 165ff., 188, 189, 246
— as Correspondence, 115–16, 182–3, 186, 189, 232
— — — and Philosophical Truth, 186
— as Genuineness, 186, 192, 246
—, Formal and Material, 123–4, 131, 186–7, 188
Truth-functions, 130, 139

Universal, The, 27–8, 32, 53, 54, 106, 110–11, 131, 146, 166, 180, 187, 191, 196, 198–9, 200–1, 233, 242
Usage, Linguistic, 150, 152, 154–6, 157
See also Language-games
Utilitarians, The, 61, 62, 68, 208, 210, 211

Vacuum-cleaner, The magical, 55–6, 75, 137, 167
Vagueness, 103, 107, 109, 110
Validity, 123–4, 186
Value, Subjectivist Theory of, 81, 171–3, 175–8, 182, 193, 200, 205, 208
Verification, 114, 135, 138, 139

Will, 58–9, 61, 119–20, 178–80, 194, 218–9, 222, 223, 232
Words, 104–9, 130, 154–6. *See also* Language

INDEX OF PROPER NAMES